# Acclaim for *No*

"Many people either misunderstand spirit____ _____ or choose to ignore it altogether. You've done us all a great service!"

—Pastor Jim Tolle, Church on the Way
(Foursquare International), Van Nuys, CA

"I'm always eager to hear from Gordon Dalbey's heart and to read from his pen. Like Nathaniel, he's a man in whom there is no guile. His discoveries on his journey into spiritual warfare may cause your eyebrows to rise, but they will also sharpen your spiritual wits. The solutions to the world's problems are found first in the spiritual realm. Gordon helps us to see that realm and to access our victory in Christ."

—Dudley Hall, Successful Christian
Living Ministries, author *Grace Works*

"This subject is often one of confusion, fear, or ignorance for Christians. Dalbey, however, has shared here his significant experience, wisdom, and sound doctrine, bringing clarity and confidence where it is much needed. Definitely a beneficial resource to further equip us all for the journey ahead."

—Dr Lisa Guinness, Director, Living Waters
Discipleship & Healing Trust (London, UK).

"With profound insight, Gordon Dalbey opens our eyes to the spiritual warfare raging right under our noses. His courageous journey leads us beyond the distraction which pits Liberal versus Conservative/pacifist versus warrior, to an authentic third option: being united at last in the overcoming power of God before a common enemy."

—Jonathan Brink, Managing Director,
Thrive Ministries

"Gordon Dalbey is a longtime friend and brother. I am happy to confirm my part in his story. He has been a courageous and honest searcher after God and, as a very successful creative writer, he tells a fascinating and compelling story of discovering incredibly important truth."

—Rev. Bob Whitaker,
Presbyterian Church USA

"This book is a wake-up call—clear, concise, and compelling. Combining personal vulnerability, biblical reliability, and spiritual acuity, Gordon Dalbey has gifted the Christian community—and the oldline church in particular—with a book that is both disturbing, in that it graphically warns and challenges our complacency regarding the forces of evil, and encouraging, because it provides a road map to spiritual victory. "

—Rev. Tom Rothhaar, United Methodist Church

*"No Small Snakes* fills a void in the Christian library of spiritual warfare books. Most works I've seen have focused on the dutiful steps to victory rather than the relationship with the General. I'm praying for God's richest blessing on this much needed work. Gordon Dalbey is one of our era's most important Christian authors. His writing exposes the deepest dynamics of the human psyche so as to bring the soul into the healing light of Christ. Now, one of the most erudite Christian minds in the body of Christ dares to expose his journey into that which transcends the intellect—the supernatural realm of victory over demonic powers. *No Small Snakes* is no simplistic handbook for dabblers, nor is it fodder for the sensationalism that surrounds the subject of demons. It is, instead, a rare interweaving of real life, rich theology, and profound insights for deliverance, freedom, and joy. The victory and liberation described on these pages emerges from the authentic ministry of Gordon Dalbey—a ministry that has blessed and changed my life along with countless others."

—Rev Alan Wright, Reynolda Church,
Evangelical Presbyterian Church, author of *Shame off You*

"Once again, Gordon Dalbey has shown us what an outstanding writer he is. Here is authentic spirituality on every page, honest searching for answers. From the Peace Corps to Harvard to the parish, his story is guaranteed to draw you out of your comfort zone into the epic contest at hand today!"

—Rev. Paul Anderson, Director,
Lutheran Renewal/Alliance of Renewal Churches

"Scriptural, practical, and personal, this book holds a wealth of knowledge in how to wage spiritual warfare—something which much of the church has not acknowledged or understood. Gordon's honesty and courage leads us to victory in this battle of life and death which engages us all, whether we acknowledge it or not."

—Rev. Michael Evans, American
Baptist Association/Wholeness Ministries

# NO SMALL SNAKES

# Other Books by Gordon Dalbey

*Healing the Masculine Soul*

*Sons of the Father*

*Fight Like a Man*

Gordon Dalbey may be contacted
for speaking engagements or further resources at:

Gordon Dalbey
Box 61042, Santa Barbara, CA 93160
www.abbafather.com

# NO SMALL SNAKES

## A JOURNEY INTO SPIRITUAL WARFARE

### BY GORDON DALBEY

THOMAS NELSON
*Since 1798*

NASHVILLE   DALLAS   MEXICO CITY   RIO DE JANEIRO   BEIJING

Published in Nashville, Tennessee, by Thomas Nelson. Thomas Nelson is a registered trademark of Thomas Nelson, Inc.

Thomas Nelson, Inc., titles may be purchased in bulk for educational, business, fund-raising, or sales promotional use. For information, please e-mail SpecialMarkets@ThomasNelson.com.

Unless otherwise noted, Scripture quotations are from Today's English Version. © American Bible Society 1966, 1971, 1976, 1992.

Scripture quotations marked MSG are from *The Message* by Eugene H. Peterson. © 1993, 1994, 1995, 1996, 2000. Used by permission of NavPress Publishing Group. All rights reserved.

Scripture quotations marked NIV are from the Holy Bible: New International Version®. © 1973, 1978, 1984 by International Bible Society. Used by permission of Zondervan. All rights reserved.

Scripture quotations marked TLB are from *The Living Bible.* © 1971. Used by permission of Tyndale House Publishers, Inc., Wheaton, Illinois 60189. All rights reserved.

Scripture quotations marked RSV are from the Revised Standard Version of the Bible. © 1946, 1952, 1971, 1973 by the Division of Christian Education of the National Council of the Churches of Christ in the U.S.A. Used by permission.

Scripture quotations marked NKJV are from the New King James Version. © 1982 by Thomas Nelson, Inc. Used by permission. All rights reserved.

Scripture quotations marked NLT are from the *Holy Bible*, New Living Translation. © 1996. Used by permission of Tyndale House Publishers, Inc., Wheaton, Illinois 60189. All rights reserved.

Scripture quotations marked NRSV are from the New Revised Standard Version of the Bible. © 1989 by the Division of Christian Education of the National Council of the Churches of Christ in the U.S.A. All rights reserved.

**Library of Congress Cataloging-in-Publication Data**

Dalbey, Gordon, 1944–
   No small snakes : a journey into spiritual warfare / by Gordon Dalbey.
      p. cm.
   Includes bibliographical references.
   ISBN 978-0-8499-1984-8 (trade paper)
   1. Dalbey, Gordon, 1944– 2. Christian biography. 3. Spiritual warfare. I. Title.
BR1725.D34A3 2008
235'.4—dc22

2007052324

*Printed in the United States of America*

08 09 10 11 12 RRD 7 6 5 4 3

*To Mary*
*My gracious, wise, and loving battle partner*

# CONTENTS

Introduction
# BAD ANGELS

Bring down your warriors, O LORD!
—JOEL 3:11 NIV

On a sunny, tropical afternoon in 1965, between classes as a Peace Corps teacher in rural Nigeria, I stopped under a large, shady palm tree to chat with the school carpenter. To my surprise, he soon began telling of dark, fearful "spirits" that had invaded his house the night before, punctuating his tale with animated gestures of his hammer.

Freshly anointed with a college degree in math, I laughed. "Oh, come on," I said, smirking. "You don't really believe in that 'spirits' stuff, do you?"

Hesitating, weighing his words as an illiterate laborer before this highly educated American teacher, he put down his hammer and wiped a sawdust-speckled hand on patched shorts. And then he looked me firmly in the eye. "There are no small snakes," he declared.

Puzzled by his words and disarmed by the confidence in his gaze, I balked. "Wh . . . what do you mean?" I managed.

Graciously, he explained that all snakes in that area are poisonous and not easily seen in the bush. One bite from the smallest, newly hatched snake can surprise and kill instantly the toughest man.

His message, foreign then to my Western ears, was nevertheless clear: be humble when you approach things of the spirit.

Thus, an African carpenter taught me it's arrogant to discount spiritual power. At the bright, robust age of twenty, however, I wasn't ready yet to learn the full lesson: not only is the spirit realm real, but it's also dangerously naive to believe that all spiritual things are good.

Today, we're beginning at last to engage the first part of that lesson. Angels, for example, have in recent years begun to enjoy widespread popularity. From magazine articles to popular talk shows and greeting cards, celestial messengers and spiritual guardians soar freely among us. In fact, rare is the list of best-selling books that does not include at least one title about paranormal phenomena, from miracles to spiritual codes.

The scent of something remote but vaguely familiar, even compelling, is wafting about our culture, and the media have picked it up.

This growing fascination with supernatural experience promises a refreshing turn from the spiritual dead-end to which our Western, rational, scientific worldview has led us. Much as we enjoy the labor-saving devices of modern technology, its premise of materialism— that all reality is limited to the natural, physical world—bears a heavy price tag for the human psyche.

To acknowledge nothing beyond what the senses can perceive and the mind can explain is to deny spiritual reality. Yet no matter how intelligently our minds would persuade, our hearts are not convinced. From nightmares to death itself, the truth intrudes relent-lessly: something greater than our natural abilities can discern or control—something literally *super*natural—is at work both within us and without.

Meanwhile, this unsettling truth borne by spiritual power—that we're not in control—has surfaced palpably in our daily lives. From data overload to busy schedules, the natural world we live in becomes more complex daily and is often overwhelming. The silver lining in this darkening cloud is that in the face of our human inadequacies, we become open to powers greater than our own—and thereby we become more real and, indeed, more human. We look beyond our unmanageable natural world for *super*natural help that human effort cannot provide; hence, the interest in angels. It's good to know that greater resources are at hand.

At the same time, however, experience has convinced me that—contrary to popular sentiment—not all spiritual powers that respond to our brokenness and need seek to serve our best interests.

Decades later, after considerable experience that you will read about here, I know that my African carpenter friend was right. Not all angels are good.

In fact, bad angels—spiritual entities that lie and destroy—not only are described clearly in ancient texts, but are being experi-enced with increasing credibility in our modern lives. These harm-ful supernatural agents historically have been portrayed as masters of deception, who enlist us as accomplices in their destructive schemes by manipulating our fear of weakness and shame of losing control.

Often in the ancient texts, the conflict between good and bad angels is portrayed as spiritual warfare, the consequences of which are borne out in our everyday, natural world. If true, this battle between the forces of good and evil would be discernible even today as we dare to recognize the fullness of spiritual reality beyond our natural selves and our human ability to perceive it.

Like the proverbial small snake, however, the subtle yet dominant power inherent to spiritual reality can overwhelm our egos with surprising ease. That's why we can celebrate the good angels and yet not dare acknowledge the bad angels. Our powerlessness and fear allow us to accommodate spiritual power only insofar as we imagine it to be good—or at least less powerful than our human ability to master it.

A small boy, for example, is acutely aware that he's much smaller than the host of adult "giants" around him, both at home and out in the world. Powerless among these towering beings who daily manifest over him the power of joy or pain, peace or panic, even life or death, he nevertheless must make his needs known and met among them.

How does he manage the fear of being overwhelmed by these huge creatures that dominate his natural world?

Enter the dinosaur: a gigantic beast, utterly powerful, manifestly destructive, patently uncontrollable—and, therefore, intensely fascinating to a small boy in a giant world. Even more compelling, the dinosaur is real—it actually lived—yet is nowhere visible in the natural world today. Except, of course, in hidden, hauntingly mysterious bones.

Thus, the boy reimages dinosaurs as good, if not easily controlled. His fear of powers greater than himself and his consequent need to master them prompt a market for model dinosaurs small enough to fit firmly in a little boy's fist. In play, he animates; he controls; he manipulates the figures.

The cuddly, smiling TV dinosaur with the unassuming name Barney secures the charade with friendly, hug-me songs. Cartoon films such as the Land Before Time series contribute loving grandparent sauropods and cute, high-voiced kid raptors, who always emerge victorious from their adventures.

To know promises the ability to master. And so the little boy reads, he studies, he learns, and, like Adam, he names—especially six-syllable species. His spirit, borne by his fragile three-foot frame, thrills with deliverance: *Voila!* Mastery over the fear! I can control this awesome power. In my hands, in my vocabulary, in the grip of my imagination, the beast is subdued.

I am lord of the mystery. I am safe.

Now fast-forward from the child to the adult—to an unsettling dream, news of an untimely death, a sudden accident, a frightening impulse. All beg the question, *Where did this come from?*

The list of possible answers always includes a larger destructive and uncontrollable source lurking behind the scenes—something more credible, more tangible than mere "bad luck" or the hot chili you ate before bedtime. Something real but not visible, like a dinosaur. It's terrifying, overwhelming if you think about it.

It's delusive if you don't.

Unlike dinosaurs, agents of spiritual evil are not extinct but frighteningly extant. No lifeless bones here but, indeed, animate power without form.

Enter the adult counterpart of the prehistoric beast: the devil caricature with red suit, pitchfork, and horns. Witness the occasional sports mascot who frolics around the stadium on behalf of the home team Blue Devils, Sun Devils, or Demon Deacons. Or consider synthetic Halloween witch costumes and plastic goblin masks. Devils and demons mean party time: hocus-pocus and superstition, great for laughs, all in good fun.

All in childish denial—a pathetic attempt to gain mastery over our deepest, most primal fears.

For here at last is the terrifying truth that our materialistic mind-set not only is incapable of grasping but also conspires to suppress: the problem is not that our childish imagination gets hooked into foolish fears but that *something real is evil and we can't control it.*

And so, manageable evil sells. Big-time. In recent years, Halloween has approached Christmas in holiday business volume. The material sales competition suggests the deeper contest that the two holidays reflect, as dark masks and the effort to conceal versus bright lights and the effort to reveal. Our dark Halloween caricatures foster the comforting deception that spiritual evil is so ridiculous, so manifestly foolish as, for example, to parade around easily recognizable as a red-suited devil or black-caped witch. It's reassuring: We can see it, so we're safe. It doesn't look like us, so we're apart from it. It's ridiculous, so we're still normative and in charge.

In fact, to wear the very costumes is to declare, "We're more powerful than these things. We can put on their appearance, but they can't put on our appearance. We can manipulate their character, but they can't manipulate our character."

As if there were small snakes in the jungle.

It's easy to believe in good angels, those reassuring guardians and messengers of light. They don't threaten our human power. Good, after all, needs to be loosed; only evil needs to be leashed. People who fear losing power must cast as wholly good what they can't control; otherwise, their weakness and vulnerability will be exposed and the evil will overwhelm them—if only through the shame of their inadequacy.

How then do we begin to escape the narrow confines of our materialistic, scientific, Western worldview to move through and beyond our fears to the full truth of spiritual reality?

That very truncated worldview dictates its own, myopic answer. Trapped in its grip, we fancy that materialism is overcome by denying material, physical pleasures and luxuries. A generation of us tried that during the 1960s. We dropped out of the corporate bucks, scorned our parents' post–World War II prosperity, dismissed their chrome Buicks, and drove beat-up VWs to San Francisco to live off peace and love. "Flower power," we declared, would overcome the materialism that had suckered our parents.

This heady mix of youthful anger and righteous idealism, however, made a toxic blend. Our San Francisco hippie sanctuary, Haight-Ashbury, quickly became a drug den—nicknamed "Hashbury"—with beggars, prostitutes, and drug dealers battling for the turf.

Flowers and peace signs, it turned out, not only could not exorcise the demons of our heritage, but in fact gave them new avenues of destruction. "Next time you're getting mugged," as one right-wing bumper sticker put it, "call a hippie." That stung. Not because it came from those who condemned our lifestyle, but because it pointed to a serious flaw in our worldview, namely, that we could not recognize genuine evil and take steps to overcome it.

The well-to-do idealize poverty because they've never suffered its reality. Meanwhile, the need for food, clothing, and shelter often forces the poor to obsess on material things. The hungry poor think more about food than do the satisfied rich.

Only the well-endowed corporation children among us could

afford to be hippies and drop out—while blue-collar sons went to Vietnam. The whole social revolution of the 1960s was as much about class as about war or racism.

Contrary to bourgeois fantasies, *the true counterpoint to materialism is not poverty and deprivation but authentic spirituality.* Asceticism and self-denial are helpful disciplines only to those wealthy enough to have given themselves over to worldly consumption and greed—and even then, only insofar as they reestablish a healthy balance of the material and spiritual life.

We're saved from the emptiness of self-worship neither by the abundance nor by the lack of material goods, but by refocusing our worship appropriately on ultimate spiritual power. Thus, I can worship the God who is not me but is indeed the true Other.

Nothing you smoke, snort, drink, eat, couple with, or sacrifice can conjure relationship with such a Power—or thereby restore you to your true identity and purpose in life.

Without a deliberate spiritual life that integrates the natural and the supernatural, our self-centered desires rule us; we either pursue them in sinful greed or flee them in self-righteous disdain. We're truly lost, unable ultimately to grasp any greater purpose beyond animal self-preservation and pleasure or inhuman self-denial.

Appetites, whether indulged or scorned, thereby co-opt the true focus of our destiny.

Unbalanced, we fall.

Disintegrated, we fall apart.

And only two responses to supernatural bad angels emerge.

Like children grasping after model dinosaurs, we can pretend to reduce these awful powers of darkness to a manageable size. That is, we can fabricate a sense of control—if not by mascot devils, then by attempting to manipulate spiritual power through New Age or more traditional "religious" practices. One fancies, *If I visualize it as such, so it will be*; another, *If I sacrifice enough time, energy, and money, God will give me what I want.*

On the other hand, we can simply deny spiritual power altogether.

Together, basking in our dazzling intelligence, we snicker.

As lying alone at night, we shudder.

Both polarities of manipulation and denial are designed to cover our fear of spiritual power and the loss of control that it reveals. We don't have to be afraid, as long as we're in charge; thus the compulsion to believe that our natural perceptions and powers define and comprise reality.

But what if our human fears have colored our perceptions?

What if neither the frantic emptiness of self-worship nor the steadfast motions of religion deliver us from evil?

What if there *are* bad angels?

Then at last another choice must emerge: neither to deny nor to domesticate the mystery, but rather to confess and engage it with bold humility.

The ancients called it "faith," that is, a trust that no matter how unwieldy or dire our outward circumstances may appear, the powers of good are ultimately greater, and that as we struggle against evil, the good will win out.

In this choice, we press on—not without loss, not without pain, but in fact trusting that the very struggle itself strengthens, instructs, and matures us for our intended life tasks.

Some years ago, during the early stages of writing this book, I was strangely drawn by "holy coincidence"—as I once heard another preacher term such occasions—to two real-life adventure classics.

In *Kon-Tiki*, Norwegian scholar-turned-seafarer Thor Heyerdahl in 1950 sails his log raft more than four thousand miles from Peru to the South Pacific islands. Challenging orthodox anthropology of his day, he proposes that the Pacific islanders' family tree is rooted in South America, not in Asia.

And in a downtown thrift shop, I stumbled across a dusty paperback copy of *The Oregon Trail*. Therein, twenty-three-year-old Harvard graduate and journalist Francis Parkman treks from St. Louis to the Northwest in 1846, living with Native Americans and witnessing the dangers and wonders of frontier America.

Today, the natural world is properly cataloged and subdued. Supersonic jets, packed with tourists, daily fly Heyerdahl's course from South America to the Pacific islands; six-lane interstate highways stretch matter-of-factly along Parkman's route from St. Louis to Portland. The frontier, it would seem, has been ably explored, documented, and tamed.

From our collective Western soul rises a psalm of praise to the gods of good planning and sturdy construction: Whew! For a minute there, it seemed as if we might not be in control after all!

Yet even as the caged lion loses the exigency of its roar, our self-proclaimed victory over the natural wilderness and its mysteries has truncated our vision and betrayed the explorer—even the adventurer within us all.

True explorers blaze trails not just to entertain or to make our lives easier, but to inspire an openness to truth not visible from the village. Indeed, their exploits call the villagers themselves to recognize and pursue that truth in the face of the unknown. "Find the wilderness that beckons your own uncertainties," the true adventurer proclaims, "and trek it." That is, "Listen for the mystery that stirs your deepest passion, and pursue it. For therein lies the key to your destiny."

In 1960 President Kennedy called my generation of young Americans to a "new frontier." Some went to the moon; I went to rural Nigeria as a Peace Corps volunteer. Today, the new millennium has called us to a newer, spiritual frontier—the likes of which neither I nor the late President Kennedy could have dreamed only a generation ago.

If attention to the good angels has blazed a trail to spiritual reality and power, let us then press on further in our journey to the full truth.

Let us face the bad angels.

Even as I exhort the adventurer, however, I must note that the excitement of the journey arises partly from the legitimate fear of its risk. Like the ancient prophets and today's outdoorsman guides, I'm obliged not simply to promise, but also to warn.

Where I live in California, the Santa Ynez Mountains offer relaxing creekside hikes and spectacular views of the ocean. Preparation for the enjoyment, however, must include some talk about rattlesnakes, which are not uncommon up there. We want to spend most of our time talking about the fun ahead, because that's why we're going. But if we don't talk openly and realistically about the rattlesnakes, the fun can quickly turn to tragedy.

Similarly, religious communities too often tell stories of the wonderful things God does and exhort members to proclaim the benefits of the faith without teaching them about the rattlesnakes, the genuine evil in the world.

And along the trail, many fall.

This book is not designed for the armchair tourist, the casual

Discovery Channel viewer, the vicarious Internet surfer. The powers that you read about herein are not confined to Heyerdahl's Pacific Ocean or Parkman's nineteenth-century Wyoming prairie.

They're literally at hand. Here, now, and, yes, within us all.

Even as the natural oceans and wilderness threatened past adventurers, manifest dangers lurk today in the supernatural realm. A generation of pioneers who once needed physical strength, endurance, and vision today need persevering character and keen spiritual sensibilities—traits that our materialistic worldview is hell-bent to dull and anesthetize.

In spite of our most refined and intelligent efforts, the spiritual realm that beckons us today has not been technologically sanitized and reduced to a comfortable tourist attraction. Rather, it yet stirs with a host of dark, even deceptively bright counterfeits and seductive diversions, which would obscure the path to truth and divert travelers from their intended destination.

In this journey, therefore, no mere escapist desire for "peace and love," no happily conjured visual images, no pretense of moral goodness, mental intelligence, or physical strength, nor any human fabrication no matter how deliberate or sincere can ensure your safety and guide you into your destiny.

The story you read here has been twenty years in the making. The incidents may well stretch your credulity—as they certainly stretched mine. With university degrees from Duke, Stanford, and Harvard, I often found myself pausing amid the journey to wonder, *Can this be real?*

As time and again experience overwhelmed my doubts, I realized that my academic training in critical thinking—even my BA in math and my scientific background—only fueled my curiosity and determination to examine the evidence humbly and to seek plausible conclusions.

Accordingly, my adventure begins not with great battles and greater victories, but with curious experiences and likely observations. I caution the "spiritual enthusiast" from the temptation to bypass this initial leg of the journey.

At the outset, for example, Heyerdahl's chopping down his own balsam trees for his fabled raft seems an inglorious labor, even to read. But his labor—and the reader's—allows us to own the larger vision and thereby to persevere amid the later storms that threaten it.

To short-circuit the mystery is to abort the destiny that it beckons. Rushing to the last chapter of a mystery story not only robs the reader of entertainment; it's unreal.

And that, in fact, may be the deadliest sin we face on this journey.

In another of my thrift-store books, *101 Wacky Kid Jokes*, I found this unlikely exchange:

"Gee, it's dark out tonight, isn't it?"

"I don't know. I can't see."[1]

*To see the darkness, or to be blinded by it?* That is the question.

This book is one explorer's answer.

# Part I

# THE CALL: ENGAGING THE MYSTERY

## Chapter 1

# DRAFTED BY THE SPIRIT

I have called you by name–you are mine.

—Isaiah 43:1

It started out like any other meeting at our denomination's regional office. But as I was called upon to report for my local cluster of churches, I was suddenly catapulted into the center of a mystery that had baffled me for years.

After several other area representatives had reported, the head conference minister—who had known me throughout my seven years in his conference—turned to me and said, "And how are things with our churches in your area, Roger?" Then he caught himself as the others around the table chuckled. "Gordon," he declared, shaking his head in dismay and smiling at his apparent blooper. "Did I just call you Roger?"

I nodded, lost in amazement.

"Now why in the world would I do a thing like that?" he asked rhetorically. Smiling and shrugging his shoulders, he turned back to his agenda.

Quickly, almost desperately, I interrupted. "I don't know why you called me Roger," I blurted out, glancing uneasily at the other pastors around the table, "but I know one thing: I'm going to find out, once and for all, because it's happened all my life. Whenever somebody mistakes my name, whether new acquaintances or even people like you, who've known me a long time, it's always the same wrong name—Roger."

The others paused briefly in mild interest, and the meeting continued. But even as I went through the motions of my report, my mind whirled with memories and questions.

It was true. No one ever mistook my name for Bill or George. It was always Roger. A fuzzy image of being introduced at a party crossed my mind; then a seminary classmate's greeting in the hall. The double take, embarrassed laughter, and apologies were all too familiar. "Well, you do sort of look like a Roger," some would say afterward, prompting others to remark how "some people just look like a Nancy or a David."

It once occurred to me that in military jargon, *Roger* communicates an affirmative message, as in that staple of war films: "Roger, Captain! We're on our way!" I happen to have a pronounced square-block jawbone, and I wondered if maybe people were subconsciously making a connection between the popular firm or solid sense of such a face and military decisiveness. My speculations, however, never produced a plausible explanation, and I had come to regard the whole thing as simply an amusing coincidence.

Now, I began again to wonder.

I strained to remember the first time it had happened. College in North Carolina? Peace Corps in Nigeria? Grad school in San Francisco? High school teaching in Chicago? Seminary in Boston? I drew a blank. How many times a year does the average man hear his name mistaken? Again my questions seemed to lead nowhere, and the strange consistency of the name Roger left me with a single, haunting, why?

Indeed, as I left the denominational offices that afternoon, the amusing coincidence had become a compelling mystery. Sitting alone moments later in my parked car, I sighed and shook my head in wonder. *This Roger business is just too much to be a coincidence,* I prayed. *Lord, what in the world is going on here?* Awed and humbled by this powerful mystery—both terrified and excited by its life-defining potential—I was overcome by an electric sensation that I can only call a true "fear of God," not from danger, but from awe at being in the presence of so much power that all you can do is worship.

In that moment, I knew that the name Roger reflected far more than mere coincidence. And having grasped my attention so publicly at last, the mystery therein held the very key to my destiny. I would not—indeed, I dared not—let go. Trembling, I sighed again and yielded. "Okay, Lord, lead on," I whispered—and knew at last that I had turned a corner, never to turn back.

## Chapter 2
# CALLED BY NAME

When the baby was a week old, they came to circumcise him,
and they were going to name him Zechariah, after his father.

–Luke 1:59

Determined to find some clue to the "Roger" mystery, I pondered over my given name.

At birth, I received my father's name and became Earle Gordon Dalbey Jr. My father went by Earle G. Dalbey, and he told me that as a toddler I enjoyed announcing myself as "Berle Bobby Boomer." (Those who speak toddlerese will recognize that as Earle Dalbey Jr.) My family, nevertheless, was confused over what to call me. Clearly, I could not be called Earle, the same as my father. "How is anyone going to know which of them we're talking about?" my mother rightly asked.

For a while, I was called E. G. Then Earlie was tried briefly, as well as Junior—and all were mercifully discarded. For some time before going to school, I was called Brother, likely because of my year-older sister's influence. At last, when I did go to school, my middle name, Gordon, seemed the obvious choice, and it stuck.

In 1964, after college, I joined the Peace Corps and was sent to Nigeria, where to my surprise I discovered the source of my surname, Dalbey. Exploring a jungle road one day on my motorbike, I turned off onto a smaller bush path and was startled to see up ahead a blond white man standing in front of a house, beside a NORCAP sign.

Assuming the man was British, I puttered over and waved to him. Stopping my cycle, I alighted and extended my hand. "Hello," I said, "I'm Gordon Dalbey."

To my amazement, the man immediately smiled broadly, pumped my hand, and began speaking a language I had never heard before—definitely not the local Igbo dialect, which I spoke. Begging his pardon, I held up my hand in a "stop" gesture and shrugged my shoulders in apology. "I . . . American," I said. "Speak English?"

"Oh, I am so sorry," he said graciously and clearly. "When I heard your last name, I assumed you were Norwegian, like me."

"Norwegian?" I echoed, confused.

"Yes, of course," he said. "Dalbey is not an uncommon name in Norway." Genially, he put his arm around my shoulders and welcomed me into his home, explaining that NORCAP stood for Norwegian Church Agricultural Project. He then led me to a big table and unfolded a map of Norway, pointing out places where the Dalbey name is most common.

He explained that the name itself was a combination of two Norwegian words: *dal*, meaning "valley," as in the English "hill and dale," and *by*, meaning "city." Hence, my name meant "city in the valley." We speculated that the *e* was added by anglicizers as Viking conquerors settled in England.

*Amazing!* I thought. *I travel halfway around the world to learn about Africans and end up learning about myself!*

On returning home from Nigeria, I entered journalism graduate school and began publishing magazine articles. I needed a pen name and decided upon "E. Gordon Dalbey Jr." in order to avoid confusion as to my preferred first name.

At thirty, after working as a newspaper reporter and a high school teacher, I yielded at last to the call and enrolled in seminary. I had never preached a sermon before, but during my first-year homiletics class, I decided to enter the seminary preaching competition with a sermon about Jacob and his dark night of the soul, wrestling with God's angel in the river gorge at night (Gen. 32:22–32).

The all-important names in the story fascinated me: Jacob, "the one who grabs from behind," that is, the cheater who won't look you in the eye and fight fair—the mama's boy who hides out in the tents while his macho brother, Esau, hunts the family meat—is finally called to account by God and must wrestle it out at last with an angel face-to-face, man-to-man. And wonder of wonders, he digs in and comes up with the strength to win!

His wrestling match with the angel is the defining point in Jacob's life, for through it emerges not simply an improved Jacob, a slightly better cheater, but, in fact, a new man. The whimpering loser has become a fighting winner. Clearly, the name Jacob no longer fits. And so this former wimp, whose only apparent hope lay in cheating, receives the blessing of new life—indeed, the revelation of his divine destiny—through a new and more appropriate name. Jacob becomes Israel, literally, "one who struggles with God," that is, the "man of ultimate determination," indeed, the "winner."

My sermon won the first-place award. Some years later, the

university dean of the chapel, who chaired the award committee, told me, "I will always think of you in connection with Jacob's story."

Thereafter, I became increasingly uncomfortable with my first name. I was proud to be my father's son and a Dalbey. But I had begun to appreciate the biblical understanding that each man's name must reflect God's unique, individual calling.

John the Baptist's unique mission, for example, demanded a special name, different from that of his father, Zechariah. The common Hebrew Bar-Zechariah, or "Son of Zechariah," might suffice as a surname for the one chosen to announce the Messiah, but not Zechariah Jr. as a first name. A first name must reflect God's call rather than mere human tradition or desire.

In Hebrew, Zechariah means "God remembers," that is, He does not forsake His people. This kinetic name fosters expectation for God's deliverance—something Israel groaned for under the Roman yoke in Jesus' time. In so critical a moment in Israel's history, the coming generation would need a vanguard to herald not simply what God had done, but what He would do now. A messenger named Zechariah Jr. would suggest the anticlimax of a fearful, stuttering God, whose word cannot proceed.

Indeed, it is the mother—whose pregnancy beyond the natural age of childbearing has delivered her from self-centered desires into the awe of God's goodness—who first apprehends God's purposes ahead. Elizabeth insists that her son be named not after his father but John—the Hebrew Johannon, meaning "God is gracious."

Zechariah, meanwhile, has been disciplined with dumbness for not trusting God's power to act sovereignly and bring a son through his aging wife. His indignant relatives urge him to overrule Elizabeth, protesting, "You don't have a relative with that name [John]!"

(Luke 1:61). But divine discipline has caused this father to yield his own agenda for his son to God: "Zechariah asked for a writing pad and wrote, 'His name is John.' How surprised they all were! At that moment, Zechariah was able to speak again, and he started praising God" (vv. 63–64).

Above all other character traits, God is determined to establish His grace—His unmerited favor and blessing—as the authentic base and channel for proclaiming the Messiah. As God's grace grows out of His remembering our needs, so John grows out of Zechariah and is the appropriate platform for redemption and the refining of God's purposes in history—even John's history.

In our culture, a glance through any professional directory, such as for physicians, lawyers, or clergy, reveals an inordinate number of "juniors." Such identification with his earthly father may well motivate a son to achieve as a way of pleasing or emulating Dad. But biblical faith understands that apart from the intention of the *heavenly* Father, our lives can only "miss the mark"—the root meaning of the verb *to sin*.

In my own case, I had trained in seminary to be a parish "general practitioner." I nevertheless wanted to fine-tune my call, to discover what special gifting or aspect of ministry God had designed me to pursue. If, indeed, as the biblical stories testify, God fashions a person's name to reflect His unique purpose in that person, then to assume my father's entire name as my own—like a Zechariah Jr.—seemed an abdication of my call, if not a withdrawal from God's timely purpose through me.

No man is so unique that his life's meaning and purpose can be divorced from those who came before him. In John's case, coming from a priestly household surely prepared him for the fiery convictions necessary to his task as herald of the Messiah. Although John's particular call grew out of his father's call, it nevertheless bore its own uniqueness, which could not be entirely contained by his father's name.

With this new perspective, I decided that as a first effort to step out in the direction of my own unique calling—whatever that might be—I would drop the "E." and the "Jr." from my manuscripts, checkbook, and all other documents. Instead, I began writing only "Gordon" for my first name and leaving blank the space for my middle name. Without a clear vision of my own call, I could not at that point affirm my father's profession as a navy officer and his life convictions as its seedbed, but could only trust that revelation would follow. And as we shall see in a later chapter, it did.


SOON AFTER ARRIVING IN SOUTHERN CALIFORNIA TO PASTOR MY first church, I made a strange discovery that caused me to think even then that my birth name was not sufficiently unique. At our annual regional pastors' gathering for the denomination (seven years before the Roger incident noted before), I was introduced to the larger body along with the other new pastors. Later that evening, someone came to me and asked, "How long were you in San Diego, Gordon?"

Confused, I said that in fact I had never lived in San Diego but had only recently arrived in the Los Angeles area from seminary in Boston.

"That's funny," the person said. "I know I've heard your name around here for years, and I could swear you were in San Diego."

"Are you sure you mean Gordon *Dalbey*?" I asked, hoping to clarify the mistake.

"Oh," he said, smiling even as he knit his brow, puzzled. "I thought you said Gordon Dalbeck."

I confessed that I was still thoroughly confused.

"I guess you don't know that one of our fellow pastors in San Diego is named Gordon Dalbeck," he explained.

"No kidding!" I exclaimed. "What a coincidence!" I made a mental note that someday it'd be fun to get in touch with this fellow pastor with a name so similar to mine, not knowing the shock that awaited.

SOMETIME LATER I RAN ACROSS A BOOK TITLED SIMPLY *HEALING*, in which then-Catholic-priest Francis MacNutt declared that the supernatural workings of the Holy Spirit are alive today even as described and promised in the Bible two thousand years ago. This notion seized my imagination, and in my pastoral calls, I began to pray for physical healing quite specifically. To my amazement and wonder, several persons experienced dramatic recoveries that their doctors could not explain.

Worried I might appear crazy to my family, church, and fellow pastors, I told no one about my experiences. Yet I longed to share them with someone from my oldline church tradition who could validate those experiences and reassure me that I was not only sane but in fact growing into a deeper, more authentic Christian faith.

One day, a flyer appeared in my church mail from the national Parish Renewal Council offering spiritual growth resources through its several regional coordinators. Excitedly, I searched the flyer for a Southern California connection and was delighted to see listed a Rev. Bob Whitaker, the pastor of a Presbyterian church about an hour's drive away.

I called Bob that day, and he reassured me that my experiences were quite biblical and that many in oldline denominations were rediscovering the power of the Holy Spirit as I had been doing. In fact, he said, a group of such pastors had been meeting for several years in the Los Angeles area, and would I like to come to the meetings with him?

I eagerly accepted the invitation and was not disappointed. To talk openly with fellow oldline pastors—Presbyterians, Methodists, Episcopalians, Lutherans—about the present-day reality of Jesus and the Holy Spirit soaked my spirit, which had become parched by rational, intellectual religion. Together we praised Father, Son, and Holy Spirit; together we shared stories of healings; and together we prayed for one another with great expectation.

At one of the first meetings I attended, a pastor spoke on the gift of prophecy, a gift of the Holy Spirit mentioned and described often in the Bible, as in 1 Corinthians 12:10. During ministry time, he prayed that God would release His Spirit to prophesy among us, and then, to my surprise, he immediately came and stood beside me.

Laying his hand on my shoulder, he spoke for perhaps a minute. The only words I recall were: "You are My warrior, and I shall send you forth in My name to overcome and to conquer. You shall lay hands upon My servants and the enemy shall flee from sight; the heavens shall open and you shall see the hosts of heaven rejoicing!"

When the prophecy had been spoken, another pastor remarked, "Man, that was sure some anointing!"

Uncertain myself, being only recently exposed to such activities, I was nevertheless impressed by the general consensus among the others that in those words God had indeed anointed me, that is, had called me to a ministry and given me the power to do it.

But what did it mean to be God's "warrior"? Assuming that the words spoken were, in fact, from God, what sort of overcoming and conquering did God have in mind for me to do? The term *spiritual warfare* had been used occasionally in the group, and I decided that someday I would investigate that.

Not long thereafter, ongoing problems in my marriage began to overwhelm me, and I asked Bob Whitaker if I could come to him for counsel and prayer. Graciously, he agreed to meet weekly with me. Several weeks into our counseling sessions, I attended the previously mentioned denominational meeting during which my supervisor called me Roger.

Though Bob and I originally focused on my marriage issues, when the question of my name appeared so dramatically at the meeting, I was anxious to seek Bob's wisdom.

I recall fairly bursting into his living room for our next counseling session, immediately pouring out what had been happening. "What in the world," I asked finally, "do you think all this business of the name Roger means?"

Bob paused, mulling over my story. "Well," he said finally, "it could mean one of two things. The first is simply that there's someone who looks like you named Roger, and people are getting you confused with that person."

"But that's impossible!" I declared. "I've been mistaken for Roger pretty much everywhere I've lived as an adult, and that means Boston, San Francisco, Chicago, Los Angeles. Nobody named Roger who looks like me could be following my path that closely!" I shifted to the edge of my chair. "So what's the other possibility?"

Bob hesitated, then shrugged his shoulders matter-of-factly. "The other possibility is simply that Roger is your name."

*"What?"* I exclaimed.

"Sure," Bob retorted. "Think about it: at confirmation, Catholics always give young people new names to mark their coming of age and joining the Church."

"You mean, to signify that they belong to the family of God and not to their parents any longer?"

"Of course, that's part of it. But don't forget it's all entirely biblical. Remember when Abram became Abraham? There are all kinds of examples in Scripture where—"

"Like when Jacob became Israel!" I interrupted excitedly.

"Exactly. When God called them into a new sense of mission or direction for their lives, He often did it by giving them a new name. If He can do it for Abraham and Jacob, He surely has the right to give you a new name, too, if He wants to!"

Strange as it sounded at first, it was beginning to make sense. In fact, my parents had not asked God what to name me, even as Zechariah and his relatives simply assumed his son would be named Junior. But even if it was God's will for my parents to name me Junior, God could sovereignly change my name at any time to suit His purpose.

"I'm beginning to see what you mean," I said. "But what do you think I should do about it?"

Excited himself now, Bob leaned forward. "The first thing you need to do is go and find out what Roger means," he smiled. "And then call me!"

Of course! Why hadn't I thought of that years ago? As I sat there, my confusion gave way to excitement—and then fear. Whatever I was to discover in the name Roger defined my life. Up to this point, the issue of my name had been like a treasure hunt, full of adventure and promising to reveal at last who I was created to be. Yet suddenly I was not so sure I wanted this "treasure" to be found. It was clearly no chest of money to be spent in any way I desired, but a definition of my very self in the Creator's terms—no do-as-you-like fantasy, but a commandment, a yoke. Was I ready for this new identity, this ultimate purpose God had ordained for my life? Would I like it? I had not chosen it myself from any list of options; it had been chosen for me. As Bob and I talked further, I remembered Jesus' words to His disciples: "You did not choose me; I chose you."

I knew then that what was happening to me squared with biblical faith. My human nature was balking, but when I looked up the full text of Jesus' words, I was heartily encouraged: "You did not choose me; I chose you and appointed you to go and bear much fruit, the kind of fruit that endures" (John 15:16a).

Certainly, I wanted my life to be fruitful, to accomplish what would truly count for a long time. And then I read Jesus' ultimate assurance immediately following: "And so the Father will give you whatever you ask of him *in my name*" (v. 16b, italics mine). If, therefore, I accepted the call God was placing upon me, I could trust Him to provide whatever I would need to fulfill it—precisely insofar as I called upon Jesus in His *name*, confessing its literal Hebrew meaning, "God is my savior."

Exhilarated, I began to sense what Jesus meant when He said, "The Kingdom of heaven is like this. A man happens to find a treasure hidden in a field. He covers it up again, and is so happy that he goes and sells everything he has, and then goes back and buys that field" (Matt. 13:44). The treasure, I knew, lay before me, for what could be more valuable than knowing why you're here, that is, the Creator's design for your life?

I sighed decisively and turned to Bob. "Where's the nearest library?"

And so, on the brink of a new year—at 4:55 p.m., December 30, 1982—I pulled into the Glendale Public Library parking lot, raced inside to the reference desk, and asked for a book on names.

"We're closing in just a minute," the attendant noted, keys in hand.

"Yes, I know," I said quickly, puffing from my sprint, "but this is very important and will just take me a second."

Glancing at the clock, the attendant reached behind her desk for the name book and handed it to me.

Thanking her, I took it behind a shelf of books and sat down on the carpet, cradling it in my hands. Trembling with excitement, I looked at the book. A mere turn of the pages and I would discover my destiny!

"Attention. The library will be closing in two minutes," boomed a voice over the loudspeaker.

My heart drumming against my ribs, I opened the book and my fingers flew through the pages to *R*.

Ralph . . . Richard . . . and at last, there it was: Roger.

As I read what followed, my jaw dropped and my heart drew up in silent amazement: "Roger: Norse, *Hrothgar*, 'Famous Spear.'"

"Norse!" I exclaimed.

"Attention, the library is now closed. Please bring all books to the counter immediately."

I sat there stunned. Knowing that Dalbey was Norwegian, I could hardly believe my eyes at the apparent coincidence that Roger was also of Norse roots. What could this possibly mean—that I now had two Norwegian names?

*"Attention!"*

Quickly I let the pages flip closed and stopped as my eye caught a "List of the 100 Most Popular Names" at the beginning of the book. I looked, and there at the very end was Roger—number 100, the least popular. One row of overhead lights went out, and I leaped up, sprinted the book back to the reference desk, and headed for the exit.

*Incredible!* I thought, leaning into the library door. Whatever task the Lord was calling me to, a major clue would likely be found in Norway. Furthermore, it would not likely be a popular task.

I had never been to Norway in my life; in fact, the only Norwegian I had ever met was the missionary agriculturist years before in the Nigerian jungle.

*Norway?* I puzzled over this surprising development but could see no possible future scenario for such a trip. As the library door click-locked behind me, I decided to put Norway on a back burner and concentrate on the meaning of the name itself.

A public telephone on the corner ahead caught my eye, and I raced over to make my call. "Hello, Bob?" I burst out. "This is 'Famous Spear'!"

## Chapter 3

# CONFIRMED BY THE BODY

The Spirit gives one person a message full of wisdom, while to
another person the same Spirit gives a message full of knowledge.

—1 CORINTHIANS 12:8

A t our meeting the following week, Bob recalled the pastors' spiritual renewal group and the prophetic ministry that I had received.
"Didn't he say something in his prophecy about you being a warrior?"

"You're right!" I exclaimed. "He talked about my being used to
conquer and that the enemy would 'flee from sight' when I laid
hands on people."

"Well, that seems a very likely confirmation of the Roger name
and 'Famous Spear,'" Bob declared. "Still, I would just begin praying
that if all this is from the Lord, He would continue to confirm it
through other people or situations. Certainly, this is pretty important to the Lord as well as to you—the kind of thing He would want
to make very clear."

On the way home that afternoon, I stopped at a Christian

bookstore to pick up a book on the gifts of the Holy Spirit. As I approached the counter to ask the clerk if he had it, I saw behind him dozens of postcard-sized name posters arranged alphabetically on the wall, each with a common first name followed by its meaning and a related Bible verse. Excitedly, my eyes darted along the letters to *R*, and there it was: "Roger: 'God's Warrior,'" followed by "For the weapons of our warfare are not carnal, but mighty through God. 2 Corinthians 10:4" (KJV).

"Can I help you, please?" the clerk was asking.

"Yes, indeed," I replied, shaking my head and smiling in wonder. "I'll take one of those name posters—the one that says 'Roger.'"

Moments later, I sat quietly amazed in my parked car, the Roger poster propped up on the steering wheel before me. *Lord,* I prayed finally, *if this is really my name, the name You have given me now instead of Earle Gordon, show me in some clear way.*

As I pulled out of the parking lot and headed home, Rev. Gordon Dalbeck came to mind, and I decided to write and ask him how he got his name. In addition, it occurred to me that I had not yet submitted the issue of my name and calling to anyone in my own church for confirmation. I had started a Wednesday evening prayer group a year earlier as part of my growing interest in healing prayer, which drew about five persons regularly; I decided to bring up the issue at our next meeting.

At home, I found Rev. Gordon Dalbeck's address in my Southern California Conference ministers' directory. Curious whether we might be close in age, I decided to check the national directory as well, which lists more detail, including the minister's ordination date.

I leafed casually through the first pages, arrived at the *D*s, and pointed to the top, where the *Da*'s began. Dropping my forefinger from Dack to Dakens, I saw at last the name Dalbeck below it, just above my own. I was about to slide my finger quickly across the line to the date of ordination, when to my utter astonishment I caught the entire listing: Dalbeck, Gordon Earl.

I sat there stunned.

Years earlier, when I had first encountered the name Gordon Dalbeck, it had never occurred to me that he might have another name—and certainly not my very own Earl! In my lifetime, I have known very few Gordons and even fewer Earls.

Not in my wildest imagination would I have thought there might be another man with Earl and Gordon as his first two names— much less one with a last name only two letters away from Dalbey! The fact that there was such a man, and that he was a fellow clergy- man in my own denomination and regional conference, was beyond comprehension. Statistical odds would not allow this as mere coinci- dence. All my rational training as a mathematician and a theologian rose up in protest within me: *This cannot be!*

And yet lying open before me at page 487 was the 1981 national directory of *United Church of Christ Ministers in Full Standing* with the listing "Dalbeck, Gordon Earl." As I sat there, the sensation of biblical fear passed over me yet again, and I knew that I was in the presence of such power, such mystery, that I dare not do anything but follow it.

Pulling myself together, I wrote a letter to Gordon Earl Dalbeck in San Diego, introducing myself as a fellow UCC minister in the area and gingerly telling him how I had occasionally been mistaken for him because of our similar names. I then shared with him my amazement at our having the same two first names and asked if his parents had told him where they got those names and what signifi- cance they might have in his family.

"My parents simply liked the two names," Gordon Earl replied after asking his older brother.

I wondered whether the striking similarity in our names—as clergymen in the same denomination and region—simply underscored the need for a distinctive name for my life and ministry. In any case, it was time to submit the whole issue to my prayer group.

At the next Wednesday night church prayer group, I sat patiently through the others' concerns, wondering how I would bring up the issue of my name. Many of our deep personal needs had surfaced during the months of praying together, and a very special trust had risen among us. But still, this name business could seem pretty bizarre. At one point, it occurred to me that the others might think their pastor had gone crazy for even considering such strange things; maybe it would be better not to bring it up at all.

"Well," I began after we had ministered to all the others, "is there anything else we might want to be praying about?"

The others looked at each other in silence and then shook their heads. "I guess not," said one.

I plunged in.

"Well, I do have something in my life I'd like you all to be praying about," I said. Looking around, I saw the same care and openness in everyone's faces that I had come to trust, so I continued. "I know this may sound a little strange, but I have a sense that the Lord is calling me to a new sort of focus in my ministry, and on top of that, He's giving me a new name to go with it."

I was about to tell them the whole Roger story but drew up as a strange notion occurred to me. "Rather than tell you outright what the name is, why don't you just pray for me now?" I said, pausing.

"And what if I ask that God might show some of you that name, without my telling you, if it's really from Him?"

The group stirred uneasily. "But—of course, there's no way we could know," one said.

"I'm not asking you to know," I explained gently, "but only to be open to the Holy Spirit's showing you. I realize you can't know anything like that in your own human power; that's why we're asking for the power of the Holy Spirit. Don't try to think or imagine anything; just be open as we pray. If nothing at all comes, that's fine, but I would appreciate it if we could just try this—okay?"

Puzzled looks, murmurs, and then finally nods of agreement spread around the group. "Okay," said one. "Let's try it!"

We bowed our heads and waited. "Lord, we thank You for Gordon," one began, "and we ask You to help him with this concern about his name."

More silence. And then another spoke up. "I'm feeling a little uncomfortable praying to know the name the Lord might be giving you," she said. "In fact, I'm sensing that you might be too anxious to give up your name, as if you might need to deal with some troublesome feelings toward your father first."

*Oh no!* I sighed in disgust. *This wasn't what I expected, Father!* I sat quietly, praying for understanding.

"I had the same sense," said another in the group.

Two witnesses. I was busted. "Well, Lord," I prayed out loud, "if I do have some unresolved feelings toward my father that I need to face and deal with, bring them up so I can." In the moments that followed, several past events and feelings came to mind, and the group prayed with me about each. Finally, we sat quietly, and it seemed clear the prayer time was over.

Feeling good about the newly resolved feelings for my father, I was nevertheless disappointed that no answer to the question of my name had come forth. I struggled to give my disappointment to the Lord and trust that what had taken place was in fact appropriate and more important than my own agenda that night.

Later, out in the church parking lot, I saw that two remaining members of the group were saying good-bye and heading for their cars. One of them was a woman who had been particularly responsive to my teaching on the Holy Spirit; in fact, during our prayer times over the months, she had demonstrated a remarkable gift of what the early church called simply "knowledge": "The Spirit gives one person a message full of wisdom, while to another person the same Spirit gives a message full of knowledge" (1 Cor. 12:8). Often when the group seemed stumped and didn't understand what God was doing in a particular situation, much less how to pray for those involved in it, the silence would be broken by this woman. During frustrating moments of long silence in prayer together, I had come to anticipate her quiet "Hmm . . ." as a tentative opening before offering matter-of-factly, "I'm sensing that . . ."

When she shared her perception at that point, inevitably the rest of us would nod in agreement: "Yes, that's what's going on here!" Her initial uneasiness with such prayer—"It's pretty different from what I was used to growing up in church!"—had diminished with experience in the group. Nevertheless, I had not yet told her that I saw this gift of the Holy Spirit at work in her, for fear of short-circuiting her growing into it.

The temptation to do so that night, however, was overwhelming amid my anticipation and disappointment. In a word, I succumbed and called out to her as she was reaching for her car door.

"Before you take off," I blurted, jogging over to her, "I'd appreciate it if . . . maybe you could just pray some more about my name and, you know, maybe ask the Lord if He might show you a name."

"Oh, I don't know," she said hesitantly, stepping back. "I mean, I'm pretty new at all this kind of prayer, and I really don't know much about it."

"Well, in all honesty, I'd rather somebody prayed for me who had so little confidence in themselves, like you," I said, smiling. "That way I'm more likely to get a word from the Lord and not from the person."

We laughed and then fell silent. "Well, actually," she ventured at last, "when we were praying inside, there *was* a name that came to me."

"What?" I exclaimed and then quickly drew back, straining to control my excitement. "I mean, could you . . . maybe just tell me what the name was?"

"Oh, I don't know," she said uneasily. "It just sort of was tumbling around in my mind, and of course I don't know if it's the name you're thinking of."

"Well," I offered evenly—as my heart was pounding, "it's not like I'm putting you personally to the test or anything. I mean, it can't hurt just to tell me what name came to you."

My efforts to restrain my excitement were not well veiled, and she felt the pressure. Nevertheless, she took a deep breath and exhaled nervously. "Well," she offered, "the name I got was Roger."

I smiled thinly and lifted my hands in surrender. "That's it," I said as much to myself as to her. "That's the name!"

"Oh no!" she said, laughing uneasily. "You mean Roger is the name you were talking about, that you think the Lord has given you?"

I nodded, speechless.

"That's amazing!" she exclaimed. "Now how could it be that I would get just that name in my mind?"

"That's the gift of knowledge from the Holy Spirit that I've been teaching about from the Bible," I said, smiling even as the now-familiar biblical fear swept over me. "And it's really true, even today," I added, shaking my head in wonder, "isn't it?"

# Part II

## THE JOURNEY: ENTERING THE BATTLE

## Chapter 4

# BUT THE FIGHTER STILL REMAINS

> Otherwise, I will soon come to you and
> will fight against them with the sword of my mouth.
> —Revelation 2:16

Two years after Pearl Harbor exploded into World War II, amid the joy of a Thanksgiving furlough and the fear of a planet ablaze, I was conceived. From the womb, I learned that war is not an option, but the reality of life in this world.

My father was a career navy officer, and I treasure early memories of his bending over in military khakis to pick me up and hug me after returning from sea duty. Clinging to his neck and dangling high above the ground, I longed to be like this giant man, and the thrill of angling his khaki officer's hat over my forehead and strutting about the kitchen was glorious indeed.

Growing up in the postwar years meant hours of playing war with the other boys—digging foxholes and making broomstick rifles, woodblock walkie-talkies, sand-filled paper-bag grenades, dirt bombs, and a host of other makeshift war materials—all designed to make us feel a part of our fathers' heroic exploits. On rainy days, we went to war indoors, setting up dozens of brown two-inch toy soldiers behind couch pillows, clocks, and picture frames and then moving around "firing" at one another's "men."

When I became old enough to read and then to visit the library, I found myself captivated by magazine photos of battle, from rolling tanks to facedown bodies half covered by sand on D-day. Along with my friends, I cheered at the old John Wayne war movies, and after television arrived—when I was in the second grade—the *Victory at Sea* program.

Unlike today's space-war fantasies spawned by Star Wars and blasted forth on Xboxes, the battles we watched on TV as boys had actually happened, less than a decade earlier, and in fact, our very own fathers had participated. Manly combat in my boyhood was not *apart from*, but manifestly *a part of*, the real world—not divorced from the father, but in fact, defined by him.

Visiting a war-surplus store was therefore a thrill hardly to be matched. Rusted machetes, survival kits, life rafts, combat boots, bayonets, field hammocks, and such stirred a host of adventurous fantasies in my boyhood mind. Once, I discovered a few unopened cans of C rations in my grandfather's house, and several of us had a day to remember, playing war in the basement and taking time out from recon amid the furnace ducts to eat "real army food."

I grew up longing to be a soldier and fight in a war myself, as most of the men around me had done. Deep in my budding masculine soul, I hoped someday there might be another war like the one I'd heard so much about, so I could fight in it and become like those valiant men.

Yet when I entered school, my daily experience suggested that even if such a war might come, I would not measure up. In first grade, it was discovered that my IQ was above average, and after a few years of moving to new schools as a military kid, I skipped two grades. Being thereafter younger and much smaller than my classmates, I became an easy target for bullies, since fighting back was out of the question.

One day in my high school freshman math class, at twelve, the teacher called on me several times when others were stumped by his questions, and I excitedly proclaimed the right answers. When the bell rang, I walked, self-satisfied, out of the classroom—until a shout fired out from a shadowy area just down the hall.

"Hey, *you!*"

Startled, I turned to see one of my heftier classmates, who had missed several answers, staring furiously at me. In the noisy hall, not many heard his shout, but those who did paused and stared.

"You mean . . . me?" I managed very politely, then drew back as others gathered around us.

With a menacing glare, he drew closer. "Yeah, smart-ass, I mean you!"

Before I could say another word, he seized my shoulders and slammed me painfully up against the lockers with a resounding clang. "Next time, you watch out who you go showin' up in class— y'hear me?"

"Uh—sure," I gasped, wincing.

Haughtily, he jerked his head in the direction of the shadows, and several others stepped out behind him. "Let's go," he scoffed, tossing a contemptuous glance in my direction.

Undaunted by this and other similar experiences, I clung to my dream of someday fighting in a war. When I entered college just before my sixteenth birthday, the navy ROTC program promised the opportunity for me not only to fight in a war but also to wear my very own navy officer's hat. As the son of a career officer, I felt sure I would be accepted. Indeed, the director of the ROTC program told me my young age would be no problem, and when I took the written intelligence test, I scored in the high nineties.

That afternoon I reported to the hospital for my physical exam. I recognized several others there from my freshman dorm, and we began talking about last week's football game, the tough calculus course, and what the ROTC program might be like. Whatever the program held in store, I knew I was going to like being with these guys.

Soon each of us was given a check-sheet to take through the various stations of the physical, at each of which a navy doctor conducted the focal part of the examination and signed the "Approved" column. After scoring above average at all stations, from push-ups to blood work, I turned at last to the final test, for eyes. I'd always had excellent vision, and with a full list of approval signatures so far, I strode confidently toward the eye doctor's room.

Brian, one of my dorm mates, was just coming out smiling broadly. "Good luck!" he shot out crisply.

"Thanks!" I fired back, hoping my confidence showed.

Inside, the doctor greeted me quickly and pointed to a chair. Sitting down, I noticed a strange-looking instrument on the table beside him—about a foot high and half as wide, dark gray, with two tiny holes aligned vertically, resembling a small stoplight. When he had pronounced my distance vision 20/20, he asked me to stand across the room and watch the instrument on the table. He noted that the holes had lights in them—white, red, or green—and that he was going to flash them randomly. Turning off the room lights, he flipped the machine switch.

"Just tell me what two colors you see," he instructed.

Two small spotlight holes appeared. Both looked alike, though to my surprise, I couldn't tell what color they were.

"Just tell me the color," the doctor said again, noticing my hesitation.

Puzzled, I balked. "Both look white," I allowed, as a strange uneasiness crept over me.

"We'll try two more," he said, pushing a button. Another click, and the two lights fell dark and then bright again.

Knitting my brow, I focused intently on the twin beams. *Were they light green? The top one looked sort of white—the bottom one might be red. . . .*

"Can you tell me the colors?" the doctor asked, his voice ringing out impatiently.

Desperately, I squinted hard, then shook my head. "Could you maybe just show me a white light by itself, so I could tell the difference, and then a green and—"

"I'm sorry," he said, "but you'll have to tell me as you look at them."

"I . . . I don't know what . . . to say," I stammered. "They all . . . seem the same color . . . to me."

The doctor switched off the machine, turned on the lights, and pulled a small book off a shelf, then opened it and laid it before me. On each thick cardboard page lay a large splattering of dots, variously shaded and sized, arranged in a circle. *What's going on?* I wondered. *What's this got to do with being a navy officer?*

"Tell me what number you see when you look at these dots," the doctor said.

To my relief, I saw a "39" formed by several dots and said so.

He turned the page, and I reported a vague "24." *Whew!* I thought. *At least I can see the numbers!* On the next page, however, I saw nothing discernible among the cluster. Just dark and light shaded dots.

The doctor flopped the book shut with a loud, decisive thwack. "I'm sorry," he said, turning to sign my sheet, "but you're color-blind." As he handed the paper out to me, I saw the long line of signatures broken at the bottom by a single scrawl in the "Negative" column.

Stunned, I drew back, afraid to touch it. "Wh-what do you mean?" I mumbled.

"You're color-blind," he repeated. "Both tests showed it clearly."

"B-but I saw the numbers in the dots!" I protested.

"Those are the numbers you see if you're color-blind," he noted. "People with normal color vision see different numbers in those dots than you did."

Bewildered, I panicked. "Does that . . . I mean, what . . . difference does that make?"

"Well, a lot of difference." He shrugged matter-of-factly. "Navy ships have green lights on one side and white on the other. If you're standing deck watch at night and you see another ship heading toward yours, you need to be able to tell which direction it's coming from or the ships could collide."

I stood there frozen in shock, my heart pounding furiously. "Oh," I murmured finally, "I . . . I guess that makes sense." Unwilling to leave, unable to stay, I gazed in terror at the sheet of paper in the doctor's outstretched hand.

"I'm sorry," he said. "But others are waiting outside."

Mechanically, I reached out and took the paper. "Uh . . . yeah," I muttered. Quickly I turned and left.

Out in the hall, I paused in disbelief. How could this be? I'd been driving a car for almost a year and never had trouble making out stoplight colors. Sure, other kids had teased me once in a while when I didn't see some colors just right, but—

"How'd it go?"

Jarred, I turned and saw Brian stepping toward me from the group of dorm guys. In the background, the others were punching each other good-naturedly on the arm and chattering about the day's adventure.

"Well, not so good," I said. A burst of laughter rang out at someone's joke in the group behind, and I looked. "Actually, I, well, I didn't make it."

"Gee . . . I'm sorry," Brian offered sincerely.

"Well . . . see you back at the dorm," I muttered and turned away, fumbling with the paper. Moments later, from the other end of the hall, more laughter echoed as I grasped the knob, leaned into the heavy door, and stepped outside.

On that day, in that moment, all my hopes of becoming a man and a warrior—like my father—exploded in an undifferentiated flash of red, green, and white light. I could not allow myself to grieve that loss, because I knew then, as did every boy in my generation, that real men don't cry—unless, of course, they wanted someone to give them something to cry about.

A few weeks later, I was startled to feel numbness beginning to spread along my left arm and the entire left side of my body. As this tingling sensation left and returned randomly, I became frightened and eventually made an appointment to consult the dean of students. Seated uneasily on the far side of his huge mahogany desk, I told this heavy, dark-suited, white-haired man that I wasn't doing as well in my studies as I wanted to and described the sudden sensation of numbness that had struck me.

"What you need, son," he declared, smiling quickly, "is a schedule." From one of several broad drawers, he took a sheet of paper crisscrossed with a matrix of clock times and blank spaces. "You just fill in these spaces for every fifteen minutes of your day, and come back and see me in two weeks."

Dutifully, I returned to my dorm room and, calculating my study time, filled in the grid. Two days later, however, I not only hadn't kept my schedule, but also felt ashamed for not keeping it. In a moment of hopeless anger, I balled up the paper and threw it into the trash can.

I never went back to see the dean.

Soon afterward, I began looking for some way to sublimate my wounded energies. My course work offered the most likely opportunity, although it was not at all clear to me where to focus. When I was a high school sophomore, Communist Russia had launched *Sputnik*, the first spacecraft. Thereafter, career counselors did not ask good male high school students, "What field do you want to major in at college?" but only, "What science?"

As valedictorian of my high school class, I had struggled with this question and decided that I would major in mathematics. My father, who had received his MBA as part of his navy training, had told me of a new company he had heard about called IBM, which was developing something called a computer. He encouraged me to prepare for "a great opportunity to work there."

I recall, therefore, being startled in the second week of my college career as my freshman English professor handed back our first essay assignments. When all in the class had apparently received theirs, I had not. I was about to raise my hand to ask for my essay when he proceeded to remind the class of his writing standards—and began reading from my essay as a model example.

Confused, I balked. This was not the plan at all. I was supposed to be a mathematician and scientist, to save America from Russian domination—not a writer!

As THE SEMESTER UNFOLDED, HOWEVER, I FOUND MYSELF RUSHing through my calculus and chemistry assignments, then sneaking over to a corner of the Student Union lounge and struggling hour after glorious hour with ideas and sentence structure for my weekly essay assignment. And those were the days of liquid ink pens, before not only computers, but typewriters. When eventually I finished the term with an A in English and only a B in calculus, I felt embarrassed, if not ashamed. *How will I explain the A in English?*

Later, I considered majoring in English instead of math. After several other English courses, however, I realized that the academic literary discipline focused mostly on criticism of noted authors and not on original writing by students themselves. And so, because I had come to enjoy writing so much, I majored in math. In 1964 I graduated with one of the few bachelor of arts degrees in that major—and confounded the math department with my C average in course work and score of 99 on the math Graduate Record Examination. For decades thereafter, I had nightmares of facing a coming final exam for a course in which I had enrolled but rarely, if ever, attended.

It never occurred to me that writing could in any way address my urge to become a warrior—much less serve as a weapon itself. Even as my graduation approached, I wanted very much to serve my country. But if I couldn't be a navy officer like my father, I decided simply not to join the military. No high-minded pacifist, I was just a wounded son. When my draft board signaled its intentions shortly before June, I chose instead to join the Peace Corps—and "See the World," as the navy recruitment ads proclaimed.

THE PEACE CORPS ASSIGNED ME TO TEACH MATHEMATICS AT A Catholic boys' secondary school in rural Nigeria. There, the puzzling contrast between my Western rationalism and the local spirituality soon became apparent. I recall one student—call him Peter—who came to me desperately seeking help shortly before the do-or-die West African School Certificate examination. The outcome of this test would determine whether his six years of secondary education—paid for by a host of relatives, all expecting a "return" when he graduated into a well-paying job—were a success or failure. Peter was suffering severe anxiety and headaches. "We know that America has powerful medicine," he declared and begged me to give him some "America medicine" to help him succeed in his exams.

Not far from where I taught Peter about congruent triangles, his father served as priest at a local juju shrine. "My people say that my headaches are from our family's enemies, who want to put a spell on me and make me fail my examinations," Peter moaned. Scoffing, I went to my Peace Corps medical kit and tossed him several aspirin.

My naturalistic, scientific, Western mind had many opportunities to scoff during those two years in Nigeria, as I often heard such stories about evil spirits and their oppressive tactics. As I righteously passed out aspirin, never once did it occur to me that my own perspective on spiritual reality might be prejudiced.

Nor did I recognize in Peter any part of my own self just a few years earlier as a young college student, paralyzed in fear that I might fail the parents who had invested so much hope in me. Nor, indeed, that I had myself become the very college dean who had callously tossed me a schedule organizer and dismissed my true needs as a bewildered freshman.

Yet even if I had been able to sympathize with Peter's fears and comfort him, my own Western materialistic worldview blinded me to any spiritual dimension of his problem—as it blinded me to my own. In fact, Peter frightened me, because I knew that aspirin had not healed my fears, either.

By the end of my tour in Nigeria, I was convinced that I had served my country better in the Peace Corps than in any way my draft board might devise. Accordingly, I maintained my military deferment by studying journalism in graduate school. During that summer of 1967, I volunteered to join an American Friends Service Committee project to help white suburbanites in Los Angeles recognize and combat racism in their midst.

Though cordially received by community organizations, we were largely discounted as troublemakers, much to my naive surprise. With the objectivity gained by my experience in Nigeria, I saw for the first time the darker side of the white, middle-class neighborhood that had nurtured me as a boy. And I readily connected its racism to a militaristic spirit of domination over others who have less worldly power.

Torn and confused at the end of my graduate studies, I flirted briefly with the army and even sought a commission. The process included facing a panel of several army review officers. After examining me with standard questions, one noted my background.

"We often hear that Peace Corps people are anti-American when they come back," he said. "What about you?"

I drew back, surprised, then took a deep breath and said that I regarded my Peace Corps service as an expression of my love for America. With a rustle of papers, my inquisitor passed to the others on the panel; I was soon graciously dismissed. Two weeks later, I received in the mail a packet of army orders to missile-training school, with a cover letter that began, "Dear Lieutenant Dalbey." Forced to decide on this last chance to become an official soldier, I realized that something was amiss in my warrior ambitions, something beyond mere filial loyalties. Uncertain but determined, I declined the offer and found a deferment job teaching "an essential subject in a culturally deprived community"—that is, junior high math among immigrant, Spanish-speaking Californians.

During this period, as the Vietnam War escalated amid growing protest at home, I began to hail the antiwar movement with great gusto, much to my naval-officer father's dismay. If the truth be told, I embraced the rebellious spirit of the age precisely in order to disconnect from my father and the shame of not measuring up to his standard as a military officer and businessman.

Through all the pain that my belated adolescent rebellion both surfaced and wrought, however, I knew in my heart that my authentic future could only proceed out of affirming where I had come from—even, indeed especially, the parts of me that my father's life had modeled.

As then dean of the chapel Rev. Davie Napier of Stanford

preached one Sunday morning: "Ours is a task not to curse the past but to redeem it, in the true prophetic tradition." I was so moved by that statement that I based an article on it titled "The Great White Son Turns Left," which at twenty-six I sold to the *Christian Century.*

Thereafter, I began publishing in many denominational church magazines. Perhaps my most revealing article from that time—and today the most surprisingly apt, given how little I knew then of what was to come in my life—appeared in a 1972 issue of the Quaker *Friends Journal* titled "Li'l Bad Wolf: Wm. Penn, Jr." Significantly, my byline read "E. Gordon Dalbey, Jr.," and the article itself dealt explicitly with a boy's struggle at once to identify with his father and become his own man—just as in my boyhood the popular comic book character Li'l Bad Wolf always failed to live up to his crafty father's ambition, even unto rescuing the Three Little Pigs from his father's clutches.

The Quakers are pacifists, and in that sense they represented to the antiwar movement a viable position of strength amid charges that we were "chicken" for not taking up arms. Certainly, I recognized the real pain, if not danger, in a young man's trying to cut himself off from his father. Indeed, during a brief stint as a substitute English teacher while crashing at a commune, I stumbled upon a biography of William Penn, founder of the American Quaker movement, and was amazed to discover not only that William was a "Jr.," but also that his father, William Sr., was a highly successful officer in the British Navy. This drew me personally into Penn's story, as my father had become a Quaker before World War II and maintained his membership throughout his military career and after for sixty years. This pacifist/warrior conundrum thereby framed my model of manhood, and its apparent cognitive dissonance served as the proverbial grain of sand in the oyster that spurred me after resolution into manhood.

As a reward for his naval victories, Admiral William Penn Sr. was given a large estate in southern Ireland, seized from the Irish in a forced British takeover. Even as he eventually came to disclaim the imperial rewards of his father's professional achievements, the well-bred younger Penn nevertheless fulfilled his heritage and destiny of authority. Indeed, becoming "admiral" of the Quaker forces in America consummated the identity of William Penn Jr. Just as John the Baptist fulfilled his priest father as he preached with priestly conviction, so William Penn Jr. fulfilled his loyalist, warrior father by preaching loyalty to God and commanding the pacifist "troops."

In spite of such rational published insight, in 1972 I had not yet resolved my own adolescent rebellion toward my father. Contrary to popular consensus, I found it hard to believe that either the Viet Cong or the Russians were the true enemy. Even as I recognized its repressive, totalitarian application, neither did communism seem a viable candidate—if only because its basic premises of equality and communal cooperation seemed intrinsic to Christianity itself: "They [the believers] would sell their property and possessions, and distribute the money among all, according to what each one needed" (Acts 2:45). Or as the Communists put it, "From each according to his ability, to each according to his need."

Since my adolescent rebellion had cast my military father as the enemy, a simple leap of logic led me to conclude that the enemy was simply the warrior himself. My efforts toward "peacemaking" therefore focused on undermining and eliminating the warrior. And so together, marching for "peace and love," my generation sang Native American folksinger Buffy St. Marie's "The Universal Soldier": "He's the one who gives his body as a weapon to a war, / And without him all this killing can't go on."

I soon became angry and disgusted at the many "martial" church hymns, such as "Onward, Christian Soldiers," and resolved never to sing them again. Luther's "A Mighty Fortress Is Our God" was especially suspect, for—astonishing then to my antimilitary sensibilities— not only did it decry "this world with devils filled," but it also portrayed Jesus as a warrior: "Lord Sabbaoth, his name, from age to age the same, / And he must win the battle."

The issue, meanwhile, was not simply that men were fighting, but whom they were fighting, namely, each other. Even as I sang my case against the "universal soldier," I sensed that ultimately the source of war-making was no human being, that underneath our apparent "warrior" and "peacemaker" labels, we human beings were commonly subject to some larger destructive impetus, which could lead even peace workers to become violent. The secular youth culture around me, rebelling as it was against fathers, readily identified the enemy as masculinity. Hence, the politically correct, feminine goddesses of grace and tolerance righteously displaced the religiously correct, masculine gods of judgment and punishment. Even as Mom had saved us from Dad's harshness, we looked now to the women to save us from war.

HUMAN WILL CLEARLY CONTRIBUTED SIGNIFICANTLY TO THE problem. But if our faulty choices composed its sum total, I could only focus my anger on another human being for making those choices—even the warrior—and thus fuel the very antagonism I wanted to extinguish.

What's more, even as I dismissed the warrior in my peace activism, I could not escape a deep desire within me to fight against evil on behalf of good. No matter how fiercely I now scorned the soldier's bayonet, Superman's body of steel, or the Lone Ranger's silver bullets, my boyhood impulse to fight for the good never left me. And though I rejected the world's armed soldier model, nevertheless I could not see how, in this violently broken world, my becoming a passive milquetoast—no matter how holy—could serve God's purposes.

As a frustrating counterpoint to "The Universal Soldier," I sang Paul Simon's "The Boxer"—who, spent and empty, lays down his gloves and declares that he is leaving the ring, "but the fighter still remains."

My dilemma was as frustrating as it was clear. As a boy, I had rejected the bully model of soldier, who fights to hide his own inadequacy. As I became a man, my father's "Greatest Generation" World War II soldier, who fought against fanatical regimes, seemed to cry out for a more redemptive, even enduring victory. And the pacifist, who never fought, didn't register in my heart at all.

More than ever, I was determined to fight for the good. But I could never quite discern just what evil I was to fight against.

And that deadly shortsightedness, as we shall see, undermines the true warrior today.

## Chapter 5

# JESUS, THE WARRIOR KING

But the LORD is with me like a mighty warrior.

−JEREMIAH 20:11 NIV

I dentifying the genuinely evil enemy was not easy for me as a young man. The only war I knew going on at that time was in Vietnam, and it was not at all clear to me, in spite of our national involvement, that we were fighting the true enemy there. Not only had President Johnson fabricated the Gulf of Tonkin incident that prompted it, but Viet Cong leader Ho Chi Minh also had long before expressed his admiration of the U.S. Constitution. Even after the war, the feared repressive Communist regime never materialized there.

Logically, the peace movement's view of the warrior as the enemy could only make me want to destroy warriors—and thereby become myself the very destroyer-of-life that I wanted to overcome. The bombing of draft boards, for example, which some promoted, seemed to me the selfsame violence that I scorned in the military. How was I to wage peace without being destructive?

Not until the late 1970s was I freed from this dilemma by Holocaust survivor Elie Wiesel in his essay "The Jew and War." "When men go to war," Wiesel wrote, "God is their first victim." From the very first war between brothers Cain and Abel, war has "always represented absolute evil and chaos. . . . War is an aberration, a denial of God's name, which is . . . Peace."[1]

*Amen!* I thought.

Striking closer to home, even at my boyhood fantasies of soldier heroics, Wiesel then warned that war must never be glorified:

> We must never endow [war] with a loftier meaning, a spiritual dimension that would embellish it. Even in ancient times, when other nations looked upon war as an exciting, romantic, or mystical adventure, Jews looked upon it as a curse. War does not elevate, war is not an ideal, and we must not idealize it.[2]

While I could not then acknowledge the authentic spiritual dimension of warfare any more than Wiesel, his basic point made sense. If, indeed, God is against war and wants His people to proclaim that, then the very geography of the promised land ensures they must. Insofar as Israel lies between the ancient warring superpowers Egypt and Babylonia/Assyria, no nation so battered about on all sides by such military giants could affirm war-making. Americans, on the other hand, geographically removed from the great wars in Europe and Asia, are particularly tempted to idealize war—as in Rambo movies, GI Joe and Star Wars toys, Xbox combat games, and the like.

My boyhood enthusiasm for war-making was fueled not only by

such fantasies, but also by the simple fact that my father and his fellow American soldiers won their war. As a boy, I knew that games are far more fun when you win—especially war-games, because their life-or-death stakes are the highest of all contests. Wiesel cut even that prop out from under me: "It is easy to hate war when one is defeated, but Jews have hated war even when they won. We never seem to hate the enemy; it is war we hate, it is war we consider the enemy."[3]

As I read those words, a floodlight burst forth in my mind. *Of course! The warrior is not the enemy; war is the enemy!* If, as the old adage declares, God hates the sin but loves the sinner, then God hates war even as He loves the warrior. This confirmed my own basic conviction that I did not want to destroy warriors, but I did want to eliminate wars. Indeed, soldiers, whom war kills, cannot be the enemy but are, in fact, the manifest victims!

Even as it excited me, this new insight led me to further unsettling questions:

- If, indeed, the enemy of God's people is war, then why does God send His people into war throughout the Old Testament?
- How do you focus a fight against so vast a human enterprise as war itself without succumbing to its very murderous impulses?
- If war is the ultimate enemy, the agent that most deeply frustrates God's purposes in this world, then what about other equally viable candidates, such as hunger, poverty, and disease, which often kill more people than wars? And what about human character traits such as jealousy, hate, and pride, which seem to fuel most armed conflict? Indeed, a

variety of evil takes place even in countries that are not fighting military battles.

- As a tool of evil, war certainly contributes heavily to poverty and hunger by diverting resources, and it fosters hatred and pride. But war itself cannot account for all evil in the world.

Clearly, something even more evil must underlie war.

Militant "hawks" had often hurled the first question at me. I could only respond that Jesus was clearly against killing in any form and blessed the peacemakers as the true "children of God" (Matt. 5:9 NLT). "Nevertheless," my challengers would say, "you can't cite Old Testament texts like 'beat their swords into plowshares' to support your disarmament position and conveniently overlook the many other times when God sends His people into armed battles!"

Good point. I could, of course, simply eliminate the Old Testament witness entirely from my peacemaking ministry. Yet I've always been suspicious of "Christians" who, like the ancient Marcionite heretics, are anxious to exclude the Jewish texts. The Old Testament was Jesus' Bible, and He declared that He did not come to abolish its precepts but to fulfill them. Somehow those stories of God sending His people into armed battles had to be redeemed, not discounted. But how?

On the one hand, the religious hawks affirmed ancient Israel's war-making as a license for Christians to wield weapons against other, presumably less righteous nations—as in the Crusades. On the other hand, the pacifist "doves" wanted to dismiss the Old Testament wars altogether as primitive and to exclude from the faith any notion of enemy and battle—from "martial" hymns to demons.

In the old covenant, God was training His people for the coming of the Messiah, preparing them for a new covenant as the ultimate revelation of His presence and power on earth (Jer. 31:31–40). The Israelites, oppressed militarily by large surrounding nation-enemies, accordingly looked forward to a messiah after the model of David, the warrior king, to save them.

While flirting with pacifism, I had decided that in Jesus, the joke was on Israel; instead of a military savior, God had sent a noncombatant lover as a surprise, to call into account His people's shortsighted, human-centered worldview. In the Old Testament, that is, God had used available historical props, such as kings and wars, to teach His people the elementary lessons of morality and faith. But when Jesus comes, clearly the warrior must go, for the Messiah manger-child proclaims that God's way is peace and love, not war and hate.

From this perspective, Jesus is the antithesis of the warrior, who thereby becomes the enemy of God. But Elie Wiesel had convinced me that any argument that allowed such a conclusion was spurious, that war—not the warrior—is the enemy.

My reasoning had led me to a dead end.

PUZZLED, I REALIZED THAT MY CONFUSION HAD BEEN PROMPTED by the Old Testament wars, so I decided to reexamine those stories. In doing so, I was convinced yet again that, indeed, the God of Israel scorns any reliance whatsoever upon physical military power. Nevertheless, I was still baffled by the apparent contradiction that this same God often orders His people into battle, even to take the offensive at times.

For example, when the Israelites return to the promised land after being exiled generations before by the murderous Babylonians, the prophet Zechariah proclaims to King Zerubbabel, "The angel told me to give Zerubbabel this message from the LORD: "You will succeed, not by military might or by your own strength, but by my spirit" (Zech. 4:6).

Again, from Isaiah: "Woe to those who go down to Egypt for help and rely on horses, who trust in chariots because they are many and in horsemen because they are very strong, but do not look to the Holy One of Israel or consult the LORD!" (31:1 NIV).

The message is clear: In the battles of this world, God's people are not saved by guns and bombs; but neither are we saved by abstract ideologies such as pacifism or tolerance. Indeed, all of these are human fabrications. The issue for God is not correctness, whether religious or political, but faithfulness.

That is, nothing human hands make nor human minds conceive can save us. From this view, peace is defined not by the absence of conflict but by the presence of God, and peace can therefore become an idol as readily as war if it does not proceed from surrender to Him.

Jesus does not bring us peace; "he *is* our peace" (Eph. 2:14 KJV, italics mine). He did not come simply to stop wars but to restore the kingdom of God on earth as it is in heaven. He is first and foremost not the way to peace but the way to the Father (John 14:6). This does not mean that God is a bloodthirsty tyrant who thrives on making war. It simply means that He is God. In biblical faith, victory begins with wholesale focus on God and ends not with the mere cessation of hostilities but with His active rule.

Yes, Jesus taught, the peacemakers receive the blessing of being called God's true children (Matt. 5:9). But to a Jew, to make peace meant to be agents of shalom, that is, those who—as John the Baptist exhorted—prepare the way for God to come and rule (Matt. 3:1–3). Seek first to establish His kingdom, Jesus declared, and circumstances will then follow according to His will (Matt. 6:33).

In fact, peace is a fruit of the Holy Spirit (Gal. 5:22). As such, it's not the natural result of our efforts but the supernatural result of God's efforts. God will therefore take care of external circumstances insofar as we are surrendered to and trusting in Him to act in and through us.

This does not mean simply pulling the covers over your head and expecting God to do it all, but rather stepping out as He calls, trusting Him to provide the resources and weapons necessary to do it together.

The Old Testament story of the weak-kneed Gideon, whom God called as judge to destroy the enemy Midianite army, portrays this truth graphically. Gideon, who in his fear tested God several times with a wet-and-dry fleece before advancing the army, raises a huge contingent of some thirty thousand Israelites for the battle. But God pares it down to a mere three hundred men, explaining to Gideon, "The men you have are too many for me to give them victory over the Midianites. They might think that they had won by themselves, and so give me no credit" (Judg. 7:2).

The God of Israel tells His people to distrust military power—not because it's intrinsically evil, but precisely insofar as it keeps them from recognizing and trusting in His power instead. Again the overriding issue here is neither increased firepower nor disarmament, but idolatry—attributing saving power to either weaponry and soldiers or pacifist ideology instead of to God.

Disarmament thereby becomes idolatry insofar as it stems from a rational ideology rather than wholesale dependence on God to reveal His battle plan. Laying down arms bears no more saving power per se than taking up arms—and could well be patently foolish, if not suicidal.

Under the old covenant, therefore, military battles remained a common, appropriate context for God's saving action. Yet to affirm the new covenant witness in the life of Jesus—who never took up arms and who said, "Blessed are the peacemakers"—would necessarily mean to renounce killing and physical violence as means of achieving God's purposes.

I could see only one way out of this dead end, only one way to redeem warfare as a modern context for God's saving action, namely, that *God must be calling His people today to some other war besides armed military conflict.*

What that other war might be, I couldn't say precisely, but it would have to be essentially, even manifestly, spiritual. From this perspective, the battles of ancient Israel could be affirmed as a preparation, a training exercise for this other, spiritual battle to be revealed in the messianic age to come.

This is not, as Wiesel warned, to embellish guns and bombs with "a spiritual dimension," but rather to engage an entirely new dimension of war itself, in which guns and bombs are subject to God's purposes, if not irrelevant. "The weapons we use in our fight," as the apostle Paul put it, "are not the world's weapons, but God's powerful weapons, which we use to destroy strongholds" (2 Cor. 10:4). Neither atomic bombs nor disarmament alone can mediate sufficient power to accomplish God's purposes for humankind.

From this view, Israel's biblical history could be seen as a prototype, a revelation of God's personality, a model of God's relationship with His people for all time. The natural, historical events that the Bible records among the Jewish people must therefore reflect a more pervasive, timeless spiritual reality, namely, that what happened to the Jews happens to all who seek to identify with their God.

In the Jewish people, the transcendent thereby becomes historical, the spiritual becomes physical, Jacob becomes Israel, God becomes human, the Word becomes flesh—and, at last, the very particular call to one small nation long ago becomes the universal call to us all today.

In the biblical worldview, not only does sacred become flesh, but flesh becomes sacred—a patent impossibility within our Western dualistic mind-set. As the communion bread and wine herald supernatural reality, so what happens in the natural world can be seen, as the traditional definition of *sacrament*, as "an outward sign of inward, spiritual grace."

In this melding of the natural and supernatural, the old covenant war stories become *a handbook for spiritual warfare in the messianic age*—a physical reflection of a spiritual reality recognizable only to those who acknowledge the new covenant Messiah and the consequences of His coming.

This interface between physical and spiritual reality in the old covenant wars became more plausible to me as I considered the positive side of the coin: *God is love.* But God did not demonstrate that simply by raining down warm, fuzzy feelings on His people; He sent His Son, the flesh-and-blood Jesus of Nazareth.

Even now we understand that God is the source of love (1 John 4:7), which is fundamentally a spiritual reality that takes on flesh in human responses. So God often responds to our emotional/supernatural need for love by sending another physical human being to manifest it.

Christians pray regularly for physical events to reflect spiritual reality: "Thy Kingdom come," Jesus prayed, "*on earth* as it is in heaven" (Matt 6:10, italics mine). Jesus did not come to bring us to heaven but rather to bring heaven to us. Good acts in this world—from charity gifts to affectionate touch—may reflect the larger theater of God's spiritual victory among us.

Similarly, physical military battles under the old covenant may reflect *the larger theater of yet-to-be-resolved conflict that hinders God's kingdom rule and purposes among us on earth.*

The Messiah—in whom God's Spirit takes on natural flesh, through whom His Spirit is actively revealed and released into the natural world—must be the appropriate focus of resolution in that conflict. And if, indeed, Jesus yet lives, then the spiritual battle that He came to reveal two thousand years ago is still at hand. What's more, His victory is at hand even today for us to appropriate. Indeed, the power we need in order to claim victory in that battle must have been accessible to us all those years since His coming.

The more sensible these conclusions became to me, the more chagrined I became to realize how blind I, like the historic church, had been to this basic reality. I knew that the Messiah brought special power into the world, ostensibly to perform some special, even ultimate, accomplishment. A simple change of enemy nations, however, as from Philistines to Nazis to Communists to Taliban, would not suffice the advent of such all-encompassing power.

If Israel was called to be a "light to the nations" (Isa. 42:6), a revelation of God's nature and power to humankind, surely it was called ultimately to herald victory over a far greater enemy than simply another nation, such as the Philistines—or even over war itself, as the redemption of humankind encompasses not simply the cessation of hostilities but also surrender to God's kingdom rule and enactment of His purposes. Armed military conflict must therefore signal an even more pervasive, foundational saboteur.

Whatever destroys life opposes the Creator of life; war is not the only context for such destruction and cannot, therefore, in itself comprise the ultimate enemy of God's purposes. Insofar as the Messiah came to fulfill God's purposes on earth, He came to destroy all the enemy's works of sabotage—not just war-making (1 John 3:8).

With this understanding, I faced a startling conclusion, one that upended both my boyhood war cry and my adolescent peace-marching: *Ancient Israel's battles are a prototype of the larger, spiritual conflict that the Messiah revealed.* What's more, *Jesus is indeed the Son of David*—neither the Eternal Pacifist come to proclaim that wars have ended, nor the Immanent Tyrant come to destroy all who disagree with Him.

In fact, *Jesus is the warrior king* come at last to summon God's people to the true and ultimate spiritual battle at hand, now as from the very genesis of humankind.

It made sense. When Jesus healed a man "who was blind and could not talk because he had a demon," everyone was amazed—not primarily at what He had done, miraculous as it was, but at who He might be by virtue of His firepower. "'Could He be the Son of David?' they asked" (Matt. 12:22–23).

At first, I balked at this notion of Jesus as warrior king, mostly because my image of David, the warrior king, was prejudiced by my own antimilitary rebellion against my father. Of David's battle exploits, I could remember only swords and blood. When I reread David's first recorded battle, however—against Goliath—I was surprised to find him portrayed explicitly as a spiritual warrior and, thus, an altogether appropriate forebear of Jesus.

I had heard the story often as a child in Sunday school and

thrilled in my little boy's body to think that a kid my size could whip such a big bully as Goliath. Like tiny Israel taunted by the great superpowers Egypt and Babylonia, I longed for that kind of power amid the playground tough guys. Upon rereading the story as an adult, however, I was startled to hear young David proclaim to Goliath that he claimed no power of his own for the victory:

> You are coming against me with sword, spear, and javelin, but I come against you in the name of the LORD Almighty, the God of the Israelite armies, which you have defied. This very day the LORD will put you in my power; I will defeat you and cut off your head. And I will give the bodies of the Philistine soldiers to the birds and animals to eat. Then the whole world will know that Israel has a God, and everyone here will see that the Lord does not need swords or spears to save his people. He is victorious in battle, and he will put all of you in our power. (1 Sam. 17:45–47)

Gruesome, yes—but the basic orientation of a true spiritual warrior.

From a purely physical, military perspective, it clearly was no contest—like Jesus against the giant Roman Empire. Yet even as Goliath fell before David, the Roman emperor lay prostrate at the cross of Jesus by the fourth century AD. And no Christian had lifted sword, spear, or javelin against Rome.

I SAW NO WAY AROUND IT: AS THE SON, AND THEREBY SPIRITUAL heir, of David's kingdom, Jesus came to proclaim precisely the God of David who is "victorious in battle"—yet "does not need swords or spears to save His people." He came among us primarily not to announce peace on earth but as the first step toward that end, to declare outright and manifest war against God's enemy—that is, to show God's people the true battle in the spiritual realm, which we dare not recognize until we have the power to win it.

At last, I saw it: Jesus is no Grand Facilitator of the flower children such as I was, flashing peace signs and scorning the warrior: *He is the Commander in Chief of God's army, come into the world to recruit and empower spiritual warriors in this, the messianic age.*

The people of Israel did not recognize Jesus, therefore, not because they had wrongly expected the Messiah to be a warrior king, but because *they did not recognize the war He had come to win.* Insofar as Israel is God's prototype of larger humanity, this is why people don't recognize Jesus even today.

When people do not recognize the spiritual battle at hand, they cannot recognize Jesus. Indeed, the enemy of God takes advantage of their myopic vision by ultimately causing them to misfocus on each other as enemies. The shameful division in the larger church today is thereby a clear indication that Christians are mostly blind to the reality of spiritual warfare.

Nothing obviates division and promotes unity like the danger of a common enemy. Communist Russia and capitalist America, for example, were allies when the Nazis threatened, and they became enemies after Armistice.

Peace defined apart from surrender to God can become an idol, an easy diversion from His purposes, even a wolf in sheep's clothing. In a diabolic irony, insofar as various Christian denominations and factions deny the reality of evil and fancy that "the war is over," peace can become a license to compete and battle with each other—instead of at last joining forces against their common spiritual enemy. "They dress the wound of my people as though it were not serious," as Jeremiah scoffed. "'Peace, Peace,' they say, when there is no peace" (Jer. 6:14 NIV).

When the Pharisees accuse Jesus of driving out demons by the power of "their ruler Beelzebul," Jesus turns to military language and declares:

> So if one group is fighting another in Satan's kingdom, this means that it is already divided into groups and will soon fall apart! . . . No, it is not Beelzebul, but God's Spirit, who gives me the power to drive out demons, which *proves that the Kingdom of God has already come upon you.* (Matt. 12:26, 28, italics mine)

As I entertained this notion of spiritual warfare, I knew that my rational, human-centered, modern mind could all too easily patronize it as simply a figure of speech, a new label with no power to make any real difference in human lives. If war is the enemy, I could rationalize, that's fine; we'll continue with our peacemaking efforts as always and call it "fighting against war". If poverty is the enemy, fine; we'll continue helping the poor as always and call it "war against poverty," as President Johnson said in the 1960s. An advertising agency might call it good copy, a novel way to boost interest in peacemaking or charity.

I knew, for example, what fighting poverty meant, both physically, in community organization, fund-raising, and political action; and emotionally, in building self-esteem in the poor and reassuring the fearful rich of their nobility in giving. Indeed, if pressed, I could even portray a spiritual dimension of the poverty issue: The rich need to ask God and the poor for forgiveness for their greed and insensitivity to others less fortunate and to invest their resources, clearing the economic path to overcome poverty. The poor need to forgive the rich, discover their God-given talents, and prepare to develop and exercise them for His purposes.

Working toward all these goals is, of course, often frustrating, simply because human beings are by nature nearsighted and unable, if not unwilling, to discern spiritual reality. A secular mentality, therefore, could easily portray the overall struggle against poverty as a spiritual battle and then seek to win it exclusively through such natural means as education and political clout.

Such trivialization of the term *spiritual warfare*, and hence continued ignorance of the reality it reflects, would be precluded if a larger, more pervasive enemy were identified lurking beneath not only war-making and oppression of the poor, but the entire spectrum of ungodly, destructive human behaviors. Yet my educated, "sophisticated" sensibilities balked at once. Surely, I scoffed, any intelligent person knows that any such business as a "devil" or "demons" is pure superstition, and that Jesus' own mention of these was simply His concession to the more childish, parochial mentality of His era.

I believed that war and poverty, like all destructive circumstances, are the result of wrong human choices, plain and simple, and they can be eliminated only by those who are intelligent and educated enough to recognize that and make the right choices. Any notion that human choices might be affected by spiritual powers of evil seemed patently irresponsible—as in "The devil made me do it!"

Yet I was not comfortable denying the existence of something just because I didn't like the consequences of acknowledging it. Indeed, what if some evil spiritual power was in fact frustrating all physical, emotional, and spiritual goals in the war against poverty, for example? The existence of such evil would not preclude human responsibility but rather demand it—namely, to diligently study the nature of that evil and seek power to overcome it.

My usual approach to social justice and peacemaking was thereby preempted by this entirely new perspective: for the past two thousand years, God through Jesus Christ has been calling us not simply to lay down physical arms but to take up spiritual arms—even after the model of ancient Israel's battles.

Granted, no snake, devil, or spiritual enemy manifests itself in those Old Testament battle scenes. Yet neither does the Messiah. *For the true spiritual enemy cannot be revealed and unleashed for the final battle until the true Savior has come*—that is, until the power to overcome that enemy is available to the people of God.

Thus, when the risen Lord appears to His disciples, they ask, "Lord, will you at this time give the kingdom back to Israel?" Instead of responding to their human-centered view, Jesus deftly refocuses them to wait for God's power before telling others about Him:

> The times and occasions are set by my Father's own authority, and
> it is not for you to know when they will be. But when the Holy
> Spirit comes upon you, you will be filled with power, and you will
> be witnesses for me in Jerusalem, in all of Judea and Samaria, and
> to the ends of the earth. (Acts 1:7–8)

Clearly, the power of God's Spirit is set to accomplish something even greater than restoring the political fortunes of Israel. And that power, that new kingdom, is at hand, even for us to establish as God's spiritual warriors.

While human beings—even His own disciples—confuse Jesus' mission and debate who He is, the demons recognize Him at once:

"Demons also went out from many people, screaming, 'You are the Son of God!'" (Luke 4:41).

In the face of these radically new ideas, wholly foreign to the church and faith of my boyhood, I grasped after any familiar ideas that would help me navigate such strange but compelling waters. The most adaptable notion was simply that war is idolatry, insofar as it leads people to look for saving power in their weaponry instead of in God.

Yet my new understanding had revealed a dimension of idolatry in the peace movement as well, namely, in its secularized notion of disarmament. We are saved, I now understood, neither by taking up nor by laying down worldly arms, but only by surrendering to the God who in Jesus has called us to take up spiritual arms.

To LAY DOWN ARMS WITHOUT RECOGNIZING THE ESSENTIAL SPIRI-tual dimension to human conflict is to proclaim a false, and there-fore dangerous, "peace"—a myopic fantasy that only renders us more vulnerable to a spiritual enemy. Furthermore, a cease-fire in itself cannot establish God's shalom—that is, His very presence and thus the intended fulfillment of all that the human heart longs for and all that our loving Parent God longs to give us.

Jesus, therefore, is no more the foremost advocate of disarma-ment than He is the champion over God's spiritual enemy—and, indeed, no less. As Christians today, we must call into account not only shortsighted national defense policies, but also a Christianity that in the name of open-mindedness discounts the very spiritual reality upon which it is based and thereby blinds itself not only to the destructive power of evil, but also to the saving power of God.

The question is not: Shall I spend my energies working for

disarmament or praying, promoting peace candidates or fasting, reading the editorial page or the Bible? The question is: How can I be so wholly submitted to God that I can both hear and respond when He calls me to any of these?

And so I have concluded that the spiritual rearmament to which God has called us in Christ can begin only with a renewed acceptance of God's authority over our lives—that is, as we acknowledge Him as King and facilitate His kingdom. War ceases not when vanquished surrenders to victor but rather when all of us surrender to Jesus.

Indeed, this is precisely the focus of God's efforts to make us stop warring against each other. As the psalmist proclaims, "[God] stops wars all over the world; he breaks bows, destroys spears, and sets shields on fire. 'Stop fighting,' he says, 'and know that I am God, supreme over the nations, supreme over all the world'" (Ps. 46:9–10).

This text has been scandalously domesticated by its more common translation, "Be still and know that I am God." This is no gentle invitation to quiet meditation, but in fact, a sharp rebuke from the Parent God who refuses to sit idly while His children have turned away from Him to kill each other. It's a call to disarmament as much as a call to worship.

Our childish human pride, meanwhile, makes excuses: "He hit me!" "They attacked us first!" or "But I'm just naturally superior." But would a loving parent accept *any* excuse if his or her children were fighting each other to kill? More likely, the parent would seize their weapons and smash them angrily—as indeed God threatens in this psalm.

If, as this Scripture insists, human war-making distracts His children from God's authority and destiny, then yet another startling conclusion emerges: the "other side" in any human conflict—from husband-wife arguments to national wars—is not the enemy but rather a fellow victim of the greater enemy who seeks to divide and destroy us all.

Today when my wife, Mary, and I speak at conferences together, we're occasionally asked, "Do you and your wife ever fight together?"

"All the time!" I reply, tongue in cheek. "We fight together, side by side, against the enemy who would divide and destroy us."

Jesus, that is, came to eliminate war between human beings in order that we might turn back to God and fight together against our true spiritual enemy.

*God seeks physical disarmament through spiritual rearmament* by refocusing our energies on the true war being waged in the realm of the spirit. In order to recognize the authentic battle, we must discern the authentic spiritual enemy of God, who has for millennia seduced proud human beings into fighting one another instead of him.

During the civil rights movement of the 1960s, for example, virulent racism festered among working-class whites in the South. At the same time, most white, Southern laborers had no unions and hence no bargaining strength against wealthy management executives. The large-family-business owners found racism to their advantage; as long as working-class whites were focused on "keeping the n—rs down," they were not focused on how bad their own working conditions were and would not threaten the privileged, white aristocracy. As long as working-class whites and blacks were fighting among themselves, they could not see their common enemy, who profited from their infighting.

Racism, per se, was not the enemy in this case, but rather a tool of the enemy, used to cause division, blindness, diversion, and destruction. In the same sense, neither is war God's true enemy, but rather a tool used by the enemy, who delights to see God's children killing each other instead of turning on him.

At least two major consequences of this new perspective became clear to me.

First, to ignore the spiritual dimension of military conflict among us is to ensure that you will fall victim to the evil that perpetrates it—whether you win the war or not. As Elie Wiesel declared, only evil wins in war-making. Second, any effort to eliminate physical weaponry from the world—from handguns to nuclear weapons —must be undergirded at all times with a deliberate engagement of the spiritual enemy, using every spiritual weapon that God has provided by pouring out His living Spirit among us.

A purely secular call to disarmament, therefore, is not only naive but potentially suicidal.

The conclusion was inescapable: *Effective peacemakers in the world must first and foremost be warriors in the kingdom of God.*

And this revelation unveiled my next question: If the battle underlying all human conflict is indeed spiritual, what sort of spiritual enemy are we up against, and what sort of spiritual weapons has God made available to us for victory?

Obviously, I needed some clear-cut demonstration to bring this apparent spiritual battle out of the conceptual realm and into my daily, physical world. I did not realize then that in order for that to happen, I first needed to be open to spiritual reality. For— embarrassing as it is for me to admit, as an ordained clergy with years of parish ministry experience—I really did not believe that God could manifest spiritual power in the physical world, much less that some enemy of God could do so.

"If you haven't met the devil," as the saying goes, "it's because you're going in his direction."

To my amazement, I did not have to wait long for the demonstration that flipped the power switch from idea to reality.

## Chapter 6
# MEETING THE ENEMY: A FIRST SKIRMISH

No, it is not Beelzebul, but God's Spirit, who gives me
the power to drive out demons, which proves that
the Kingdom of God has already come upon you.

—Matthew 12:28

The social upheaval of the turbulent 1960s made it easy for me to believe that some kind of enemy was alive and well within me. In fact, my own personal, adolescent rebellion always seemed to hamper my efforts to combat the external evils in society.

As a journalism graduate student at Stanford, for example, living in an African American neighborhood across the freeway from the university, I was outraged by President Nixon's 1970 invasion of Cambodia and was prepared to join a boycott of classes in protest. To my surprise, however, the Black Students Union issued a declaration refusing to support the boycott, on the grounds that it did not speak to the black predicament but represented a mere "family squabble" between disillusioned white youth and their affluent parents: "You have responded to the napalming of . . . non-white Asians by throwing a temper tantrum, as if suddenly discovering that your father was a liar, a racist, and a murderer, after he told you that he represented the best humanity had to offer."[1]

Stung, I did not join the boycott. Indeed, I began to question the motives in my radical political loyalties. Was I a "wannabe," using people of color to shield my emotional wounds, even my own racism? Eventually, I moved out of the black community and stopped dating African American women and desperately seeking friends of color. I knew something was not right in my heart, and my frantic efforts to identify with African Americans were a cover-up for whatever that might be.

To sort out my confusion, I went to a psychiatrist. A major clue to my problem surfaced in one of the first sessions, when I mentioned a particularly upsetting event in my life and the psychiatrist asked matter-of-factly, "How do you feel when you remember that?"

To my utter embarrassment, I had no idea how to respond to such a question. *What difference could my feelings possibly make?* I wondered. For several minutes the psychiatrist persisted in asking the question, and I continued to balk. Finally, he said, "I think you're angry right now."

Immediately, I denied it. Yet by the end of the hour, I not only knew he was right but also was beating his office pillow furiously, with a rage that shocked me. Realizing how deeply I had suppressed my feelings, I began beating a pillow at home—with increasing fury, day after day. Eventually, however, I felt less release and even greater tension afterward.

SIGNIFICANTLY, AT THIS POINT IN MY LIFE, NOT ONCE HAD IT EVER occurred to me that God might be able and willing to give me any help I needed in order to move in His direction for my life. Through years of churchgoing—sermons, Sunday school classes, Christmas pageants, Easter celebrations, communions, hymns, Bible studies, picnics, and potlucks—not once did anyone suggest to me that God is alive and well and speaking even now to whomever might have ears to hear.

I had attended chapel services regularly as a college freshman. At one point, the entire incoming class took a battery of required psychological tests. One particularly disturbing sequence of questions stands out in my memory: "Do you have fantasies of murdering someone?" asked one. "Do you wish you could wear clothes of the opposite sex?" asked another.

And then, right up there with all manner of mayhem and perversion, followed the question: "Do you hear God talking to you?" In fact, I did not. I hunched over my desk and glanced around furtively before deciding that it was definitely safer to continue marking no, that I never hear God talking to me, either. I wonder today how Jesus would've scored on that test.

Years later, when I taught religion at a Catholic high school, we studied the ancient prophets and one student asked, "How come God doesn't speak to people now like He did back then?" Even at that point in my life, I was jarred enough to balk at the question. I replied that God does speak to His people and is speaking to us now—but we simply don't hear Him. Not because He's silent, but because too often we are not silent, and our ears are plugged with our own agendas.

I asked the young man if he heard classical music on his radio. "No," he replied. "I don't tune in to that station."

"It's like invisible radio waves," I explained to my class. "God is broadcasting, but we're not tuned in to His station" (Matt. 13:14–15).

All this made rational sense to me. And yet it never occurred to me actually to "tune in" and ask God directly for the knowledge and wisdom I needed to overcome my overpowering anger. I had never really given God a chance to speak—mostly because I doubted that He was real enough to do so, and I wasn't about to risk losing a lifetime of Christian faith, no matter how flimsy.

And then one day, sweating and exhausted after pounding out my anger on a sleeping bag stuff sack, I slumped over in dejection and tossed the sack aside in disgust. In that moment—helpful as it had been in surfacing my problem—I knew I could never beat another pillow in my life. There had to be another way to resolve my deep anger. But how?

As I sat there panting, I recalled Francis MacNutt's book *Healing*. *Didn't he say something about emotional healing, as well as physical?* Leafing through the chapters, I turned to one titled "The Four Basic Kinds of Healing." There, the author described three basic kinds of sickness:

1. Sickness of our spirit, caused by our own personal sin
2. Emotional sickness and problems (for example, anxiety) caused by the emotional hurts of our past
3. Physical sickness in our bodies, caused by disease or accidents

To my surprise, I then read, "In addition, any of the above can be caused by demonic oppression, a different cause that requires a different prayer approach, namely, prayer for exorcism."[2] A chapter titled "Deliverance and Exorcism" was included, and I turned to it in curiosity.

Anticipating my surprise, MacNutt began:

> One might wonder what a chapter on praying for deliverance from evil spirits is doing in a study on healing. To tell the truth, I did think of leaving it out—especially since it is such a controversial subject. Nevertheless, it is a part of healing in the broader sense of freeing us from all evil that burdens us and prevents us from being fully alive and free.[3]

I paused. Should I bother with a writer who entertained such bizarre notions? MacNutt had some very well-reasoned teachings on healing, however, and again he anticipated my reservations with his closing remarks, which were soon to be seen as prophetic:

> For those who have had no experience in any kind of deliverance ministry, some of what I have written in this chapter may seem problematic if not downright medieval. I would only ask that you put it all on the back burner, as it were, until such time as you have a chance to see for yourself.[4]

With a sigh and shake of my head, I condescendingly set such foolishness aside to reflect on the three sicknesses and my own unresolved anger.

I had no apparent physical sickness, so I eliminated number three from consideration at once. For years I had been dealing with emotional hurts in my past, but MacNutt said healing in that area requires forgiving the one who hurt you. *Have I done that?* I made a list of persons and hurts that I had already identified and spent several days recalling the pain they had caused me, crying out to Jesus, and forgiving them in my heart.

I waited several more days, and though I felt my anxiety ease a bit, it still remained. Returning to MacNutt's list, I read in his explanation that personal sin might include holding a grudge, that healing requires you to ask God's forgiveness for not having forgiven the person who hurt you.[5] And so I reviewed my list, asking God's forgiveness for not having forgiven those persons.

Again, I experienced a noticeable, though limited, relief. My edgy anger still remained. Maybe I needed to forgive more to be forgiven more. I expanded my list of wounds and wounders and tried again—but several days later, little had changed. Frustrated, I reread MacNutt to see if I had missed some important instruction. But no, I had done all that he had indicated as necessary.

And then it struck me, as a strange sensation of both fear and hope crept over me. *Wait a minute,* I thought. *There was one more thing, but surely that couldn't be—*


SOMEWHERE IN MY MIND, A WHISTLE BLEW, A YELLOW LIGHT flashed. Granted, MacNutt had pretty sound credentials and his other suggestions were helpful, but I'm an educated man—a college math major, in fact, with a minor in physics. Any sensible person knows there's no such thing as evil spirits or a devil. Why, even the nickname of my undergraduate alma mater, Duke—founded by Methodists—was the Blue Devils, and we'd all had great fun at ball games watching the blue-suited mascot with tail and horns climb the goalposts and shake his pitchfork at opponents!

For two years in the Peace Corps, I had scoffed at the idea of evil spirits to my African friends, even as they staunchly witnessed to that reality. Sure, the Bible stories said that Jesus often cast out demons, but like the stories of physical healing, any intelligent person knows they're just figures of speech to accommodate popular ignorance.

I sighed as the sheer desperation of my circumstance interrupted my protest. It occurred to me that my undergraduate degree in math and physics dictated a scientific openness to new data—and demonic encounter would certainly be something new. The security of all my theological training, even my controlled, well-ordered worldview, hung in the balance. I sat at my desk for some time, stymied, with MacNutt's book on my lap.

Finally, I unleashed the question: *Could there be a demon in me?* My stomach turned noticeably at the very thought. Uneasily, I decided to read the entire chapter titled "Deliverance and Exorcism."

MacNutt used several clear biblical references to note that demons are not expelled by praying a petition such as, "Lord, please take this demon away," but by calling their names and ordering them to leave in the name of Jesus.

*All right,* I said to myself. *I'm game! I'm fed up with all this anger in me. Nothing else works—let's try it.*

*What could be the name,* I wondered, *of this evil spirit tormenting me?* As I sat uncertain, the obvious word *anger* came to mind—and immediately, I felt a tightness in my chest. *Could that be the name of the demon?* It seemed too simple, but it made sense after the psychiatrist's observation and my pillow-beating rage. I took a deep breath and closed my eyes. "Okay," I said out loud. "In the name of Jesus, you spirit of anger in me, be gone!" To my surprise, at once I saw in my mind a dark shape growing larger, and a cloudy heaviness began filling my mind. Quickly and more forcefully, I ordered again, "In the name of Jesus, you spirit of anger, get out of me!"

Suddenly, the picture in my mind changed, and I saw a curving, tunnel-shaped path, as a train might wind through a mountain, with a snakelike figure moving within it. Watching, I thought of a bowel movement. Once again, I commanded the anger to leave in the name of Jesus, and the snakelike shape moved out of the tunnel, as if unwinding from the mountain or being eliminated from a bowel, and disappeared.

A slight shudder passed through me, followed by a cool freshness.

I sat quietly as an unusually comfortable peace settled over me. No pillow beating, no screaming, just peace. I smiled and then hesitated. Something clearly had happened that affected not only my emotional state, but also my body. *What in the world could this mean?*

"The Kingdom of God has already come upon you" flashed in my mind (Matt. 12:28). With a sigh, I found myself smiling again— and then hesitating again. *Could it be true? Was there really a demon in me?* I shook my head in wonder. *Apparently so!*

At once, I drew up: *Could there be other demons in me?*

After years of desperately searching for emotional healing, I had a long list of problem areas in my life, and I proceeded to attack them afresh with this new spiritual approach. Soon, I had identified other demons at work in me and expelled them similarly, by asking God their names and wielding the name of Jesus against them. The perceptible shudder that accompanied these experiences demonstrated that whatever I was seeing in my mind's eye during my deliverance prayers was not only real, but also foul by nature—as suggested by the bowel movement motif—and not to be retained in any aspect.

Power over such demons clearly lay in the authority of Jesus, for they obeyed and left whenever I addressed them in His name.

That these things looked like snakes awed me. The shape I saw in my mind was not a sphere, a flat sheet, or even an elephant or shark, but a snake. The connection with the ancient biblical imagery was unavoidable. Never in my years of theological training had it occurred to me that the serpent in the garden of Eden might bear any reality whatsoever beyond mere literary device. Now, I wondered.

I had believed that evil was simply a reflection or consequence of wrong human choice, not an independent entity with its own effi-cacy. After all, even in the Genesis creation story, Adam and Eve did *choose* to turn away from God, didn't they?

Yes, I realized, but the serpent put the idea in their heads. The snake initiated the process that bore ungodly fruit and in that sense was the source of evil, not the humans.

Granted, the humans bit—literally—on the snake's offering, so we clearly have a basic flaw: an easily seduced nature that makes us vulnerable to the evil one's initiatives. At worst, we're accomplices, but not the mastermind of evil, which has a spiritual source beyond human nature and intentionality beyond human will.

In the face of such graphic evidence, I knew I would have to go back to the Bible, not with the theological microscope of my semi-nary days, but with the wide-angle lens that my immediate situation required. I would need a special measure of the open-mindedness that I had always affirmed out of my higher education—but that, as I had come to discover, was mocked as much by its rational natural-ism as by any dogmatism among the legalists.

I had read the Bible before but never took seriously its portrayal of evil as a spiritual entity. I rarely thought of the garden of Eden story in relation to Israel's history, the coming of Jesus, or the church. How did this character, which appeared as a snake in the garden of Eden and now in my own personal deliverance prayer, fit into the overall story—even my own?

As the freeing effect of my deliverance prayers increasingly confirmed the biblical accounts, I knew I needed to begin allowing the Bible to draw me forth and confirm my experiences, that is, to portray ultimate reality itself. When I turned to look at the Bible through this new lens of openness and faith, here's what I saw.

# THE BIBLE AS A WAR STORY

Then war broke out in heaven.
—Revelation 12:7

In the beginning, God created the world and decided as well to bring forth creatures a "little lower" than Himself (Ps. 8:5 NLT), who would reflect His image much as a child reflects that of the parent. Maybe God was lonely and wanted relationship with creatures like Himself—even as His creature Adam longed for "one of my own kind" in the woman (Gen. 2:23).

Since "God is love" (1 John 4:16), these human beings were created out of love and designed primarily to receive love from God and share it with each other. Of course, God could have wired them like love robots, totally incapable of anything else. But as a good parent, God knew that love from children who feel coerced into it, or otherwise have no choice, cannot be genuine. And so God included in the human makeup a free will, that is, an awareness of what it would be like *not* to love Him—a willingness, even a readiness, to turn away from God and regard one's self, instead, as the proper focus of devotion.

Any parent of a teenager knows what lies ahead.

In spite of this divine flaw in us, the overall design worked well at the outset. Adam and his wife, Eve, received the bounty of their Creator's love and returned it freely. The choice not to reciprocate did not emerge in this idyllic garden. In order to secure the blessing, however, God commanded them not to eat the fruit from the Tree of the Knowledge of Good and Evil, which would let them see fully how to exercise their freedom not to love Him. So they didn't eat it, and together they lived happily ever after.

The End.

Maybe God planned the story to go like that. Still, it's boring. No book publisher would buy it, and no film producer would give it a second glance. Who wants to read or watch a story about two happy people frolicking around in Paradise forever? Such a tale doesn't stir our human imagination, because in our God-created, free-to-choose hearts, we know it's unreal. A story without danger, threat, or conflict doesn't engage our hearts, simply because it lacks evil—and thereby doesn't reflect the definitive, archetypal story that has shaped us all from our very genesis.

Maybe God Himself became bored. Perhaps He was brutally honest with Himself and finally admitted that if love from others is only as genuine as their freedom to turn away, Adam and Eve's wholly naive love for Him had to be false indeed. Anyone can love you purely if they have no other choice—a contrived devotion hardly worthy of the almighty Creator's dignity and handiwork.

To possess free will before the Creator is heady stuff and leaves the creature vulnerable to pride. But for love's sake, it would be better to risk the creatures' turning away by allowing them knowledge of their options. Sure, the consequences for creation would be devastating if they did *not* choose God—but if they *did* choose Him, how much more would their faithfulness reflect a deep and genuine love for Him!

Clearly a test, a temptation, is required—one worthy of the almighty Creator's workmanship and His creatures' trust.

Here at last is risk, danger, and promise. A story beckons. The eternal drama is set. Our hearts lean forward.

And so another character appears onstage, distinct from God and from the human being and distinguished at the outset as one dedicated to separating God's child Adam—literally "humankind" in Hebrew—from his Father.

This new character is the enemy of God, and his tactic, impure and simple, is to seduce the child from the Parent. To accomplish this he must stir distrust in the creature toward the Creator, and he will do so by distorting and misrepresenting God's character. The enemy clearly has access to God-like knowledge, for he knows the creature's essential divine flaw in having free will to say no to the Creator. Not surprisingly, he directs his attack precisely at that weak spot.

He scorns the Father's love to His face: "You think these children of Yours will choose You with their free will? Ha! I may be the deceiver, but You can trust me on this: they won't care a fig about what You say, no matter how badly it hurts them. Go ahead, tell that fifteen-year-old boy to wear sunscreen lotion and a big hat at his friend's pool party to protect himself from skin cancer! Tell that lonely woman to honor her heart and not have sex until the man commits to her for life! They'd rather die—and I'll make sure they do!

"Young or old, they're all the same—just wait and see. A little shame here, some fear there, and I'll have them destroying themselves. Ha! And here's the clincher: the more You command them to stop it, the more they'll do it, just to show You they control their own lives!"

The essential nature and motivation of this evil character were revealed to me when ministering to a middle-aged mother who sought my help for her teenage daughter, whose father she had divorced when the girl was very young. The mother had a limited income and was troubled when her gifted daughter, as a high school senior, wanted to attend a particularly expensive college where several of her best friends were going. The girl had applied and was accepted. Uncertain of her resources, the mother nevertheless began saving for the necessary funds.

A few years earlier, the mother had quarreled publicly with an unscrupulous businessman in town and the man had been appropriately discredited. In revenge, this man began reaching out to the woman's daughter. An older man, he played upon the young woman's longing for the caring father she never had, and finally, he offered her the college money.

The mother, meanwhile, had scraped together the necessary funds; outraged at the man's offer, she forbade her daughter to accept it. Influenced by her "benefactor," however, the girl blamed her mother for taking her father away from her, rose up in rebellion, and took the money from her mother's enemy, thus creating a lasting rift between her mother and her.

The evil one also seems motivated by revenge—as if God had at one time rebuked him publicly, and so, being powerless to retaliate directly against the Almighty, he seeks instead to seduce God's beloved children away from Him. As any parent knows, that's a pain unto death—which appropriately beckons the cross.

The fact that the enemy has supernatural knowledge, that he knows the truth well enough to decorate his lies with it, suggests a previous association with or closeness to God. In that sense, he's like a disgruntled ex-employee, eager to tempt other workers into disloyalty to the boss.

And, indeed, the enemy is quite good at his craft, mixing sufficient truth with his lies to tempt the human creature into turning away from the Creator. He takes the truth of what greater knowledge the forbidden fruit will bestow and twists it so that God's prohibition sounds like mere jealousy—when in fact it was the Father's loving effort to protect His children:

> The snake asked the woman, "Did God really tell you not to eat fruit from any tree in the garden?"
>
> "We may eat the fruit of any tree in the garden," the woman answered, "except the tree in the middle of it. God told us not to eat the fruit of that tree or even touch it; if we do, we will die."
>
> The snake replied, "That's not true; you will not die. God said that because he knows that when you eat it, you will be like God and know what is good and what is bad." (Gen. 3:1–5)

God knows all too well that the divine flaw He instilled in human nature renders us dangerously prone to misuse such knowledge. And so He is predictably upset when His children seize it against His will and eat the forbidden fruit. He punishes them with severe consequences in this world: pain of childbirth for the woman; hard work for the man; and for both, expulsion from the paradise of innocence and finally, death.

If the punishment was designed to draw the children back to their Parent-Creator with willing love, clearly it failed. Outside the garden generations later, the human creatures continue to rebel. This time, God drastically disciplines His wayward children with a flood that wipes out creation itself, except for Noah, "the only good man of his time" (Gen. 6:10). Afterward, however, Noah's offspring continue to be led astray by the enemy.

Frustrated, but undaunted in His efforts to win His children's love, the Creator decides upon a radical move: He will set one man, Abraham, apart and devote His finest efforts to him and his descendants, even as a father to a son, and lift that people up as a model of Himself among the other human creatures—a "light to the nations" (Isa. 42:6). He will give Himself wholly to these people, revealing His true self to them in all aspects, so that they in turn can reveal Him to the others—thereby exposing and overthrowing the enemy's scheme and restoring His children to their created destiny in Him.

The enemy could seek no more bitter revenge—and tout his power no more convincingly—than to discredit and destroy these people, chosen to reveal God's presence in the world. For if these people fulfill their call and shine before others, then God shines before the world. But if they fall, God's image and manifest character reference fall—and the whole world will see His failing.

Hence anti-Semitism.

Moses uses this fact almost as blackmail to save the people when God, frustrated at their constant complaining in the desert, contemplates eliminating them altogether: "Now if you kill all your people, the nations who have heard of your fame will say that you killed your people in the wilderness because you were not able to bring them into the land you promised to give them" (Num. 14:15–16).

In a major effort to show His people clearly where they have turned away and to draw them back—to distinguish His own path from that of the enemy—God reveals Himself as directly as possible in human terms: He gives His people the Torah, the Law, the teaching, through Moses on Mount Sinai. His children now have a manifest list of self-destructive behaviors that will turn them away from God, written in stone for all to see, so that they might no longer stray proudly in the darkness and fall prey to the enemy.

Yet the Law is literally so concrete, so divorced from the Father's heart, that its coming bears more than a trace of exasperation. In the desert, the people whine about having to eat pigeon meat, and God punishes them by sending a deluge of pigeons to gorge themselves until they throw up.

In giving the Torah, God seems to be saying, "So you want the knowledge of good and evil, do you? Fine! I'll give you law after law, down to every jot and tittle, to remind you of your sin and keep you in constant fear of blowing it." This knowledge of good and evil comes with a consuming fear of choosing evil—but significantly, not with the power to choose good. Moses tells the people at Mount Sinai. "God has come to test you, so that the fear of God will be with you to keep you from sinning" (Ex. 20:20 NIV).

Again, the apostle Paul wrote: "Now we know that everything in the Law applies to those who live under the Law, in order to stop all human excuses and bring the whole world under God's judgment. For no one is put right in God's sight by doing what the Law requires; what the Law does is to make man know that he has sinned" (Rom. 3:19–20).

In teaching us where we have turned from God's intention, the Law acts as a counterforce to the divine flaw that impels us to pride. The Law calls God's people to accountability as an ever-present reminder that we have missed God's mark and must humbly rely on His mercy in order to walk in it.

The enemy, however, also remains undaunted, continuing to excite the human creature's will to say no to God. For hundreds of years, God struggles to bring His children into willful obedience by reminding them of their sin through the Law, then punishing or rewarding them accordingly.

But the punishment-reward system of the Law eventually sabotages the very heartfelt relationship it was designed to facilitate. His children continue to stray. Exasperated, God eventually loses patience and decides that He has not punished them severely enough. Wielding the armies of Babylon as a whip, He once again disciplines His children with exile—this time, from the "Eden" of their promised land.

During this period when the people are smarting from the consequences of their rebellion, God gives them several brief glimpses of the enemy. His name is revealed as Satan—in Hebrew, "the opponent"; in the legal parlance of the Torah, "the accuser."

In Job, Satan is portrayed as having considerable latitude in world affairs: "When the day came for the heavenly beings to appear before the LORD, Satan was there among them. The LORD asked him, 'What have you been doing?' Satan answered, 'I have been walking here and there, roaming around the earth'" (Job 1:6–7). *The Living Bible* describes Satan's activity in military terms, as "patrolling the earth."

Again, the scene in which Satan sets out to harass Job indicates that he seeks to turn us away from God, that he would do so by taking advantage of our weak spots—especially those times of misfortune, when we are most likely to doubt God and question whether our faith in Him has any positive value or effect:

> Satan replied, "Would Job worship you if he got nothing out of it? You have always protected him and his family and everything he owns. You bless everything he does, and you have given him enough cattle to fill the whole country. But now suppose you take away everything he has—he will curse you to your face!" (Job 1:9–11)

God's response to Satan indicates clearly that biblical faith is no Manichean dualism, in which both the good and the evil have equal power. Satan must receive God's permission to act and must act within God's restrictions: "'All right,' the LORD said to Satan, 'everything he has is in your power, but you must not hurt Job himself'" (v. 12).

Generations later, as visions of reclaiming the promised land stir, the prophet Zechariah offers another glimpse of the enemy: "In another vision the LORD showed me the High Priest Joshua standing before the angel of the LORD. And there beside Joshua stood Satan, ready to bring an accusation against him" (Zech. 3:1). Significantly, the name Joshua is the Hebrew rendering of Jesus.

The enemy, as the ultimate tattletale, opposes God's intention to redeem the people by seeking out and highlighting their wrongdoing. He's not limited to bringing false accusations, however. His most diligent attacks focus not on lies and easily disproved charges, but on our *true and actual misdoings*, in order to stir shame and justify extreme, even eternal, punishment against us as a permanent guilt trip.

As a counterforce, Jesus urges His followers not to defend their sins but to confess them readily and to "settle matters quickly with your adversary who is taking you to court" (Matt. 5:25 NIV).

Meanwhile, God knows that natural human ability is no match against the enemy's supernatural cunning, that we are incapable in our own strength of choosing good over evil. Amid temptation, we can't trust that God's restrictions are for our own good and act accordingly. We buy the snake's lie that God's Law is designed not to protect us from pain but to deprive us of pleasure. And so we rebel.

Because love originates in God and not in us, we can't love ourselves as much as God does. His millennia of punishment are designed to bring us to that confession. "I will abandon my people until they have suffered enough for their sins and come looking for me. Perhaps in their suffering they will try to find me" (Hos. 5:15).

Clearly, the divine flaw is so fatal as to require drastic reshaping by the Creator:

The LORD says, "The time is coming when I will make a new covenant with the people of Israel and with the people of Judah. It will not be like the old covenant that I made with their ancestors when I took them by the hand and led them out of Egypt. Although I was like a husband to them, they did not keep that covenant. The new covenant that I will make with the people of Israel will be this: I will put my law within them and write it on their hearts. I will be their God, and they will be my people. None of them will have to teach his fellow countryman to know the LORD, because all will know me, from the least to the greatest. I will forgive their sins and I will no longer remember their wrongs. I, the LORD, have spoken." (Jer. 31:31–34)

In this new plan, God would implant His standards of loving protection and fulfillment in His children's hearts. Not by installing in each of them a robotic "morality microchip," but by stirring a holy memory of their Father's saving love. This would restore their innocence in the garden, as it unmasks the snake's distortion of God's character. That revelation of the Father's heart allows them to turn from fearfully striving to save themselves by doing good, to surrendering to the Father and trusting Him to save them. Thus, we turn from old to new covenant, from Law to Jesus, from the Tree of the Knowledge of Good and Evil to the Tree of Life.

It's a new and wholly gracious dispensation. "They will know in their hearts when they've turned away from Me," God effectively says, "and just so they won't be afraid to turn back to Me for fear of My punishment, I'll wipe the slate clean and forgive all their wrongs."

God's wholesale amnesty strips the accuser of any power over God's creatures, rendering his threats of the terminal guilt trip empty. "Go ahead and accuse me, Satan!" the creature can now scoff. "Even if what you say is true, we can take it to the Father and He'll forgive us, give us what we need to make amends, and set us back on His good path for us." The enemy becomes a toothless, declawed lion, able to harm God's people only insofar as they fear his accusing roar, distrust God, and turn away from this new covenant.

As Peter urged:

> Be alert, be on watch! Your enemy, the Devil, roams around like a roaring lion, looking for someone to devour. Be firm in your faith and resist him, because you know that other believers in all the world are going through the same kind of sufferings. But after you have suffered for a little while, the God of all grace, who calls you

to share his eternal glory in union with Christ, *will himself perfect you* and give you firmness, strength, and a sure foundation. To him be the power forever! Amen. (1 Peter 5:8–11, italics mine)

With this ultimate plan in mind, God finally calls His people home from their "discipline of disaster":[1] "'Comfort my people,' says our God. 'Comfort them! Encourage the people of Jerusalem. Tell them they have suffered long enough and their sins are now forgiven. I have punished them in full for all their sins'" (Isa. 40:1–2).

Joyously, a remnant returns to reestablish Israel as a home for God's people in this world, a lighthouse for the beacon of His saving grace to a condemned and dying world—as Israel herself has experienced it. For a while it appears that the people have learned their lesson and the nation is restored.

THE ENEMY, HOWEVER, REMAINS PERSISTENT. AS THE GENERATIONS pass, memory of the disciplinary exile fades and the people stray from God yet again. Six hundred years later, under Roman rule, Israel is destroyed a second time and the land given over once again to pagans. Score another one for the enemy.

In the generation before that event, when it became clear to God that His people had not learned their lesson from the first exile and yet another would be necessary, God must have sighed in dismay: "It's no use. I've tried every form of discipline, from flood to exile, and they still fall prey to the enemy's lure. They still think they can save themselves from his lies and destruction, without Me."

Indeed, even the Law, originally designed to draw people back to God by showing how they had turned away unto danger and destruction, offered the enemy a splendid opportunity. Capitalizing on the creatures' shame, he can lead the people astray by making them believe they have indeed fulfilled the Law's requirements in their own natural ability, apart from God. Seeing themselves as exclusively righteous, the people then drop their guard against unrighteousness.

In C. S. Lewis's *The Screwtape Letters*, the apprentice demon laments to his master that the human he has been assigned to bring down is unassailably righteous. The master demon urges, "Make him know it"—even as the primal snake assaulted Adam and Eve's innocence and urged them to eat from the Tree of the Knowledge of Good and Evil.[2] As Jesus said:

> How terrible for you, teachers of the Law and Pharisees! You hypocrites! You are like whitewashed tombs, which look fine on the outside but are full of bones and decaying corpses on the inside. In the same way, on the outside you appear good to everybody, but inside you are full of hypocrisy and sins. (Matt. 23:27–28)

Furthermore, their pride leads the people to accuse others who do not equal their apparent moral standard—like the Pharisee who "stood apart by himself and prayed, 'I thank you, God, that I am not greedy, dishonest, or an adulterer, like everybody else. I thank you that I am not like that tax collector over there. I fast two days a week, and I give you one tenth of all my income'" (Luke 18:11–12).

As agents of division and condemnation, these religious leaders reflect the image of the accuser instead of the merciful Creator, and thereby become at last children of the enemy. Jesus charged them, "You are the children of your father, the Devil, and you want to follow your father's desires" (John 8:44).

Sadly, anti-Semites in the church, who have sought to hide their own sin by applying it exclusively to Jews, have scurrilously misappropriated this text. Jesus is not saying that all Jewish people are children of the devil, but rather that any who claim to be children of God—which certainly includes Christian Gentiles today—but proclaim their own righteousness instead of humbly confessing their sin to God have allied with God's enemy. Legalistic "Christians" who point the finger at Jews most assuredly fall under Jesus' judgment here.

For the heart of God is not to destroy His people but to redeem them: "'Do you think I enjoy seeing an evil man die?' asks the Sovereign LORD. 'No, I would rather see him repent and live'" (Ezek. 18:23). And again: "For God did not send his Son into the world to be its judge, but to be its savior" (John 3:17).

Yet even this chosen community of Israel, into whom God has poured Himself for thousands of years, has not learned to "repent and live" as He desires—any more than the church has today.

Clearly, the Creator is faced with a momentous decision. He could, of course, destroy the whole experiment, blow up the planet, and be done with these rebellious creatures once and for all. But such vengeance, while entirely human, would be for God to admit defeat. What's more, it does not reflect His Father's heart:

> When Israel was a child, I loved him
>     and called him out of Egypt as my son.
> But the more I called to him,
>     the more he turned away from me.
> My people sacrificed to Baal;
>     they burned incense to idols.

Yet I was the one who taught Israel to walk.
I took my people up in my arms,
  but they did not acknowledge that I took care of them.
I drew them to me with affection and love.
I picked them up and held them to my cheek;
  I bent down to them and fed them. . . .
How can I give you up, Israel?
  How can I abandon you?
Could I ever destroy you as I did Admah,
  or treat you as I did Zeboiim?
My heart will not let me do it!
  My love for you is too strong.
I will not punish you in my anger;
  I will not destroy Israel again.
For I am God and not man.
  I, the Holy One, am with you.
I will not come to you in anger.
(Hos. 11:1–4, 8–9)


Any father of a teenager can understand Father God's feelings here.

After millennia of ping-pong rebellion and punishment, this compassionate God at last determines to deal with the fact that His creatures turn away from Him largely because He fashioned them with a free will to do so. No amount of punishment can heal that literally fatal flaw in human nature—required for genuine love, yet so easily preyed upon by the enemy through pride. The enemy will seduce the creatures away from their Creator and claim the victory, as long as that root potential for self-centeredness is not overcome.

Even the Law, given as a light to protect us from the enemy's mis-leadings, becomes distorted as an opportunity to fabricate righteousness rather than to confess sin.

Obedience has been revealed as a false goal, simply because human nature isn't capable of it. "I know that good does not live in me—that is, in my human nature," as the apostle Paul put it. "For even though the desire to do good is in me, I am not able to do it. . . . When I want to do what is good, what is evil is the only choice I have" (Rom. 7:18, 21). If we could obey God, then we could save ourselves and would not need a Savior.

Only when you're honest enough to confess, "I can't obey God," can you see that the only choice you've ever really had beyond rebellion is to *trust* God. For people who have grown up in a broken and wounding world, as with emotionally untrustworthy parents, this is an overwhelming task. Often, we avoid it until we "hit bottom"—that is, until trusting in our own human power becomes so fruitless and destructive as to leave us no choice but to trust God.

Like a virulent cancer, the parasite sin has permeated the creature. A radical solution is called for. The creature must be re-created in order for the new covenant to function. But how do you re-create the species without destroying it? Can a pot be reshaped without being shattered? The host creature must die in order to starve off the parasite sin. But a flood, a Babylonian holocaust, and other literal destructions of the people have not proved effective—nor can the God of love countenance destroying His children yet again.

The enemy's power over the creature must be broken from within the creature's heart. But how?

Certainly, God is wholly capable of crushing and eliminating Satan altogether, at any time. But in divine irony, this would be

God's defeat, an admission that He cannot make a creature who loves Him authentically, in full view of the choice not to.

The only remaining solution becomes clear, the one God has hoped to avoid and has therefore delayed until all other options have been exhausted. For the cost will be great: take off the gloves and let the battle between God's people and God's enemy take place at last. This is, indeed, the "Final Solution"—a term that to the enemy means the utter destruction of God's people, as manifested by the Nazis in the Holocaust. To God's people, however, it means the utter destruction of evil.

God's Final Solution is Jesus.

No battle is more basic, no conflict more ultimate, no victory more enduring, than Jesus versus Satan. History has reached its focal point, the fulcrum upon which the destiny of humankind turns. This is the battle of battles for which God has been preparing His people through the ages, from Philistine chariots to Roman centurions.

The Creator's battle plan is open and straightforward: Expose Satan fully before the people; let them clearly see his dark deceptions and evil workings. Then give the people power to battle and destroy the enemy; put the weapons in their hands to defeat Satan once and for all. Without the power to destroy Satan's works, the people dare not recognize him, and even if they do, they must fall to him. But with God's power in their hands to battle victoriously, the people can recognize the evil one and choose to take up arms.

Such a plan lifts the people from the childhood punishment syndrome to a mature position of full and genuine responsibility. No longer is the battle between rebellious child and commanding Parent; now it is between the mature, faithful adult and the enemy who would destroy the entire family.

Parent and children can now be drawn together against a common enemy, instead of fighting each other. With God's power available to them, the children respond to the Father's call not from fear of punishment but rather out of a primal longing for victory over the enemy, for freedom at last to be one with the Father again— as in the beginning—and thereby restored to their true identity and created purpose.

But what about the "divine flaw"? Surely a loving Father dares not unleash the enemy before children who remain so hopelessly vulnerable. Indeed, once the enemy knows he has been exposed and the people of God have been empowered to destroy him, he will attack viciously, especially at this, their weakest point. If the enemy cannot make the creature cover up this self-centered sinfulness, he will push the creature into a terminal guilt trip of condemnation.

In order for people to die to their self-centeredness and be reborn into God-centeredness, they must know both their sin and the Father's mercy. But there's the rub. *If my self-centeredness dies,* they fear, *there is no more me. The End.* In other words, Death holds the greatest power and must, therefore, be feared and respected above all other powers.

Thus, the enemy's threats have cowed us into believing he is greater than God. Someone must be sent to demonstrate otherwise— that when our natural self dies and we trust God instead, the person is not obliterated but is in fact transformed by the Spirit of God, resurrected at last into the new life and person God has always intended.

In order to bear credible witness, that Someone must carry the divine flaw Himself—be entirely human flesh and blood—even as He carries the nature of God to those who hearken. He must, therefore, suffer the real and awful pain of death in this world, the conse-quence of human sin from creation.

Yet He must be the very nature of God; otherwise, He would be as overwhelmed by the enemy as the other creatures. It's a tall order that only one Person can fulfill, the Father's Son:

> Since the children, as he calls them, are people of flesh and blood, Jesus himself became like them and shared their human nature. He did this so that through his death he might destroy the Devil, who has the power over death, and in this way set free those who were slaves all their lives because of their fear of death. (Heb. 2:14–15)

In the earliest gospel accounts, Jesus therefore wields His power first against one of Satan's minions, who recognizes him at once. In the opening chapter of Mark, the war line is drawn:

> Just then a man with an evil spirit came into the synagogue and screamed, "What do you want with us, Jesus of Nazareth? Are you here to destroy us? I know who you are—you are God's holy messenger!"
>
> Jesus ordered the spirit, "Be quiet, and come out of the man!"
>
> The evil spirit shook the man hard, gave a loud scream, and came out of him. The people were all so amazed that they started saying to one another, "What is this? Is it some new kind of teach-ing? This man has authority to give orders to the evil spirits, and they obey him!" (vv. 23–27)

As I discovered two thousand years later, they do indeed obey Him. From the moment Jesus begins His ministry on earth, it is crystal clear to the enemy that D-day has arrived, that the Creator has launched His ultimate offensive to reclaim the earth and its people as His own.

BUT SATAN HAS DONE HIS WORK WELL, HAVING SUFFICIENTLY seduced creature away from Creator as to prompt a universal conceit— in every age, as in the garden—that says, "We can do just fine by ourselves, indeed, better for ourselves than by submitting to God." And so while some of God's people believe, most do not, and the enemy sneers in contemptuous delight as we strut into the jaws of Death. Thus, Caesar's pagan legions overrun the people of God.

*The End.*

Not.

If you thought only the enemy was persistent, read on. The story's not over yet. Other enemies of God's people have sneered: big, awe-some men like Goliath—nine feet tall with a spear as thick as a "weaver's beam," who scorned and taunted the people of God, "Here and now I challenge the Israelite army. I dare you to pick someone to fight me!" (1 Sam. 17:10).

But although the people of God are "terrified" by such an enemy (v. 11), God is not impressed, for the power of God is not the power of human beings. To prove that, He anoints the shepherd boy David and sends him forth to proclaim the victory.

And so—to minimize the carnage—God determines that the final battle should not simply pit God's people against Satan's min-ions. Rather, as in the David-and-Goliath face-off, let the represen-tative champion of each side come forth and battle it out, one-on-one. As David stepped forth on behalf of Israel against the Philistine,

Goliath, let the messianic Son of David step forth on behalf of humankind against Satan, the enemy of God.

To conquer an enemy, you must enter his territory. Let the Champion of God's people therefore meet the enemy head-on in the very stronghold of death itself and emerge victorious in the fullness of God's intention for us all. Indeed, let Him be crucified by human beings in the power of death, and let Him be resurrected by God in the triumphant power of life eternal.

And thus it was accomplished.

Freed at last, the people of God rang the church bells of victory and rushed out rejoicing into the streets to spread the news, and humankind lived happily ever after.

Here, at last, is a story that would sell. Conflict with evil—plenty of it—has added the necessary credibility to our original, idyllic garden scenario. Yet something essential is still missing.

Sure, people will pay good money to hear about a heroic deliverer who single-handedly wipes out the enemy on their behalf, then rides off into the sunset leaving them safe and content in their little town. They will not pay so readily, however, to hear about the expert marksman who comes to teach the townsfolk how to shoot so that they can overcome the enemy not only in their own little town, but in other towns as well.

And there lies the rub for the creatures—liberated from the enemy by Jesus, but largely blinded to His victory by their self-centered nature.

For God's champion, Jesus, does meet Satan on the latter's own turf. Three days and three nights the battle rages in the dominion of death. Jesus' followers, meanwhile, become discouraged and disband when they see Him die. The Son of David, they had believed, would destroy Israel's current and apparent enemy, the Romans (Luke 24:21).

Yet in fact, Jesus is the Son of the warrior-king David. He defeats Satan, the Goliath of the spiritual world, the enemy of God's people. To everyone's awe, Jesus returns victoriously in the resurrected body, as God's showcase of what is to come for all who would receive the boons of His Spirit and follow in Jesus' footsteps. "Come, follow Me in My victory!" the resurrected Messiah calls.

The people of Israel, however—blinded by their shame and desperation to keep the Law, and unable to trust their relationship with God—do not recognize their spiritual enemy. They do not see what Jesus has done, and therefore they cannot know who He is.

Certainly, the physical Jesus of Nazareth could not have walked over all the earth in the same flesh-and-blood body forever, demonstrating God's power to humanity. And so His death and resurrection released the Holy Spirit, unbound by physical and temporal restraints, to come and do the job in our bodies unto today. Jesus told His followers, "But I am telling you the truth: it is better for you that I go away, because if I do not go, the Helper will not come to you. But if I do go away, then I will send him to you" (John 16:7).

His mission on earth accomplished, Jesus returns to the Father who sent Him. Fifty days later, on the day of Pentecost, the harvest of Jesus' victory over the enemy pours forth and the believers receive the Holy Spirit. Now, the followers of Jesus have His supernatural power not only to discern and cast out the enemy, but also to build God's true fellowship of shalom—that is, the peace of knowing that the almighty God is with you, regardless of circumstances.

With this commanding evidence of God's Spirit animating them, the believers set out to tell and demonstrate for others the victory

God has won in Jesus. "I am telling you the truth: whoever believes in me will do what I do—yes, he will do even greater things, because I am going to the Father" (John 14:12).

In the coming of Jesus, the beachhead has been established. In the coming of the Holy Spirit, the warriors are equipped to press ahead and recapture the world from the enemy.

And thus God's mission is being accomplished in and through the lives of the believers.

To be continued . . .

## Postscript: The Non-Acts of the Latter-Day Apostles

As an ordained clergy, I'm embarrassed that it took me so long to see this wide-angle, "war story" view of the Bible and dismayed that so few churches proclaim it. For in fact, not to recognize the battle upon us is blindly to capitulate to the enemy. Pretending there's no thief in your house does not protect you from being robbed; it only gives thieves free rein to steal whatever they want.

The story, therefore, is indeed "to be continued" in our churches today, and God's question today is as always: "Will of the Son of Man find faith on earth when he comes?" (Like 18:8). That is, will they turn from their natural impulse to do it themselves and instead come to Me for saving, overcoming power? Or will they proudly disdain such humility and continue blindly on their path of self-destruction?

The answer will not come easily. For even if we understand and accept the wide-angle, warrior's view of the Bible, often we simply don't know how to take up spiritual arms and wage our part of the battle unto the victory God has won.

I, for one, was tempted after recognizing the biblical story as authentic to shrug it off and say, "Well, since Jesus has defeated the enemy, the battle is over—so let's just get busy loving each other and building God's kingdom of peace and justice." But while we must proclaim God's victory in Jesus and proceed with His ministries, at the same time we must beware of casting that victory in our own self-serving terms.

The promised Messiah did not liquidate the enemy any more than David's slingshot liquidated the Philistine army. David, the champion, slew one man, Goliath. And because both sides understood the terms of that face-off, when Goliath fell, the people of God rushed out to attack their enemy with full confidence of victory.

Goliath had "called down curses from his god on David" (1 Sam. 17:43), and David had responded by claiming the power of his God. When Goliath fell, both sides knew that David's God had whipped the Philistines' god; the rest was just a matter of mopping up, of going through the motions of what had already been accomplished in the spiritual dimension:

> When the Philistines saw that their hero was dead, they ran away. The men of Israel and Judah shouted and ran after them, pursuing them all the way to Gath and to the gates of Ekron. The Philistines fell wounded all along the road that leads to Shaaraim, as far as Gath and Ekron. (1 Sam. 17:51–52)

The task for God's people was not, as they justly feared, to charge out in their own strength against the enemy's forces, but rather to let their champion clearly demonstrate the victory that God had prepared for them. After that, it remained for God's people to walk in that victory, that is, to claim it, take up arms, and rout the enemy once and for all and thereby occupy the territory that God's victory had gained them.

Suppose, on the other hand, that the Israelites did not recognize the spiritual dimension of the face-off between Goliath and their champion, David. What if they saw Goliath fall and decided instead, "Well, that's one of their men down—and a big one, granted. But those Philistine soldiers have mighty sharp swords, and it's still us against them. It's great that the shepherd kid got a lucky hit, but he's sure no good to us now—what good is a slingshot against Philistine troops?"

Or perhaps, from the distance across the plain, many of Israel's soldiers could not actually see what was going on out there, and when the runner returned with the news that the Philistine champion had been killed, they scoffed, "Well, that's a nice story, all right, but I can't risk my life by taking your word for it."

In either case, we may ask, How might the Philistine soldiers be expected to react to such reluctance among the people of God? The Philistines know the terms of the contest and the terrible implications of their champion's defeat. But the Isaelites are just standing there; in fact, some are starting to turn away. The Philistines have lost their champion, but they're not fools. *"Charge!"* they shout, then sweep across the plain toward the people of God—who, having already indulged their fear, waste no time scattering in terror.

Similarly, Christians today have not recognized or understood the terms of the face-off between Jesus and the accuser of God's people. The enemy's forces, however, have known all too well what Jesus' coming as the Son of David means (Mark 1:24). They know Jesus defeated their champion on the cross. The people of God in the churches, however, have preferred to remain proudly ignorant of this spiritual reality and therefore are unable to walk out its victory.

Liberals and universalists fancy that we don't need a savior. Rather, through principled secular education, we can make intelligent choices to save ourselves. Conservatives and evangelicals say we need a savior, but through scriptural religious education, we can make biblically based moral choices to save ourselves. Human pride has blinded both camps to our absolute inability to save ourselves—and thus has blinded us to the reality of the spiritual battle about and within us.

The cross, meanwhile, serves as the supernatural transmitter of God's victorious, life-giving power won for us by defeating His enemy—and ours. Routed by the attack launched on Good Friday, the enemy's troops turned tail on Easter Sunday and began to retreat, fully expecting God's troops—that's us Jesus-believers—to be breathing down their necks like David's men with swords raised. For a brief period, perhaps for a generation or so, that was true.

But as the warriors for the kingdom of God became comfortable in the kingdoms of the world, enmeshed in property and political power, we ceased chasing down the enemy and began rather to enjoy his privileges as ruler of this world. Instead of stalking the enemy, we began following him. And he has been only too happy to mislead us.

The enemy has taken untold advantage of our pride and its incipient ignorance. Defeated, he and his minions have nevertheless swept in upon Christian churches and individuals, simply because we have chosen not to recognize either him or the Holy Spirit and have thus given him a free hand to operate among us. It's as if a wholly unrepentant criminal is brought to trial and convicted as a murderer, thief, liar, and destroyer. The jury, however, instead of sentencing him to jail, agree that the best way to deal with the problem is simply to make the criminal invisible.

In reality, Satan is that destructive criminal and we are the jury. We have the authority to bind and expel him. But we are proud and lazy: we do not want to acknowledge any power greater than ourselves, whether good or evil, and we do not want to undertake the discipline necessary to become warriors for God's kingdom. Hiding behind sophisticated tolerance on the Left and judgmental legalism on the Right, we have become lethally naive in choosing not to recognize spiritual reality and the battle at hand. Our folly is borne out as the jury abdicates and thereby sentences itself to punishment by the criminal—that is, we loose the enemy and his power of death upon us.

The warrior-king David, through whose lineage the Messiah has come, wasted no time with such foolishness:

> I pursue my enemies and catch them;
>   I do not stop until I destroy them.
> I strike them down, and they cannot rise;
>   they lie defeated before me.
> You give me strength for the battle
>   and victory over my enemies.
> You make my enemies run from me.
> (Ps. 18:37–40)

Christians today must learn to celebrate God's victory in Jesus with that same fierce determination. For as I soon discovered, the enemy is not waiting for us to come after him.

## Chapter 8

# MY BATTLE PARTNER, THE *PARACLETE*

[In Ephesus, Paul] found some disciples and asked them,
"Did you receive the Holy Spirit when you became believers?"
"We have not even heard that there is a Holy Spirit," they answered.
—Acts 19:1–2

The more I saw the battle portrayed in the Bible taking place in my own life, the more I began to see it in others as well.

Another pastor confided in me that he struggled with women in his church making sexual advances toward him. A happily married father, he had never succumbed but was becoming increasingly alarmed at the temptation before him. When we prayed about it, I sensed a dark cloud hovering inside him. Quietly, I asked Jesus to come and show me what was going on, and the image shifted to a large snake wrapped around the man.

At that point, without knowing what I was seeing in my mind's eye, the man prayed aloud for God to help him see more clearly how to rid his life of these sexual temptations. Suddenly, I "heard" in my mind the word *lust*. I then matter-of-factly spoke out: "In the name of Jesus, I bind you spirit of lust in [I said the pastor's name] and command you to come out of him!" With my eyes closed, I "saw" the snake uncoil and lift up and away from the man and out of the "picture," much as with my similar prayers for myself.

*"What was that?"* he exclaimed, jerking upright.

"What?" I asked.

"It's like . . . something sort of flew out of me!"

I explained that although neither of us had been taught about spiritual warfare in seminary, it is nevertheless real, and he had just experienced a demon's leaving him.

I had already begun to incorporate prayer for physical healing into my pastoral calls, albeit cautiously. Although nothing dramatic seemed to happen, everyone "felt better" afterward. One day, the wife of a middle-aged businessman called to tell me that her husband was suffering severe sciatic-nerve pain, and after much medication, he still had to crawl out of bed in the mornings. A staunch evangelical, he was suspicious of healing prayer.

I called the man, but he declined my offer to come and pray with him. As his pain and its crippling effect increased, and the medications' side effects left him tired and unable to keep up with his business, finally he came to me for prayer. I laid hands on his back and declared, "In the name of Jesus, I speak healing to the sciatic-nerve endings," and asked the Father to complete His work of healing in my brother. I continued by asking the Spirit to come and soak him, praising and thanking God for His goodness.

After about a half hour, the man said that the pain was still there and he had to leave for a business appointment. We were both disappointed, but we parted after a quick prayer of thanksgiving, releasing his situation to the Father. The next day, his wife called me to say that his pain had disappeared altogether. When I later talked with him, he was surprised but happy. It seemed obvious, because his wife and not he himself had called me first, that the experience so upended his cherished belief system that it stirred shame.

As I began to see positive results in praying for physical healing and deliverance, I asked God to show me how they might be connected. An answer came when I visited Mrs. Davis (not her real name), a fiesty parishioner in her early seventies who had suffered a severe leg injury in a fall one Friday afternoon. Living in a second-story apartment with no elevator, she was effectively housebound by the accident. When another parishioner called me about it, I alerted several men to pick her up and bring her to church that Sunday by carrying her downstairs to a car.

I greeted her Saturday morning as she sat with her leg propped up on a settee and encased in a temporary cast secured by Velcro straps from hip to ankle. A set of crutches leaned against the side of her easy chair. "The emergency room said the X-rays show it's probably broken," she fumed, shaking her head in disgust. "But the doctors and people who make the permanent casts won't be in until Monday to check me out, so they put me in this temporary cast and told me to just sit and stay put 'til then!" Gesturing contemptuously toward a vial of pills on a nearby end table, she snapped, "That medicine they give you cuts down the pain but doesn't do anything to make your leg better. It just makes you drowsy!"

I sat down facing her about ten feet away. After we had chatted a bit, I eased into a discussion on healing prayer. I explained that while there were no guarantees, she frankly had little to lose and much to gain if we tried it. Hesitating, she declared that she had always considered herself open-minded and was willing to see.

With that tentative agreement, we bowed our heads. When I closed my eyes, I thanked God for being there with us and wanting to heal her in whatever way He felt best. I then asked for guidance in how to pray. I had expected possibly to see Jesus come and touch her leg, whereupon I would ask out loud for Him to come and do that.

Almost immediately, however, a surprising picture came into my mind of the lady's knee tightly bound as if with black metal bands or straps. *Whatever kind of healing is that supposed to call for?* I wondered. *Come, Lord Jesus,* I begged silently, *and show us what You want to do here!*

The word *cripple* flashed in my mind. *Yes,* I thought, *she certainly has been crippled by this knee accident.* At that, I "saw" the metal straps begin to tighten around the woman's knee.

"*Oh!* My knee! It's killing me!" Suddenly, a loud and fearful cry of pain burst forth from Mrs. Davis, jarring me upright. I opened my eyes to see her bending over in her chair, grasping her leg cast with both hands. "Aaaugh!" she gasped. "It hurts terribly all of a sudden," she exclaimed, turning to me, grimacing. "It's killing me! Oh! What's happening?"

Startled, I panicked as a cold fear swept over me. *Lord,* I prayed quickly under my breath, *what* is *happening here?*

"Oh, please do something!" Mrs. Davis cried out, now rocking back and forth in agony, her face knotted in pain. "The pain is terrible!"

With a quick breath, I decided to leap ahead with all the determination I could muster: "In the name of Jesus, I command you crippling spirit to leave now, and I break those straps on her knee and set her free!" In my mind's eye, I saw the straps break and disappear.

At once, Mrs. Davis let out a loud sigh. "Ohhh . . . it's easing up now," she managed, rubbing the cast over her knee with both hands.

"That's great!" I exclaimed, amazed. I then asked God to place His healing hand upon her knee. In my mind, I saw it begin to glow red.

"Oh my!" she burst out, a note of confusion and fear in her voice. "Now it's getting hot! It's on fire!"

I had read enough accounts of healing prayer to know that warmth in a wounded area often signifies that healing is taking place. "If you can just hang in there a bit longer," I reassured, "I think the heat indicates just the healing that we're praying for."

Nodding, she agreed, and for several more minutes I continued to ask Jesus to touch and heal her leg and knee, until finally she noted that the heat had subsided.

"Lord, thank You for the healing You're doing now in Mrs. Davis's leg, and keep on doing it," I prayed. After a period of silence, Mrs. Davis shifted to the edge of her chair. "And go ahead of Mrs. Davis to the doctors on Monday," I added. "Give them supernatural wisdom, knowledge, and discernment to know how best to further Your healing purposes in her."

After a moment, Mrs. Davis sighed audibly. "Why, I feel just fine!" she announced briskly. As I smiled and nodded, she turned around to take her crutches. "In fact, I'm going to try and stand up. Do you think that's okay?"

"*What?*" I exclaimed fearfully. "I . . . uh, I mean, well, let's just wait 'til Monday and see what the doctors say," I offered.

But Mrs. Davis was already leaning forward in determination, ignoring my pleas. "Now, you just come over here, young man, and stand beside me!" she ordered.

Panicking, I nodded obediently. *Lord, is all this from You?* I thought. *What if all this is just our imagination? What if nothing's changed and she falls down on her broken leg? What will I tell the para-medics when we call them?* Standing up, I walked over and stood beside her with my arms cautiously outstretched.

Gingerly, she pulled herself up, shouldered her crutches, and then put her stiffly wrapped leg out and leaned on it slightly. I stood there, watching breathlessly. Silence. Another step. Then another, and another. Soon she was hobbling around the living room, aston-ished. "Why, the pain's gone!" she said, elated and laughing ner-vously. "I might as well take the cast off!"

"Listen," I begged nervously, reaching out to help her sit back down in her chair. "Maybe we should, you know, wait until you see the doctor. I mean, it's only two days to wait."

But Mrs. Davis was already unwrapping the Velcro straps. Setting her cast aside, she tapped her toe tentatively on the carpet—and moments later she was walking around the room just fine. As she took a few delighted hops, I thought of the cripple healed out in front of the temple in Acts 3, who began leaping and dancing inside among the amazed congregation.

"Praise God!" I exclaimed, astonished. "It sure looks like your leg is healed!"

And indeed it was.

Awhile later, I left—overwhelmed and excited about what would happen Sunday in church when she came on her own and walked around healed. Those men coming to carry her to church were sure in for a surprise! Who needs a preacher? Just her walking into the church would be a sermon right out of the Bible, two thousand years later!

But the enemy was not about to let this victory be celebrated. On Sunday morning before worship, the men told me she had called to thank them but said she would not be coming to church. That afternoon, I phoned her and she said she was doing fine, but she had "needed to talk with her sister on the phone" that morning.

Nor did she come the next week. Again I called, and again she had a flimsy excuse. Exasperated, finally I asked outright, "Mrs. Davis, I'm very happy for you that you've been healed. But won't you please tell me why you haven't come to church since then?"

After an awkward silence, she stammered, "Actually, I . . . I won't be coming back to church again."

"What in the world do you mean?" I burst out. "Why not?"

"It's just too embarrassing. What would I tell everyone?"

"Why, you'll tell them what happened, that we took authority over that crippling spirit and Jesus healed you!" I declared.

"Oh, I couldn't do that," she scoffed. "The doctors were upset enough, worried that someone had diagnosed me wrong and all. Everyone at church would think I'm crazy." And then, politely but firmly, she thanked me for being "a good pastor" and said good-bye—for good.

We never saw her at church again.

When the enemy cannot stop conception, he aborts.

It was hard enough for Mrs. Davis to believe that Jesus had healed her; to believe that we had broken a demonic hold on her was beyond her reach of faith.

Clearly, I had a lot to learn about the full range of demonic activity. I had focused entirely upon specific wounds and individual spirits, assuming that once the spirit had been cast out and/or the wound healed, the person would be so overcome with thanksgiving and joy as to witness freely and openly to Jesus' victory.

Then I remembered when Jesus healed ten lepers and only one—a

Samaritan, or nonchurchgoer—returned to thank Him. "There were ten who were healed; where are the other nine?" Jesus asked in dismay. "Why is this foreigner the only one who came back to give thanks to God?" (Luke 17:17–18). Mrs. Davis taught me the answer: because the insider has more to lose, namely, acceptance in the parochial village.

Deliverance may fix the immediate problem, such as a broken leg or paranoid fear, but to attack a single demon may provoke a counterattack from others. The major intent of evil is to separate people from God; thus, the counterattack upon Mrs. Davis aimed at keeping her away from the church and squelching her witness to Jesus' compassion and power.

Characteristically, the enemy preyed upon her shame, telling her that people would reject her if she said Jesus had supernaturally healed her. Sadly, her fear said as much about our church as it did about her. She feared not godless atheists but her fellow Christians, whom she essentially saw as unable to accept the reality of Jesus and thereby unwilling to accept her once He had changed and healed her.

It's sad when the powers of the world harm a child of God. But it's tragic when the people of God cannot acknowledge and celebrate Jesus' healing of that child—and even seek to suppress it. With a church like that, who needs the enemy? And so we have Francis MacNutt's disturbing book, *The Nearly Perfect Crime: How the Church Almost Killed the Ministry of Healing*.[1]

JESUS HEALED MRS. DAVIS. BUT WHEN, UNLIKE THE EARLY Christians, she chose to leave the church rather than "proclaim the mighty acts of God" (Acts 2:11), I found myself beginning to leave the church too. And not only my particular congregation, but also the larger body of Christ as I had known it. So graphically experiencing God's power had upended my entire worldview. Where before I had seen church as a place for me to work, to help people cope amid the pressures of daily life, I now saw it as God's own medical school—a teaching hospital, a training site wherein the healing power of the living God could be experienced, celebrated, and ministered to a broken world both in and beyond it.

My encounters with the reality of evil, which the revelation of God's healing had stirred, were beginning to suggest yet a third image of the church.

If in Jesus the ultimate battle of the ages has been brought into focus, then the church as His body is not a hotel for saints, as in the old adage. But neither is it simply a hospital for sinners. The church is also a barracks, a military base wherein the drafted warriors of God report for basic training to receive and perfect His weaponry, to study and learn to overcome the enemy's tactics.

If it's a hospital, it's not a posh recovery suite where people go to get rid of their pain and return to business as usual, but a battlefield medic center where wounded warriors are recycled for their roles in the larger combat mission.

My seminary theology and church upbringing offered me no reference point from which to see this. At our peace rallies, we sang the old folksong "Ain't Gonna Study War No More," even as the enemy capitalized on our ignorance, infiltrated our ranks, and paralyzed us.

As I searched the Bible for evidence, I found that physical healing and deliverance were the two essential ministries to which Jesus commissioned His first disciples: "Jesus called the twelve disciples together and gave them power and authority *to drive out all demons and to cure diseases*" (Luke 9:1, italics mine).

In the midst of such excitement and uncertainty, I received the Parish Renewal Council flyer listing Bob Whitaker as nearby in Pasadena. When I first called, he reassured me that many other traditional-denomination pastors like myself were experiencing and ministering physical healing and deliverance from demonic oppression. As we talked, I wondered, *Does he know about the bigger picture, which somehow includes the Holy Spirit?*

Before I could ask, Bob invited me to his church that weekend, when he would be teaching on the gifts of the Holy Spirit.

"I'll be there!" I exclaimed, amazed.

There's no word in Hebrew for *coincidence*.

Meanwhile, however, I balked. As an oldline–denomination pastor, I considered myself entirely trinitarian and would have been offended to be labeled unitarian. Yet in fact, I knew practically nothing about this Holy Spirit reported in the Bible. Sure, I had read theological articles about the subject in seminary. Every worship service at my church included singing "Glory be to the Father, and to the Son, *and to the Holy Ghost*" in the ancient "Gloria Patri," and "Praise Father, Son, *and Holy Ghost*" in the "Doxology." But I could not connect the Holy Ghost of my religious background with the healing and deliverance I was experiencing.

Certainly I never thought of the Holy Spirit as a "person," like Jesus or even Father God—though I did enjoy singing the old standard hymn "Holy, Holy, Holy" and its memorable phrase, "God in three Persons, blessed Trinity!" That the Holy Spirit might, as one of those Persons, have a *person*ality—like Father God, who became angry at Israel's sin and ached for His people's sufferings, or like Jesus, who wept at His friend Lazarus's death and lashed out at the hypocritical Pharisees—was simply impossible for me to imagine.

My marriage, meanwhile, had begun to deteriorate even further into separation. Fears, anger, pain, and confusion overwhelmed me with sleepless nights and stressful days. At that point, I did not recognize the connection between my growing openness to God's work in my life and the growing counterattack from the enemy. In any case, I looked forward to Bob's teaching, not simply to learn, but also to be healed.

When later that week I visited his church, a strange mixture of fear and hope stirred within me as I struggled to keep an open mind and take notes. His teaching focused on 1 Corinthians 12, and as he opened with verse 1, I jotted down my thoughts (here in bracketed italics):

Now, concerning what you wrote about the gifts from the Holy Spirit. I want you to know the truth about them, my brothers. . . .

*[Obviously, even the Corinthians were confused on this subject!]*

I want you to know that no one who is led by God's Spirit can say "A curse on Jesus!" and no one can confess "Jesus is Lord," unless he is guided by the Holy Spirit.

*[I'd never curse Jesus! On the other hand . . . neither would I feel entirely comfortable saying, "Jesus is Lord." Wasn't that, after all, just for simple-minded people? Still, it must have something to do with healing prayer, if it's connected to the Holy Spirit.]*

There are different kinds of spiritual gifts, but the same Spirit gives them. . . . There are different abilities to perform service, but the same God gives ability to everyone for their particular service.

*[So healing is clearly not the only gift of the Spirit. Apparently, some can do it—and those who can't have some other gift?]*

The Spirit's presence is shown in some way in each person for the good of all.

*[So much for the ego trip.]*

The Spirit gives one person a message full of wisdom, while to another person the same Spirit gives a message full of knowledge.

*[You mean, the Holy Spirit can show you things that you can't know by ordinary, natural means? Yes—like the "crippling" spirit in Mrs. Davis's knee!]*

One and the same Spirit gives faith to one person, while to another person he gives the power to heal.

*[Aha! There's the power to heal. Disappointing to see it just buried in there with all the others! I guess it's not the entire focus of the Holy Spirit after all. And how is it that Paul calls the Holy Spirit "He"? What sort of personality does the Spirit have?]*

The Spirit gives one person the power to work miracles; to another, the gift of speaking God's message; . . .

*[Funny—I thought healing was miracle enough! There are more? And can someone just speak words directly from God? There's a lot more to all this besides healing bodies.]*

and to another, the ability to tell the difference between gifts that come from the Spirit and those that do not.

*[Yes! Spirits that do not come from the Holy Spirit don't serve God. They're demons. So the Holy Spirit is the key who connects healing and deliverance—each one of several, equally important, ministry gifts that the Spirit provides.*

*But wait a minute. You mean, the gifts we're talking about here can come from some other place besides the Holy Spirit? How can that be? Sure, if that's true, you'd need to be able to tell the difference, all right, so you'd know the real McCoy. But where else could gifts like this come from? Could the enemy counterfeit even the wonderful works of God's Spirit?]*

To one person he gives the ability to speak in strange tongues, and to another he gives the ability to explain what is said.

*[Uh-oh. There's that "speaking in tongues" business! How can something so crazy as that be connected with healing people?]*

But it is one and the same Spirit who does all this; as he wishes, he gives a different gift to each person. (vv. 1–11)

*[There's that "who" and "He" again—the Holy Spirit as a person. Clearly, the gifts are not from any human source, but from the Spirit "Himself," according to the way "He" wants them to be distributed. Since the Spirit gives such gifts, obviously part of "His" personality is giving and generosity, plus determination and caring enough to give us power to do what God wants done.]*

After reading this text, Bob began by underscoring that only the Holy Spirit can inspire someone to know that Jesus is Lord:

> This is the great touchstone of Christian revelation: the Spirit comes in a context where Jesus is honored and praised. . . . Wherever the Holy Spirit is mightily at work, Jesus is greatly honored and loved. Where there is some confusion as to whether or not He is . . . fully divine, or . . . is to be praised together with the Father, there the Holy Spirit is not much in evidence.[2]

No wonder I hadn't seen much evidence of the Holy Spirit at work in my church or denomination! We just didn't honor, love, and praise Jesus—nor did we share a consensus that Jesus is indeed the divine Son of the Father. On the surface, we always seemed afraid that to do so would exclude others who didn't share that belief.

I knew then in my heart that I had discounted Jesus mostly out of shame, because I didn't want to appear unsophisticated to my colleagues or parishioners. After all, I had spent a lot of time, money, and energy gaining my higher education!

Bob then noted that Paul was concerned that Christians "know the truth" about the Holy Spirit because they were constantly exposed in their pagan culture to other, quite different spiritualities, some of which apparently urged participants explicitly to declare "a curse on Jesus":

> There is a spirituality—a very potent spirituality—which was current in paganism and is seeing a revival in our own day, in the New Age, which has nothing to do with the religion of our Lord Jesus Christ. It is a spirituality which *does* have signs, wonders,

and miracles . . . where spiritual powers come upon and seemingly possess people so that they do things they ordinarily could not or would not do.

Amazing! For most of my life, through seminary and several years as a pastor, I had just assumed that all things spiritual come from God and therefore are good. I had always laughed at occult practices, such as fortune-telling and astrology, as patently phony— that is, as bearing no power beyond that of suggestion and mere superstition.

Now, I wondered.

An uncomfortable thought struck me: *If a spirit not of God could mislead our pagan Gentile ancestors to declare, "A curse on Jesus!" might a more cleverly refined spirit of similar ilk be leading me and others to balk at proclaiming, "Jesus is Lord!" today?*

You don't have to curse Jesus in order to truncate His presence and power; just patronize Him as one example of a holy man, like others who have appeared in many times and cultures.

I took careful notes when Bob explained the gift of discernment as an ability given by the Holy Spirit to recognize "the presence of spirits other than God, that is, demonic spirits": "It is the gift of discrimination, of judgment in the sense of evaluation, which enables us to see the difference between what is good and what is not good, what is of God and what is of the devil, what is of the human spirit and what is truly of the Lord."

Certainly, if all things spiritual are loyal to God and therefore good, no such gift would be necessary. But if spiritual reality encompasses an evil dimension disloyal to God and out to sabotage His work, then we must indeed have some way to distinguish the good from the evil. And that "way" must be wholly centered in the good; otherwise, the evil would by definition deceive and mislead us.

The Holy Spirit's gift of discernment, Bob therefore taught, "is desperately needed in our day, a time when there are many counterfeits of true Christianity . . . when there are many deceivers and many false spiritualities at work in the world." Amid such an "occult revolution," he urged us to study 2 Peter 2 for discernment of "false prophets," of which "there are more and more in our day, some of whom are very clever, counterfeit impersonators of true Christianity."

Even as I scribbled studiously in my notebook, I could not know then that the notion of "false prophet" was soon to become dangerously real to me.

Bob concluded by noting that discernment often bears physical cues. In the presence of an evil spirit, some people may get goose bumps; others may feel nausea. Sometimes, he added, "you can see the evil in a person's eyes"; at other times, "you just have a growing intuition that 'something's not right here, and I'd better watch out.'"

Even as I was drawn eagerly to the teaching that night, a battle was taking place in my heart. The impending breakup of my marriage weighed heavily on me, and I struggled to stay open to what I knew was God's work. At times, I fought an impulse to nod off to sleep; at other times, my mind began wandering to a host of scattered, irrelevant topics. Once, I caught myself scorning the others present as "simpletons" and quickly scolded myself for being so judgmental. Through it all, however, I felt a genuine sense of excitement and adventure—although a headache always seemed lurking nearby to cloud my vitality with mockery or contempt.

After Bob finished teaching, I stood and stretched quickly, then immediately headed toward the doorway as others joined in greetings and conversation. To my surprise, a middle-aged woman stepped between the door and me.

"I don't know you," she said with genuine compassion, "but I've sensed you've been struggling all night."

Embarrassed, I hesitated. "Well, yes," I offered. "There's a lot going on in my life just now, and all this is sure a lot different from my usual church experience. It's a lot to take in. Now, if you'll excuse—"

"I can imagine," the woman interrupted gently, not moving out of my way. She nodded to a large man standing nearby, who stepped over to join us. "My husband and I have been praying for you all through the teaching," she continued, "but we never seemed to get a hold on what's troubling you. Would it be okay if we prayed for you now?"

Obviously, I wasn't going to be able to slip away unnoticed and work things out myself. I felt ashamed to tell the woman about my marriage, but she hadn't asked for particulars. She did seem genuine, and I had no excuse to refuse her thoughtful offer.

"Well, sure," I managed. "I mean, that'd be okay with me."

The woman nodded again to her husband, who stepped around behind me. *Strange,* I thought. *Where's he going? Why doesn't he just stay right there beside me to pray?*

Meanwhile, the woman had rested her fingertips gently on my forehead. "Jesus," she prayed, "we place this man in Your hands to minister to him as You want. We don't quite understand what he needs, but You do, and we trust You to give it to him now."

Before I knew it, I felt myself leaning backward on my heels, and then I was falling. Behind me, the man caught my shoulders and lowered me carefully to the floor.

I lay there quietly, utterly amazed. Entirely conscious, I felt even more alert than I'd been all evening. All the tension and rush of thoughts—even my shame and embarrassment—had gone. I was fully aware that I could get up anytime I wanted, but I decided to lie there and rest awhile longer. Eventually, Bob came over and looked down at me, smiling. I'll never forget looking up from the floor at his reassuring face as he chuckled. "Looks as if you got a little more tonight than you bargained for!"

Indeed, I had.

Driving home later that night, I tried to make sense of it all. What in the world had happened to make me fall down like that? The woman hadn't pushed me at all. As a college freshman, I'd experienced plenty of tension and dizzy spells, though I'd never actually fainted. Still, this was nothing like a blackout or loss of consciousness; in fact, it was precisely the opposite—a cleansing, a heightening of consciousness.

A psychiatrist I once saw said I could not be hypnotized because I had so little trust. Again, this was nothing like hypnosis, as far as I could tell. If it had been a matter of choice, I probably would have chosen not to fall back onto the floor. But afterward, I was glad it happened. Everything seemed to indicate that the woman's prayer had indeed been answered, that although no one understood what was happening in me or knew how to pray about it—including me—when she asked Jesus to take over, He did.

Later, I realized that hypnosis, which renders you spiritually vulnerable, invites demons to enter and should be avoided. Ironically, God had used my distrust to protect me from that risk. Even as the enemy can harden your defenses so you can't receive the Father's blessings, he can also prop open your heart when you need to be protected from harm. That's why discernment is so important. "Just because you're paranoid," as the saying goes, "doesn't mean they're not out to get you!"

Never in all my years attending church had anything remotely like this happened to me. Never had spirituality included palpable, physical consequences in my life.


Now, my convenient division of "spiritual" into one remote category and "physical" into a more accessible one was literally being cast down. I saw that Jesus was sent precisely to bridge that gap, to bear the Holy Spirit in a flesh-and-blood body, to bring His kingdom "on [natural] earth as it is in [supernatural] heaven."

Furthermore, in myself and with others, I was experiencing spiritual powers with a will counter to God's, which could affect the physical world and even harm bodies. This stirred fear and hopelessness in me: How was I to appropriate the gift of discernment in order to distinguish the ungodly spirits and not be misled in my life and ministry?

Clearly, I would have to surrender to Jesus and rely entirely upon the Holy Spirit to do that, through His gift of discernment. And to entertain the Holy Spirit, I would need to draw close to Jesus, let Him be Lord of my life, and acknowledge Him as Lord of all creation.

Soon after Bob's teaching, I began keeping a journal account of my learning. One of my first entries notes that I had stopped jogging because of a pain in the groin: "Jogged off and on. Knee feels okay but groin needs healing. Lots of prayers that I have been 'lifting too much weight.' I let go of all to Jesus—the church, other relationships, my songwriting, article writing, ministry."

The sentence that follows indicates that I had been opened up sufficiently at the teaching evening to seek the full range of gifts from the Spirit, even the one I had scorned most: "Tried to speak in tongues, but not yet, I guess. In Your time, let it be, Lord. Heal me, Lord."

The next day was "a beautiful day, no appointments, so I walked to Christian bookstore." There in a stack of sale books, dusty and marked "$1" in pencil, I found a small paperback titled *Ministering the Baptism in the Holy Spirit*, by the late Don Basham. Eagerly I bought the book and hurried home to read it.[3] Therein I found the clearest and most direct explanation of what being "baptized with the Holy Spirit" means—and the most compelling argument for why I needed it in order to be victorious in spiritual warfare.

Basham examined five passages in Acts (2:1–21; 8:4–17; 9:1–11; 10:34–46; 19:1–6) that demonstrate "conversion is one experience and the baptism in the Holy Spirit is a second, subsequent experience." Distinguishing between the "*introductory* ministry of the Holy Spirit to the unbeliever" and the "subsequent *empowering* ministry of the Holy Spirit for believers," he said that while water baptism focuses on salvation, the baptism of the Holy Spirit focuses on "victorious Christian living." The implications here for Christianity are profound. Basham wrote:

[I see now] that all the centuries of the church of Jesus Christ have been trying to proclaim the gospel *without* the baptism of the Holy Spirit, she has been doing it in direct disobedience to the clear command of Jesus who, *after* He had commissioned his disciples to go and "teach all nations" (Matt. 28:18), nevertheless said, "wait" or "tarry" (Luke 24:19). "Don't try to go teach and preach until you have been properly *empowered*." That's what Jesus was saying. And that is just what happened on the day of Pentecost—those 120 believers in the upper room were supernaturally empowered by the Holy Spirit.

The evidence of that empowering, Basham wrote, was immediately clear when cowardly Peter, who had denied Jesus three times on the night of the Crucifixion and had led the disciples into hiding for fear of the religious authorities after the Resurrection, was so transformed that he stood to his feet and preached an anointed message that led to the conversion of three thousand people.

The baptism of the Spirit, Basham concluded, "is an empowering experience which introduces the Christian into the supernatural realm of the Christian life." As such, it is "an experience designed to equip Christians with supernatural power with which to wage an effective battle against Satan."

Reading this altogether sensible argument with its scriptural verification, I sighed in relief. The pressure was off, and I felt free to proceed with an open mind and spirit.

One final hesitation remained, one that had followed me throughout my journey with the Spirit: *What about all those negative images of "uncontrolled emotionalism" and "holy rollers"?* Granted, being slain in the Spirit after Bob's teaching was entirely orderly and without fanfare. I retained all self-will and felt free to get up anytime I wanted. But speaking in tongues pushed my hesitation to the limit. Once I started, could I stop? Would weird sounds suddenly burst out of my mouth at embarrassingly inappropriate times?

Basham reassured:

The Holy Spirit does *not* force us to do anything. You can be sure that any spirit which *compels* you to do . . . or say something you do not want . . . is not the Holy Spirit.

People, who are afraid that they might do something embarrassing or speak in tongues at the wrong time, have failed to realize that the act of speaking in tongues is always under the control of the one speaking. The person, not the Holy Spirit, decides when he will speak out, and whether he will speak in tongues quietly or aloud. The very fact that Paul gives strict instructions about how and when speaking in tongues is to be manifested in a public meeting (1 Cor. 14:27–28), clearly indicates that the one speaking is in control, for Paul's instructions would be worthless unless those he was teaching had the ability to obey his instructions.

I had no excuse now to delay seeking the gift of tongues. Often I had seen a need, whether in myself or in others, but had no idea how to pray. What a blessing it would be simply to offer the situation up to the Father and let His Holy Spirit pray through me! As Paul explained:

> In the same way the Spirit also comes to help us, weak as we are. For we do not know how we ought to pray; the Spirit himself pleads with God for us in groans that words cannot express. And God, who sees into our hearts, knows what the thought of the Spirit is; because the Spirit pleads with God on behalf of his people and in accordance with his will. (Rom. 8:26–27)

What was I supposed to do in order to receive this "supernatural Helper" and pray in tongues? Was I simply to ask for this gift in prayer and then wait for it to come?

Here again, Basham provided the bridge to understanding. Noting that "miracles are comprised of two parts: man's part (which is natural) and God's part (which is supernatural)," he held up the example of Peter's walking on water (Matthew 14). Jesus called Peter out of the boat, and Peter stepped out onto the water and walked. "Peter was not required to do anything supernatural," Basham said:

> All he had to do was get out of the boat and walk, in exactly the same way he would have done if the boat had been pulled up on shore. . . . That was his part of the miracle.
>
> And when he began his act of walking in faith, God was right there to do His part. It was Peter's job to walk, *it was God's job to hold him on top of the waves.* That was the supernatural part of the event. The miracle wasn't that Peter walked, but that he didn't sink!
>
> The miracle of speaking in tongues isn't *that* you speak, it's *what* you speak. The act of speaking is a natural, physical act, just like Peter's act of walking. . . . And when you open your mouth to begin to speak, to praise God with the sound of your voice, the Holy Spirit will provide you with the words, the syllables, the phrases with which to praise God.

Since the Holy Spirit was not about to coerce me into speaking in tongues, the ball was in my court. If I wanted this gift, it would be my job to offer myself in praise to God, open my mouth, and push air out through my vocal cords—the altogether natural part of speaking. God's job would be to provide the words. The only hesitation at that point was my lack of faith: Would God really provide the words? Or would I just be mumbling gibberish out of my own doing?

Nervous but determined, I closed the book and set it aside.

Seated there at my desk, I took a deep breath and sighed nervously. "Okay, Lord," I said aloud, "my life's falling apart, my marriage at home and my ministry at the church. I need all the power You can give me to get through this." I paused and sighed again. I knew where I had to begin. Why was this so hard for me?

"Father," I said at last, leaping in lest my hesitation overrule, "I've turned away from You many, many times, to the point where it seems pretty clear that I just don't have what it takes by myself to stop running and let You be Lord of my life. I know I deserve to be cut off from You for the ways I've turned away from you— but I thank You, Father, for sending Jesus to take care of that and keep the door open to Your heart.

"Forgive me, Jesus, for not recognizing and proclaiming You as my Savior, and even scorning You to cover the shame of my inadequacy. I praise You and confess that I need You, Jesus, that without You, I just can't live the life I was created to live. Come and take over my life now, Jesus, my Lord and Savior!" I waited . . . and a smile came to my lips. *"Bring out the fatted calf!"*—the words of the prodigal's father—burst into my mind.

Encouraged, I took another breath and sat up with renewed hope. "Lord," I said, "I need Your Holy Spirit. I want to be able to tell the difference between spiritual things that are of You and those that aren't. I want to be used to bring others Your knowledge, wisdom, and healing, and I want to be able to speak Your healing, freeing word to them. I want to be able to praise You and pray even when I don't have any words of my own.

"And so I ask you, Father, in the name of Jesus, to pour out Your Holy Spirit on me and let me speak in tongues according to Your Word."

With that I took another deep breath, pushed it out through my vocal cords, and moved my lips much as a jogger might move his legs running in place at a stoplight. Soon, strange, bumbling sounds came out—certainly nothing I recognized as any language. *Is this it?* I wondered. Again I breathed in and spoke as I exhaled. The "words" began to flow more readily after several times, and I became more confident. Before long, the "language"—though unintelligible to me—was indeed flowing, and I was lifting my hands, praising God and dancing around my study.

The next day, I began using my prayer language in my private morning devotions, simply letting the words flow for twenty or thirty minutes. Soon, I began speaking in tongues in all my prayers with others, often inaudibly under my breath. What specific, manifest difference that made in the effectiveness of my prayers, I can't say.

I only know that since then, the burden of praying effectively has been lifted from me and placed where it belongs, with God. All my fears of not performing properly or making a mistake in my prayers began to drain out of me. When my highly educated verbal skills fail me—as they often do in prayer—I know I can always let the Holy Spirit do the praying through me.

Since that time, I have seen God act powerfully without the use of tongues. It's not that you *have to* speak in tongues, but that you *get to,* as Basham taught. Tongues is not a requirement for belief but a gift to the believer. Without the Holy Spirit to guide us in the supernatural realm, we're left spiritually defenseless. The baptism of the Spirit prepares you to recognize the enemy and battle him effectively.

The gifts of the Spirit, therefore, are not parlor-game paraphernalia or spiritual currency with which to buy God's favor—or even healing or peace of mind. The gifts are weapons of spiritual warfare made available to those who have given themselves to Jesus as Commander in Chief of God's armed forces.

The enemy who would, for example, bind an old woman's knee in pain, trap a pastor in lustful relationships with his parishioners, and shroud God's people in the dark—causing us to wonder what's happening and what to do about it and, indeed, keeping us from praying for lack of words—is routed by the Spirit's gifts of healing, discernment, knowledge, wisdom, and tongues.

Thus, as John Sandford, founder of Elijah House Ministries, has noted, the Greek word *paraclete*, used in the New Testament for "Holy Spirit," is a military term, referring to a combat buddy system. Ancient Greek soldiers fought in pairs, back to back, in order to protect each other's blind side; your battle partner was called your "paraclete."

The gifts of the Holy Spirit reveal spiritual reality that we cannot see with our natural human perception—and thereby alert us to the enemy's presence and intent.

This revelation secured a missing link in my theology of the cross. I realized that Jesus had died to bridge the gap between God and me that my sinful nature had caused. But that fact alone seemed somehow partial and incomplete.

Now I understood: through Jesus' dying on the cross, God was able to pour out the Holy Spirit on and into believers. That is, all the gifts of the Holy Spirit were present and manifested in the flesh-and-blood Jesus of Nazareth, who walked a particular territory of the earth at a particular time in history. But if that Spirit and those gifts were to be released upon all humankind in all times, Jesus must die—even as a seed must be broken before germinating and reproducing. As He explained to His disciples:

I am telling you the truth: a grain of wheat remains no more than a single grain unless it is dropped into the ground and dies. If it does die, then it produces many grains. (John 12:24)

And again:

But I am telling you the truth: it is better for you that I go away, because if I do not go, the Helper [Holy Spirit] will not come to you. (John 16:7)

I saw that the Holy Spirit is the boon of Jesus' victory on the cross, God's gift of Himself to us, His undeserving yet beloved children and heirs. "As bad as you are, you know how to give good things to your children," Jesus exhorted His disciples. "How much more, then, will the Father in heaven give the Holy Spirit to those who ask him!" (Luke 11:13).

God has acted and the ball is now in our court. True to His character of love, God does not force the Spirit and gifts upon us, but awaits our response.

Meanwhile, whether we respond or not bears consequences. Fifty days after Jesus' victory on the cross, the Holy Spirit was poured out on "all flesh," as prophesied hundreds of years earlier by Joel (Joel 2:28 NKJV). God has given Jesus-believers His very own power to mop up the enemy's legions. Christians can choose not to recognize or receive the Spirit and His supernatural power, as sadly many today have done. But we thereby leave the world and ourselves unable to recognize and overcome the enemy and his supernatural attacks.

To deny the empowering work of the Holy Spirit is to go AWOL from the spiritual battle at hand and thereby capitulate to the enemy.

You can't face the reality of evil without having power to overcome it. Because Jesus is the only power who can overcome evil, to deny the reality of evil is to deny the full reality of Jesus—both His saving work on the cross and His empowering work in the Resurrection.

Significantly, Joel's prophecy of the Spirit's coming is set squarely in the context of both restoring God's people and overcoming their enemies, the unbelieving Gentile nations. Immediately following that prophecy in Joel 2, God says, "At that time, I will restore the prosperity of Judah and Jerusalem. I will gather all the nations and bring them to the Valley of Judgment. There I will judge them for all they have done to my people" (3:1–2).

God then declares explicitly not only that the outpouring of the Spirit rouses the enemy, but also that God calls the enemy forth, precisely in order that His people might proceed with the mop-up operation:

> Make this announcement among the nations: "Prepare for war; call your warriors; gather all your soldiers and march! Hammer the points of your plows into swords and your pruning knives into spears. Even the weak must fight. Hurry and come, all you surrounding nations, and gather in the valley." Send down, O Lord, your army to attack them! (Joel 3:9–11)

For the past two thousand years, God has allowed the enemy to attack His church in the hope that He has not given up His only Son in vain, but rather that Christians would walk out His victory by the Holy Spirit's power.

This perspective reinforced my determination to help my congregation see God's victory in Jesus and the enemy whom that victory empowers us to overcome. Yet I knew that these realities were virtually foreign to our church and denomination. *Lord,* I cried out, *where do I begin?*

Through much prayer, I decided to pose two major questions to the congregation: (1) Have we sought to serve God fully enough to have encountered the limits of our own human power to do so? And (2) do we trust God faithfully enough to ask for, receive, and exercise the fullness of His power?

If my own fear and reluctance were representative, then these questions were sure to stir conflict in the church. Yet I knew I had to press ahead—not out of duty or even adventure, but because by that point in my Christian journey, I simply could not turn back. I had seen with my natural eyes the supernatural power of God to dispel demons, heal bodies, and change lives—even my own. And I desperately needed more of it.

In a word, my spiritual innocence had been lost. I had no choice whether or not to acknowledge and submit to spiritual reality, but only whether to surrender to Jesus or to the enemy.

After my NROTC rejection for color-blindness and later years of draft dodging, I had been called into military service after all, as God's spiritual warrior—and the battle was on.

# POWER IN THE BLOOD—
# AND OTHER DISCOVERIES

> [Our brothers] won the victory over [the accuser] by the
> blood of the Lamb and by the truth which they proclaimed.
>
> —Revelation 12:11

How to detect and identify particular enemy spirits became an ongoing exercise for me in trusting the Holy Spirit.

I found that sometimes the circumstances suggest the demons. For example, I had noticed that in our church sanctuary, the American flag stood beside the pulpit, while the Christian flag stood on the other side of the room. Uncomfortable with my preaching being more closely associated with our nation than with the faith, I had exchanged the two flags early one Sunday morning, only to find them placed back as before on Monday. The next week, I spoke to the sexton, who said he had not touched the flags. I repeated my exchange—only to find it undone again the next day. Clearly, someone in the church wanted to keep the American flag by the pulpit as a demonstration of patriotism. Aware of the potential for conflict in raising such an issue before the church, I simply proceeded with this surreptitious game.

And then, amid all the other tension simmering in the church, at a meeting of the deacons' board, one member asked for time at the next meeting to present a special agenda item. Instinctively, I drew up in fear—and was not misled in doing so. Producing a copy of the relevant state law, the committee member pointed to the provision that in a church sanctuary, the American flag must be placed in a position of "superior prominence" at the right of the pulpit. Shocked that the state could thereby dictate to a Christian assembly its prominence over the faith, I was dealt a double blow when several of the others present wholeheartedly agreed.

A flush of fear swept over me, and I knew that the enemy was present. But how was he operating? Gingerly, I said that I had been exchanging the flags each week—as apparently the member present had also been doing. I explained that our Pledge of Allegiance to the flag included the words "under God," and that meant the symbols of the nation should never take prominence over the symbols of the faith, that to allow such is to promote idolatry.

The air in the room clouded with a heavy spiritual darkness as two others spoke indignantly about the greatness of our country. I tried to explain the danger in regarding our country as greater than God, pointing to German patriotism during the Nazi era. Even as I did so, I found myself trembling with fear.

It soon became clear that any rational debate was being precluded by the darkness among us. I prayed desperately under my breath as the others talked, and I realized that the enemy was again trying to foster his spirit of division in the church by pushing us into the wrong battle at the wrong time.

Satisfied that I had made my point as clearly as possible, I told the committee that although I disagreed with their apparent consensus, I would abide by it because of my greater concern for unity in the church.

The next day, as I prayed about that event in my morning devotions, I agonized over why I had been so intimidated during the discussion. I had unquestionably spoken the truth about God's preeminence over national idolatry. And yet I had been struck with fear as I did so. My first thought, of course, was that I simply feared rejection by the others. But I had spoken forthrightly to them, not withholding any point, and I had a strange and uncomfortable sense that my fear had been prompted more by the enemy than by anything the people might do to me.

*Why, Lord,* I asked, *was I so afraid of the enemy then—more so even than at many other times when I had encountered that spirit of division?* Somehow I seemed more susceptible to this particular attack, weakened as Superman before kryptonite. I prayed desperately for insight and finally fell on my knees in confusion.

In my silent yielding, the Lord spoke: "The spirit of national idolatry is in you too."

"What?" I exclaimed out loud. "Why, that's impossible!" Indeed, I'd fought against right-wing nationalists ever since my Peace Corps experience opened my eyes to a more international, universalistic perspective. Nevertheless, I realized that during the national anthem before ball games, my heart always soared with pride and joy unlike any feeling I experienced either in church or in prayer.

Could it be that, even as I had committed my actions otherwise, a spirit of national idolatry remained within me from my post World War II youth?

I didn't need spiritual discernment to see that spirit among many other Americans. Though my experience around the world and in my Christian walk had changed my mind, still I had never addressed any spiritual reality that might underlie it.

Sighing, I knelt and grasped the small cross on my desk. "Lord, is it true?" I asked aloud. At once, I sensed a heavy conviction. In the name of Jesus, I renounced the demon of national idolatry within me, confessed it as a sin keeping me from worshipping God fully, and cast it from me. As the "snake" unwound and disappeared, I asked God to give me a renewed submission to Him alone so I could battle more effectively in the future against such a spirit in others.

Finally, I prayed for a renewed appreciation of what He had accomplished in first establishing America and how best to use my resulting freedoms for His purposes. "Much is required from the person to whom much is given," as Jesus said (Luke 12:48).

You can't successfully combat an evil spirit in others, I learned, if in fact that same spirit is in you as well. It's as if an enemy spy were at work in Allied headquarters, beckoning the enemy's attack with precise information on weak spots. My journal concludes: "I can deal with any spirit out there through Jesus, but if it's within me, my effectiveness will be limited. I must work to cleanse myself! That will be the main job of training for spiritual warfare. I must be a clean vessel in order to go forth and do battle in God's power."

The church is therefore often ineffective in combating evil because enemy agents have infiltrated it. Far too many Christians, for example, rush proudly to wave the American flag yet balk at kneeling humbly before the cross to confess personal and national sins. The church, in that sense, is bound by a demon of national idolatry and thus cannot free others from it. Any cursory study of

European history, with its endless tribal/ethnic and national wars, indicates clearly how this spirit came to America and infected the church here.

The presence of the enemy can also prompt certain physical, mental, emotional, or spiritual cues. Physically, I might feel a tightness in my solar plexus, like a "knot" above my stomach. Sometimes I would feel a tic, or a tiny quick muscle contraction like a light bee sting, somewhere on my body. Occasionally, my stomach would turn with a slight nausea.

At other times, my mind would cloud over with a stuffiness or heaviness, perhaps with a swirling sensation or as a twisting knot in my brain. Or at the other extreme, my mind would go rigidly blank, especially when I needed to remember something important. Emotionally, a sort of static might crawl over my skin. I might feel frazzled or jangled, as if I were being torn in different directions at the same time.

When none of these clues manifested, sometimes the Holy Spirit simply would tell me directly, as a voice in my mind or a spooky sensation prompting caution—"Watch out! The enemy is near."

AFTER RECOGNIZING THE ENEMY'S PRESENCE, I WANTED TO KNOW just what particular spirit I was up against. To call someone's name bears power to gain that person's attention. What's more, in the Bible, a name reflects the person's identity before God—as Jesus is a form of Joshua and in Hebrew means "God saves." Evil loves darkness and deception; to call dark spirits by name is to expose them to the light of truth and deprive them of their foothold. Jesus occasionally commanded spirits to identify themselves, and the spirit would speak its name through the voice of the person it had entered, as with the Gerasthene demoniac:

> He was some distance away when he saw Jesus; so he ran, fell on his knees before him, and screamed in a loud voice, "Jesus, Son of the Most High God! What do you want with me? For God's sake, I beg you, don't punish me!" (He said this because Jesus was saying, "Evil spirit, go out of this man!") So Jesus asked him, "What is your name?" The man answered, "My name is 'Mob'—there are so many of us!" (Mark 5:6–9)

It's entirely biblical to command demons to identify themselves, and as I began to do that, demon names would pop into either my mind or the other person's mind, such as *divination* or *lust*. Or I might see in my mind's eye that name-word "printed" before me. Sometimes I would not sense any voice or picture, but only a subliminal awareness of the spirit's name.

As a general rule, however, I decided not to speak to demons myself, as they lie by nature. Instead, I ask the Holy Spirit to tell me who they are. In that case, I may hear a "voice" speak out its destructive message, for example, "You don't belong here!" which might indicate a spirit of alienation, often found in men today as so many are alienated from their fathers. Words like "You're nothing but a worm!" might indicate a spirit of worthlessness.

Eventually, I began to see the particular activity that the demon would seek to manifest portrayed in my mind's eye. I might, for example, see someone beating another person with his fists, which would suggest a spirit of rage, violence, vengeance, or the like. Or I might see someone walking stiff-legged, suggesting a spirit of rigidity.

This soon became uncomfortable, if not disgusting, as the workings of uglier evil spirits similarly portrayed themselves. The enemy seems to crave a theater, as it draws attention to himself and even creates a fascination. Many twelve-step addiction-recovery meetings, for example, base their drawing power on testimonies. But if not monitored, often these otherwise excellent programs can drift over the line from humble confession to war-story bravado or lurid detail.

In time, when I sensed the enemy's presence—whether in myself, in others, or in places—and commanded the identification, an increasing host responded. Whereas at first I would hear or see only one name or image, I soon began to receive two, five, ten, and then literally scores. Before long, I found myself spending exhausting hours in deliverance prayer, reeling off name after name with no apparent end in sight. When I finally shared this with a group of Spirit-filled friends, we prayed and realized that I was giving the enemy a stage, an opportunity to display himself.

I decided instead to bind the spirit in the name of Jesus and command it to make no demonstration either outwardly, as in a person's actions, or inwardly in anyone's mind—beyond what might be necessary to identify and dispel it. Then I would ask the Holy Spirit simply to tell me its name, thus depriving the enemy of any soapbox from which to exhibit himself. Now, I often get an intuitive sense of the demon's name as I pray in my prayer language and wait on the Spirit. The demon's name will sometimes pop into the mind of the person for whom I'm praying.

Not uncommonly, people have been delivered of many demons during several hours of prayer. At times, the Spirit may call forth this kind of extended ministry. My experience, however, was an overload precipitated by the enemy and focused on burning me out.

During those early days, the enemy clearly did not want me to recognize him at all. But if he could not stop me from calling him out, he tried to wear me down by too much identification, to overwhelm me with too much of his presence. This became clearer when I began to see enemy spirits everywhere. I cleansed and blessed underneath beds, down inside drainpipes.

Books that affirm and give instruction in occult practices and the like should be thrown away; but I threw out otherwise good reference books on religion that were entirely benign, without seeking discernment from others, because they "might draw the enemy." I began pulling away from other persons, all of whom seemed to have some working of the enemy about them. Finally, in desperation, I called Bob Whitaker, my older and wiser brother.

"What it sounds like to me," Bob said gently, in his wonderfully pastoral tone, "is that a spirit of 'scrupulosity' has crept into you. You find it a lot in monasteries and in places where people just get too alone and inward. It's a nitpicky, nearsighted thing."

Within a moment after hanging up, I was on my knees. Almost at once, I knew Bob was right. I bound the scrupulosity in me and cast it out, asked for God's mercy and grace to guide me—and went back out to the trash bin to see if I could salvage a few books.

As always, however, my growth in spiritual warfare prompted the enemy to dig deeper into his arsenal. Though I refused to engage in rapid-fire, drawn-out, serial deliverance prayers, the fewer but nevertheless authentic spirits I did encounter became more resistant. I might, for example, "see" the snake wound around me, but when I commanded it to identify itself, nothing happened; or if its identity were revealed, it would not budge as I commanded it to leave.

To my surprise, the necessary spiritual aid to break this impasse came through my ministry to a local nursing home.

About a year after coming to the church, I began taking several members with me to conduct a brief worship service every month at a convalescent hospital nearby. I always brought my guitar for singing hymns at the beginning, and when I asked for requests, the suggestions from residents—most born before World War I—were invariably older evangelical standards. At first, I played those hymns, such as "Amazing Grace" and "I Have Decided to Follow Jesus," with cautious embarrassment, worrying what my pastor friends of "higher education" might think of me.

In time, however, the simple melodies wooed me, and I began genuinely to enjoy them—with one exception. A wheel-chair-bound man would sit lethargic, with eyes closed as if asleep, until I asked for song requests. Then he would lift his head and shout, "'Power in the Blood!'" This, to my educated, rational sensibilities, seemed a quantum leap from "Amazing Grace," and for several months I tactfully put off his request with a variety of fabricated excuses.

And then one day, after thanking him and without thinking, I added that I just didn't have the words and music. Before I could ask for other requests, however, a nurse's aide standing by the door said that someone had left an old hymnal on top of the piano and that maybe the song was in it. There in front of thirty-five residents, I had no choice but to look. To my dismay, "Power in the Blood" was indeed there, and amid the tattered pages, it asked the unsettling questions:

Would you be free from the burden of sin?
There's power in the blood, power in the blood!
Would you o'er evil a victory win?
There's wonderful power in the blood!

Others offered to carry the melody. *Oh no,* I thought, *not another one of those gruesome old "blood" songs!* Nevertheless, I managed a gracious smile and strummed along. Thereafter, I had no excuse for refusing the old man's request, and I had to play it every visit. Even after I began ministering healing and deliverance, the old "blood" songs remained an embarrassing mystery to me.

SOMETIME LATER, AS I STRUGGLED TO DISLODGE A PARTICULARLY resistant spirit in myself, I began praying for help—and the tune of "Power in the Blood" came to mind. I was about to dismiss it matter-of-factly when the line "Would you o'er evil a victory win?" rang out clearly in my mind. I hesitated. *Could it be?* I had scoffed at "all this 'blood' business" for so long—but then, much of what I now considered customary in my spiritual life, I had similarly once scorned. And desperate situations like the present one had always forced me to change. *Well,* I sighed, *it's in the Bible. I'll give it a try.*

And so, with my mind's eye fixed on the unyielding "snake" wrapped around me, I spoke out loud: "By the power of the blood of Jesus, I break your hold on me and send you away!" To my astonishment, in my mind's eye the snake began to unwind. "The blood of Jesus cleanse me!" I exclaimed as a sense of release filled me—and the snake slithered away faster, until it was gone altogether.

Awed, humbled, and profoundly embarrassed, I knew that God

had lured me around yet another corner from which I could never turn back. If any of my rational, universalistic bias still needed to be upended, that finished the job.

I could reason that healing prayer had a certain universalistic hook; other religions and even holistic medicine advocates often promoted healing meditations. But proclaiming ultimate saving power in the blood of Jesus brought the whole issue of spirituality into a sharp and uncomfortably particular focus. Surely, my natural mind reasoned, such an arcane notion belonged where I had found it, in a nursing home—not in this brave new world that had so righteously nurtured me with congruent triangles, theological premises, aspirin, and Di-Gel.

But I had proclaimed the power of Jesus' blood and the enemy had fled. My natural mind, educated in mathematics, could only confess the logic: the blood of Jesus has power to dispel the enemy of God.

Like an old high school geometry theorem, I could only acknowledge, Q.E.D. *Quod est demonstratum*—"thus it is demonstrated."

## Chapter 10
# UNDER ATTACK

So put on God's armor now! Then when the evil day comes,
you will be able to resist the enemy's attacks; and
after fighting to the end, you will still hold your ground.
—EPHESIANS 6:13

A mid this exciting revelation and growing encounters with Jesus as warrior King, I began to notice an occasional chest pain. At first, I shrugged it off, but it persisted and I soon found myself cutting short my jogging and tennis games. For months, I endured the pain and resisted a checkup, since my health insurance had a high deductible and cardiology tests would cost me close to one thousand dollars. Certainly my stress at home and at the church could be expected to have physical effects. Still, I balked because I'd always been so healthy. I asked God to heal me but experienced little relief.

Meanwhile, at a meeting of the Los Angeles Charismatic Pastors' Fellowship, it was announced that Delores Winder, a Presbyterian laywoman healed by God of terminal osteoporosis through the late Kathryn Kuhlman's ministry, would be in the area soon to lead healing ministry events. A few open slots remained on her calendar, and would anyone like to have Delores come to his or her church for an evening healing program?

*What a fantastic opportunity for my congregation!* I thought. Leaping from my seat, I asked to schedule her at my church as soon as possible.

My chest pain was becoming worse, and I knew that I needed to see a doctor about it, no matter what the expense. At thirty-seven, I had not been to a doctor since getting a physical exam five years earlier and couldn't even remember his name. As a last-ditch effort to avoid the expense and inconvenience, I decided to wait and let Delores pray for me—vowing that if nothing happened, I would pay the price and see the doctor.

That evening after worship, Delores taught on the healing ministry of the Spirit and then invited those who wanted prayer to come forward. I encouraged everyone to take advantage of the opportunity, and virtually all did. Only toward the end of the evening did I remember my own need. Most people had already left when Delores offered to pray for me.

About six of my parishioners stood around me, and after a few moments of silence, Delores said, "The Lord has shown me that you are healthy and your body is well. But right now your body is like a battleground, attacked and torn in many directions. There is chaos in your body. The enemy is besetting you with many symptoms, but I see you have a healthy body. Do not let these illnesses in. Claim the blood of Jesus; cast the enemy away. Ask for protection. Spiritual warfare is very great in you. Satan is angry, upset, and wants you. You will emerge from this battle to teach others all that you have learned."

At these words, I sighed in relief, then heard another woman speak who had come to assist Delores: "There's a spirit of lethargy attacking you; praise will drive it away." I sensed the truth in this as I recalled my nodding off during a teaching on the gifts of the Spirit a few weeks before and my ongoing temptation to sleep late.

In the name of Jesus, I renounced the spirit of lethargy, cast it away from me, and asked the Holy Spirit to give me vitality and true rest in its place. Later that week, as a discipline to buttress my defenses, I called a close friend and covenanted with him to call each other at six o'clock every morning to pray briefly together and get me started in the day.

As Delores and the others prayed quietly for me, I took a deep breath and prayed aloud, "In the name of Jesus, you spirits that are attacking and harassing my body, be gone!" Moments later, I sensed the pain under my arm beginning to fade. Within twenty-four hours, it was gone altogether. I did visit a doctor, however, and have scheduled an annual physical exam ever since, including treadmill and other cardiology tests. Doctors have never found any physical problem with my heart. Occasionally, the chest pain returns; I pray through it, sometimes with others, until it goes away.

I hasten to add that we are dealing not with magic formulas here but with the living God who knows each person's situation. Chest pain can be caused by a variety of problems, of which demonic attack is only one. If you have chest pains, see your doctor for a checkup. Even if your problem is primarily spiritual, only the doctor can certify that you're physically okay. Warriors use all resources God has provided, including medical science.

Before Delores finished ministering to me that night, she showed me a major weapon that I've used ever since. "Read Ephesians 6:10–15," she said, "and put on the armor of God every morning." At home, I took out my Bible and read:

> Finally, build up your strength in union with the Lord and by means of his mighty power. Put on all the armor that God gives you, so that you will be able to stand up against the Devil's evil tricks. For we are not fighting against human beings but against the wicked spiritual forces in the heavenly world, the rulers, authorities, and cosmic powers of this dark age. So put on God's armor now! Then when the evil day comes, you will be able to resist the enemy's attacks; and after fighting to the end, you will still hold your ground. (vv. 10–13)

Certainly, this was the clearest definition I had seen for spiritual warfare. The particular items of armor are then listed:

> So stand ready, with truth as a belt tight around your waist, with righteousness as your breastplate, and as your shoes the readiness to announce the Good News of peace. At all times carry faith as a shield; for with it you will be able to put out all the burning arrows shot by the Evil One. And accept salvation as a helmet, and the word of God as the sword which the Spirit gives you. Do all this in prayer, asking for God's help. (vv. 14–18)

The next morning, I prayed for all this armor, one piece at a time, and continued to do so each day afterward. Several weeks later, it occurred to me that each of the armor pieces is identified with Jesus in the Bible. And so I prayed like this: *Jesus, You are truth [John 14:6]. In the name of Jesus, Father, I take up the belt of truth in Jesus for myself and my family today.*

I then prayed similarly for the breastplate of righteousness: *Jesus, You are my righteousness* (1 Cor. 1:30); for the shoes of readiness to announce peace: *Jesus, You are my peace* (Eph. 2:14a); for the shield of faith (2 Thess. 3:3); the helmet of salvation (Luke 1:69); and the Word of God (John 1:1).

During this time, I discovered another surprisingly effective weapon in spiritual warfare. A friend had given me a tape of Christian praise songs. One day while driving across town, burdened with gloom from my chest pain and trouble at the church, I tossed it into my car tape deck at a red light. A few bars into the first song, I flipped it off. "What simple-minded music!" I huffed, lurching ahead as the light turned.

Stuck later in a traffic jam, I flipped on the tape again and listened to several songs, then turned it off again in disgust. "Bunch of throwaway songs!" I scoffed. Before arriving home, I turned that tape on and off half a dozen times. The next day while driving, I caught myself humming a tune from the tape—and turned it on again.

To my surprise, the songs that just the day before had sounded awful now began to lift my spirit, and I found myself singing praises along with the tape before the end of my drive. The enemy's heaviness and darkness had tried to close my spirit to the praise songs, but God had intervened! One day, the tape deck broke and would not play properly; defiantly, I spent fifty dollars to have it immediately repaired.

Soon, I was listening to other tapes, buying songbooks, remembering worship melodies, playing them on my guitar—and singing praises joyously throughout the day. Once, I caught myself and wondered aloud, "Lord, I'm burdened with worse troubles than I've ever seen in my entire life, and here I am singing for joy. Am I crazy? Is this okay?"

I decided it was better than okay and that Nehemiah had been absolutely right when he proclaimed, "The joy of the LORD is [my] strength!" (Neh. 8:10 NIV). As I sang praises to God, the enemy fled—and clarity and brightness filled my spirit. The spirit of lethargy, as prophesied, backed off.

Similarly, in 2 Chronicles 20, King Jehosophat's small band of fighters faces a large and fearsome army. While the nation trembles, the "spirit of the LORD" comes upon a Levite who prophesies, "Your Majesty and all you people of Judah and Jerusalem, the LORD says that you must not be discouraged or be afraid to face this large army. The battle depends on God, not on you. . . . Go out to battle, and the LORD will be with you!" (vv. 15, 17).

Before the battle, the king exhorts his men to believe what the prophet has said and then executes a surprising battle tactic:

> After consulting with the people, the king ordered some musicians to put on the robes they wore on sacred occasions and to march ahead of the army, singing: "Praise the LORD! His love is eternal!"
>
> When they began to sing, the LORD threw the invading armies into a panic. The Ammonites and the Moabites attacked the Edomite army and completely destroyed it, and then they turned on each other in savage fighting. When the Judean army reached a tower that was in the desert, they looked toward the enemy and saw that they were all lying on the ground dead. Not one had escaped. (vv. 21–24)

*Amazing!* I thought. *The king sends the choir out to lead the army!* The message was clear: singing heartfelt praises to God reaffirms His greatness and power—and can thereby rout the enemy.

Soon, it occurred to me that I could fashion a double-edged sword by writing music to go along with Scripture verses I was memorizing and then playing the songs on my guitar. I particularly liked my rendition of Joshua 1:9: "Remember that I have commanded you to be determined and confident! Do not be afraid or discouraged, for I, the Lord your God, am with you wherever you go." Once while playing that verse enthusiastically, a sensation of anger came over me. Immediately, an image flashed in my mind of a rock concert guitarist holding his guitar like a machine gun—and I realized that my own guitar was a weapon against God's enemy as I wielded it in praise.

I had written music for about half a dozen Bible passages, and had at least as many more planned, when I attended the next month's charismatic pastors' meeting. A visitor spoke about intercessory prayer and "ruling spirits" that had control over particular geographic territories, citing the angel who told Daniel, "Now I have to go back and fight the guardian angel of Persia. After that the guardian angel of Greece will appear. There is no one to help me except Michael, Israel's guardian angel" (Dan. 10:20–21). The speaker then urged us to intercede for Los Angeles and battle against any ruling spirits in the city.

Stirred, I invited the speaker to visit our church the next evening and offer his teaching to our congregation. Later at home, I knelt down and fiercely began binding and casting out the demonic strongholds he had identified in Los Angeles.

For the next evening's event, I planned a brief, informal worship time to begin the program on intercession and took my guitar to church in the morning to practice. I had only a half hour for lunch and was scheduled after that to play guitar at our monthly nursing home visit at noon. Hurriedly, I tossed my guitar in the backseat of the car, drove to my apartment, parked in my stall under the building, and ran upstairs for a quick sandwich.

When I dashed downstairs twenty minutes later to drive to the nursing home, to my shock I found that my car had been burglarized. My three-hundred-dollar guitar (that's in 1979 dollars) and recently repaired car stereo were both gone. I called the police at once, but they could offer no help by that time; in fact, when I reported my address, the dispatcher was surprised. "We hardly ever get a theft call in that neighborhood!" he declared.

Hanging up in anger, I realized that the enemy had taken away two important weapons that I had been wielding against him: the tape deck with which I played praise songs, and my guitar with which I was even then writing more musical ammunition. *How could this have happened, Lord?* I cried out.

Simmering quietly, I sensed the answer: "Don't ever again step out beyond your calling as you did last night." For an individual to challenge the huge demonic strongholds over Los Angeles, as I had done, was at best naive and at worst suicidal. I was blessed only to have lost a guitar and tape deck for such foolhardiness. That night, I encouraged the speaker to clarify this point in order to save others from my jarring experience.


SINCE THEN, I HAVE BEEN CAREFUL TO STAY WITHIN GOD'S CALL, always asking Him before challenging demons, *Do I have authority in this arena?* In general, I have that authority over my wife and child and those who give it to me by calling me for counsel and prayer or attending one of my conferences. Beyond that, I pray cautiously for discernment before engaging the enemy.

Soon after the theft, a parishioner called and asked if I would be willing to include a "Questions for the Pastor" column in the next month's church newsletter. "In particular, I want to know what the Bible says about occult practices like astrology, fortune-telling, and such."

I had avoided talking so specifically with anyone in the congregation about the enemy's workings, knowing how explosive such a topic could be in our oldline–denomination church. Could the very surfacing of such a question itself be a working of the enemy? The questioner was entirely sincere, however, and I decided after considerable prayer to answer the question as forthrightly as possible by focusing simply on the Scriptures and avoiding any interpretation. (See chap. 18, "Letters from a Spiritual Warrior," p. 295.)

I was still uneasy about how the congregation might respond, and the day before the newsletter was mailed, I wrote in my journal: "Up at 4:00 a.m., lots of self-deliverance, old tongues! Like a year ago! Sweating when I awoke."

After first receiving the gift the year before, I had prayed in tongues as long as half an hour each morning but had stopped after a while. Now that the battle was intensifying, I would need to reclaim that gift and use every spiritual weapon at my disposal.

Later that morning, I received a phone call from a woman in Arizona, who identified herself as the friend of Delores Winder who had discerned the spirit of lethargy the night Delores had prayed for my heart pain. She had continued to pray for me since that time, and that morning the Lord had told her to call and say, "Today is your day to slay Goliath."

Indeed, as David had shed Saul's armor of steel, she encouraged me to "release to Jesus your desires, ambitions, talents, ministry; cut all strings to them, and give them to the Lord. He will restore them only as you release them."

Furthermore, she said, "The Lord is raising up His army, calling forth the leaders first—generals and commanders. David slew Goliath and routed the Philistines, but later in life he withdrew from battle and let his lust for Bathsheba lead him to sin. You must stay on the front line. It is good to have the conflict in the church out in the open."

Surprised at this woman's call, I was nevertheless encouraged by the words she shared—although admittedly a bit uneasy about any call to be on the front line of spiritual warfare.

Early that afternoon, I decided to take a bold step, which I hoped would be confirmed by the morning's events. Several weeks before, I had responded to an ad in a local throwaway paper for phone answering machines, paying the man for one machine that turned out not to be what I had asked for. After many calls in which he assured me he would pay me back, I had received nothing. And so I drove to his address with the unwanted machine, knocked on his door, and asked for my money back.

He tried to talk me into waiting longer, but I sensed an evil about the man and said that I would not leave without my refund. Finally, after a few moments of stalling, he returned my money and I gave back his machine.

Soon after returning home, I received a phone call from an old friend who had dropped out of sight some years earlier after a divorce. I had heard from him only a few times since, and he had clearly lost his bearing on reality; a mutual friend reported that after he had lodged him for several days, the apartment was burglarized the day he left. When he called, he asked me in a silky voice to come and meet him at a place about an hour's drive away. I sensed a demand beneath his tone and hesitated as an all-too-familiar tightness gripped my solar plexus. Rationalizing to myself that "I should be compassionate," I became defensive and eventually agreed.

After hanging up, however, the tightness turned to nausea. I tried again to tell myself I should consider the man's feelings, but at last I knew it was no use. Praying for Jesus to stand with me, I called the man back and said that I did not want to see him and was sorry to have misled him. At once, the demanding voice burst forth and he became furious at me. Asking Jesus to stand between us, I held my ground and finally hung up. Recording this in my journal, I wrote:

> Praise God! I'm free! Thank You, Jesus, for turning that corner in me. . . . "God guided the stone, but David had to throw it"! I put myself where God wanted me—at the guy's house to get my money back, on the phone to [demanding old friend]—and God took it from there! Thank You for giving me strength to stand!

Once around the corner, however, I discovered that the battle had only begun. When I went to my office Saturday morning, I found that my "creatively and comfortably cluttered" desk had been swept clean and turned into several prim and neat stacks of books and papers.

Confused and angry at such an invasion, I phoned the secretary, who told me that Kate (not her real name), a church member, had decided my desk might offend visitors and so had taken it upon herself to straighten it up. Outraged, I nevertheless fought off fantasies of vengeful anger and prayed for wisdom as to how to handle this affront. I slept fitfully that night, knowing that the next day's worship would include communion. *How,* I worried, *can I dare approach the sacrament, much less minister it, while harboring such resentment?*

The next morning, I went to church an hour before worship as usual and in my desperation prayed out loud in my office: "Lord, send Kate to church early if You want me to speak to her directly; otherwise, set me free from this resentment in order to minister the sacrament as an honor to You." Moments later, to my surprise—and not a little fear—I saw Kate's car pulling into the parking lot. *Okay, Lord,* I sighed nervously, *stay with me on this one!*

I asked Kate to come into my office and explained my feelings to her. My journal records, "She listened, was very understanding. Praise God! I could take communion!"

TWO DAYS LATER, AT A CHURCH MEETING, I HAD A SIMILAR ENCOUN-ter with a particularly frustrating member Liz (not her real name). If any situation bore a potential for conflict, she seemed to know super-naturally how to spark it. My training in psychology and knowledge of her painful childhood suggested several reasons for her disruptive manner, and for some time I compassionately tried to overlook it. Yet as she grew even quicker to assume conflict at church events, my "pure compassion" gave way to an equally pure anger.

That night, we needed to discuss forming a new worship commit-tee, and Liz—in her late sixties—urged three women over sixty-five for the three-member committee. At that, my inner leash broke, and I cried out in my spirit, *Lord, what can I do about this woman? I know You want me to love her, but what she does is making me furious!*

In that moment of surrender to God, I sensed the enemy at work. At once, I confessed and released my anger at her and asked God to show me through His Holy Spirit what was going on. The word *con-tention* came to mind, and I silently bound a spirit of contention in

Liz. She became noticeably subdued, but I could see that she was nevertheless chafing at the bit to stir further conflict.

I asked God for a spirit of wisdom and then spoke to the committee, saying simply that we needed a cross-section of worship sensibilities, which three women in the same age bracket would not provide. Liz huffed and was about to speak, but I silently bound the contention again and others picked up the discussion.

After praying for her for several weeks, I finally knew I had to talk openly with Liz and went to see her. Thanking her for her years of service to the church, I then told her straightforwardly, with no anger, that her contentious attitude was becoming an obstacle to open discussion at the church. I hoped that such a truth-telling would spur her own will to cooperate more with others at the church—though I never told her about my prayers of binding the enemy in her. As I anticipated, she was upset that I "would say such a thing," but I prayed to hold my ground, and she listened.

Thereafter, I demonstrated my compassion for her by thanking her when she was either supportive or helpfully critical in other settings, and by continuing to bind the enemy's power over her. In time, those who had before come to me complaining of Liz's manner told me how much nicer she had become.

The next week, the Charismatic Pastors' Fellowship met, and I parked my car near the freeway in a store lot in order to carpool with others. The theme for the day was spiritual warfare, and it was a "powerful as always!" meeting, as my journal reports. Later that afternoon, when the others dropped me off at my car, I waved goodbye and turned to unlock the door—only to see the handle dented and off-center. "Oh no!" I sighed in disgust. But it was true—my newly replaced tape deck had been stolen.

Driving home alone, I prayed out loud, "Lord, this is twice now the car's been broken into, each time after meeting with the pastors' group and dealing with spiritual warfare! What's going on?" Through my fuming, I sensed that the enemy hated my new walking in the Lord's strength and was attacking me—perhaps hoping I would draw away from the pastors' group and ultimately from my calling.

"I refuse to let this get to me!" I resolved aloud. In fact, I decided I wouldn't tell anyone else about it, that I could manage without a tape deck if necessary, and nothing the enemy could take from me would alter my commitment to the Lord's work.

Several weeks later, I happened to mention the second theft to a longtime member of the pastors' fellowship, and he shook his head in kindly dismay.

"Gordon, my brother," he said, "you've got to take the authority God's given you and stand against the enemy on things like this. He's got you saying, 'It's okay, no matter what you take from me,' when he has absolutely no right to take a single thing from you. Don't make any deals with the enemy, like 'You can have this, but I'll keep that.' Don't let him have *anything* of yours at all! Bind him over all your possessions and send him away!"

Chagrined, I realized that my friend was right. As a boy during recess at school, I had seen a bigger boy on the playground slapping another boy, taunting him, "Whatsamatter? You 'fraid t' fight?" I had never been a playground fighter, but it occurred to me that God was allowing the enemy to slap my face—hoping that I would reach my limit very soon and fight back—unlike the way I had shrunk from conflict during my bullied high school days.

God was teaching me to be His warrior. I was learning that simply striving to be loving, compassionate, and never angry can't bring God's peace, because it doesn't recognize God's enemy. Being "harmless as doves" is only half of Jesus' exhortation; I needed to learn as well to be "wise as serpents" (Matt. 10:16 NKJV).

During the peace movement of the sixties, I had decided that war-making is wrong and must be replaced by love. But I had now spent enough time with Jesus to see that genuine love requires deliberate, saving acts—that, in fact, the ruthless enemy of God is not dispelled by mere peace signs, flowers, or an ideology of compassion—but only by the sign of the cross and the perseverance of those who walk in God's authority.

Genuine peace, gentleness, and love are fruits of the Holy Spirit (Gal. 5:22), the consequences of surrender to God, not to our own altruistic sensibilities. These fruits were won by violent battle on the cross, and they properly supplant and occupy the territory that Christ-centered truth-telling frees from the enemy's grasp. When divorced from Jesus, efforts to proclaim peace and love—no matter how humanly sincere—are a delusion that renders us dangerously vulnerable to evil.

The enemy does not respect sincerity but only authority—which every Christian has. "Power without love is demonic," as another has said; "love without power is sentimentality."

My anger in the face of that woman's contentious behavior was altogether appropriate. The problem arose only when I did not recognize the true, spiritual enemy sparking it within her and thought of lashing back at her personally. I believe today that my anger came from God, that I was in fact sensing God's own anger for what the enemy was doing to God's church through that woman. (See the chapter "Man's Anger and God's Righteous Purpose" in my book *Sons of the Father*.) But this fact only made the enemy more determined to misfocus this anger and give the woman an excuse to reject my correction. My initial, human-centered striving for peace and love, however, would have squelched that word of God within me, for without recognizing the enemy present, I could see nowhere to focus that anger except on the woman herself.

A warrior must be angry at the enemy in order to fight. Propaganda stirs that anger in worldly war. In the presence of our spiritual enemy, the people of God will most assuredly experience anger and must be prepared to focus and wield it faithfully. We need no humanly devised propaganda to stir such anger, for God supplies it readily.

The holy anger of God, properly focused in a human being, was portrayed graphically in King Saul when the enemy Ammonite army besieged an Israeli town and threatened to gouge out the right eye of every person in it. Messengers relayed this dire threat to Saul, who reacted quickly in the power of God: "When Saul heard their words, the Spirit of God came upon him in power, and he burned with anger" (1 Sam. 11:6 NIV). Today's English Version translates, "he became furious."

The Holy Spirit is no milquetoast but deliberately and explicitly incites anger *when the enemy threatens the people of God.* This is no self-centered anger of the flesh, as if Saul were peeved at being interrupted from his otherwise comfortable day; rather, it's God's anger, bestowed in order to stir others to save His people from the enemy.

Significantly, God's anger as manifested in Saul stirred the fear of God in those who otherwise would have been consumed by their fear of the enemy. "And the LORD made the people afraid of Saul's anger, and all of them came out together as one" (1 Sam. 11:7 TLB). When we choose not to receive and express God's anger in the presence of the enemy, our only alternative is to experience our human fear of the enemy—leading to retreat and defeat.

CHRISTIANS WHO LIVE IN FEAR OF THE ENEMY OFTEN ARE SIMPLY afraid of *any* anger and therefore cannot focus a godly anger against their foe. Perhaps as children they saw anger wielded only destructively by their parents and made an inner vow never to "get angry like my father/mother." They can't distinguish between selfish human anger and God's saving anger.

The essential role of anger in spiritual warfare became especially real to me during this time when in a morning devotion I prayed for someone, and God showed me that person's inner brokenness. I felt tears of compassion for the person, and then, even as I wept, I found my fists clenching in anger. Immediately, I stopped praying and worried that I might have a "loose wire" in my emotions—but then realized I was simply feeling God's anger. I asked Him to show me how to focus His anger, and the names of several demons came to mind. I asked if He was giving me authority over these and sensed a yes. And so, angrily, I bound those spirits over the person and cast them out. On occasions when God has not given me that authority, I try to connect the person to someone to whom He has given it—his or her pastor, spouse, or prayer group leader—so that person can pray accordingly.

Since then, I recognize my initial worries as characteristic attacks of the enemy, who wants us to stop praying and not focus God's anger against him. I have also discovered that the enemy is overcome by the Word of God. In this case, a text appeared that Sunday in my denominational preaching lectionary that portrayed Jesus' struggle with exactly the same emotional contrasts I had just faced.

At first the story seemed altogether straightforward:

> A man suffering from a dreaded skin disease came to Jesus, knelt
> down, and begged him for help. "If you want to," he said, "you
> can make me clean." Jesus was filled with pity, and reached out
> and touched him. "I do want to," he answered. "Be clean!" At
> once the disease left the man, and he was clean. (Mark 1:40–42)

The word "pity" in my Good News Bible, however, was foot-
noted, and I read below: "Some manuscripts have *anger.*" *How,* I
wondered, *could Jesus have been "filled" with both pity and anger before
the leper and his plea for healing?*

In prayer later, I understood. The devil wreaks his destruction in
many forms, of which bodily illness is one. Accordingly, the text
portrays the man's disease as an entity in itself, which responds
quickly to Jesus' healing command. The heart of God is reflected in
Jesus as pity toward the diseased person, for the Father identifies
with our sufferings. But as a good Father, He is angry at the disease
itself—enough, in fact, to cast it out of His child.

The fact that Jesus addresses His command not to the disease,
but rather to the man's body suggests that the man had become hos-
pitable to the disease—as perhaps in self-pity—and needed to be
jarred into recognizing and renouncing that. In any case, the disease
(evil) leaves when the man's body and spirit hear the Creator's command to be restored as He originally intended.


I HASTEN TO ADD HERE THAT NOT ALL SICKNESS IS THE WORK OF
demons, any more than all stomachaches are the result of too much

ice cream. Some sickness may simply be the effect of living in a fallen world. Spiritual discernment is necessary to make the appropriate diagnosis and treatment. No matter what the source of the ailment, prayers for healing—as well as a visit to the doctor—are always appropriate. In any case, Christians must be alert to identify that which the enemy stirs and expel it.

Significantly, the word *compassion* stems from two root words: *co*, meaning "together," and *passion*, meaning "suffer." Jesus' readiness to suffer together with the oppressed person led Him into anger at the oppressor. I realized that although the warrior of the world's kingdom may be motivated and sustained solely by anger inflamed by propaganda, the spiritual warrior's license to do battle lies in a willingness to share in the sufferings of others.

Without compassion, warriors soon forget what they're fighting for. "A true soldier fights not out of hatred for those ahead of him," as G. K. Chesterton noted, "but out of love for those behind him." Thus commissioned by compassion, God's warrior is fit to be armed with a holy anger. The two responses cannot serve God apart from each other. Anger without compassion is destructive; compassion without a capacity for anger is to be destroyed.

I now realize that the resistance among my parishioners to healing prayer and the power of the Holy Spirit prompted God's anger within me. God is not happy when His people reject the power Jesus died to give us. But in my spiritual immaturity, I did not see that God's anger in me was directed not at those people but at His enemy, who was stirring and enforcing that resistance. I believe that God was calling me to weep for those people even as He was calling me to lift His sword in anger against the enemy.

But all too often, I wept without lifting the sword, and my pity drifted into passivity; or I lifted the sword without having wept, and marched into judgment, bitterness, and resentment.

I now realize that God is not against all anger per se, but against anger that emanates from human desire. God wants us to retain the capacity for anger—not to fortify our position against other persons, but to fortify God's position against His enemy.

As James put it, "Remember this, my dear friends! Everyone must be quick to listen, but slow to speak and slow to become angry. Human anger does not achieve God's righteous purpose" (James 1:19–20). The warrior of God learns to recognize and appropriate not man's but God's anger—and to focus or express it only as God directs.

My growing experience with God's strength within me demonstrated that too often I had hidden from an appropriate godly anger behind a false mask of "compassion." *How*, I wondered, *am I to be set free from this fearful charade and grow yet further in the strength to walk out His victories?*

All too soon, He provided the battle to teach me.

## Chapter 11

# ON YOUR GUARD: UNMASKING FALSE PROPHETS

> False prophets will appear. They will perform miracles and
> wonders in order to deceive even God's chosen people, if possible.
> Be on your guard! I have told you everything ahead of time.
>
> —MARK 13:22–23

M y efforts to rediscover the workings of the Holy Spirit and encourage others to do so continued to stir resistance. The lack of harmony in my marriage and lack of support in my church eventually led me to feel lonely and seek comfort and support from others who shared my experience. One day, I saw in a local church newsletter the notice of a Spirit-filled Sunday evening worship nearby, and I decided to try it. About fifteen people attended the first night I went, and we all enjoyed an uplifting evening of worship together.

When we gathered afterward to pray for each other, one woman seemed particularly anxious to join in. Perhaps sixty, noticeably overweight but well kempt, she seemed to take charge in a way that led me to believe she was a regular member of the church. Her quick smile seemed to betray an inner longing to be accepted, which struck a chord of compassion in me; nevertheless, her prayers assumed an air of authority that left me impressed yet strangely uneasy.

At the fellowship hour afterward, she came over to greet me and soon began telling me that she had lived alone since divorcing her child-molester husband some twenty years previously and had undertaken a freelance ministry of "healing and prophecy—just going where the Lord sends me." Jane (not her real name) did not belong to any church but occasionally referred to her "spiritual daughters"—various younger women whom she had taken under her wing and prayed for.

My pastor's heart at once saw a lonely person in great need of emotional healing and apparently with considerable gifts. As she chattered endlessly about her past spiritual exploits, I finally excused myself and left—imagining how wonderful it would be to have someone among our church body with such powerful gifts of healing and prophecy.

Several months later, I bumped into Jane at a large Christian conference in the area. I had taken a carload of parishioners with me, and we were sharing a snack in the lunchroom when Jane came over and asked if I would come with her to pray for a friend of hers. "I saw your gifts the last time we prayed," she said, greeting the others at my table with a nod, "and I know you could be a very special help."

I turned to my parishioners, trying to hide the pride and elation swelling within me—would they please excuse me?

Several weeks later, I was pleasantly surprised to see Jane in our church for Sunday worship. To my even greater surprise, I saw as well Alice (not her real name), an active member of another church, whom I had met briefly at an earlier renewal conference.

Each woman had come independently to our worship, and each

was quite different from the other. Jane was divorced, short, quick, and talkative; Alice was married, tall, thoughtful, and reserved.

Both, however, seemed quite gifted in the workings of the Holy Spirit, and I was delighted to welcome them amid the grumbling undercurrents at the church. I needed all the allies in the Spirit I could get, and each of these women seemed a clear gift from God.

After worship, Alice greeted me with a friendly smile and turned to visit with others. Jane made a beeline for me: "The Lord sent me to pray for you and your church!" she declared. Inwardly, I sighed in relief. *Thank you, Lord, for sending reinforcements!*

Before long, however, I began to wonder. Jane came to our after-worship prayer group and began at once to lay hands on people, share long accounts of past healings when she had prayed, and inter-rupt conversations with an exhortation to pray right then. Eventually, I spoke firmly to her, asking her please to take her time and allow all of us a chance to participate. Alice, meanwhile, spoke little and remained silent during the prayer time.

The next week during after-worship prayer group, Jane broke into one conversation suddenly and announced, "Wait! I'm getting a word from the Lord!" We all stopped, curious, as she broke into tongues for a moment and then offered an English interpretation. I tensed immediately. Although we had begun tentatively to study and even exercise spiritual gifts, no one had ever used tongues in our group before, and I was afraid some people might be upset.

Jane's interpretation, however, was gentle and fit in well with what we had been discussing. Later, I asked two others in the group their opinion, and both agreed that in spite of a discomfort at her aggressive style, the word she offered nevertheless seemed appropriate and helpful.

At the next Sunday worship, I announced that a new-members class was forming and invited anyone interested in joining to come. Immediately afterward, Jane came to me and said she very much wanted to join the church and signed up for the class. Alice said she was already a member of another church but wanted to continue visiting ours.

The prayer group members were willing to suspend disbelief. "Sure, Jane is a little strange," one offered, "but I guess we're all a bit weird in some way, and maybe we can help her as we've all been helped in the group." The following Sunday, Jane prayed in the group that my sermons "would take very little time to prepare and just flow from the Spirit"—and, indeed, my sermon the next week came together just like that, with many parishioners telling me how it particularly spoke to their need.

The next week, Jane prayed that my preaching voice would be strengthened and would hold up as the Lord needed it. I spoke at a weekend workshop soon after that and was surprised at how well my voice did indeed hold up, even after three Sunday morning sermons. Later, Jane drew me aside after the prayer group. "The Lord showed me that there is a polyp on your vocal cords that can only be cured by surgery or prayer." Surprised and a bit frightened, I hesitated, then consented as Jane insisted on praying for me at that moment.

As I observed Jane, I felt torn: elated over the benefits that her apparent spiritual gifts might offer the church, yet cautious of her aggressive style. I decided that an appropriate test would be if she would submit herself to the body and ask us to pray for her, instead of always being the prayer initiator herself.

The very next week, Jane spoke up in the group. "Would all of you please pray for my obesity?" she asked. "I really need help with this."

Startled and disarmed by her vulnerability, we all prayed for her. Many significant words came forth for her emotional healing, and a sense of relief filled the air. Afterward, she stayed behind to ask if I would give her spiritual counsel, especially to minister emotional healing to her. Pleased, even flattered, I remembered my first impression that Jane could benefit greatly from emotional healing.

I met alone with Jane for six weekly meetings. Often in our prayers, the Lord would lead us to a particularly painful episode in her past—yet every time I invited her to let Jesus come into her wound, she would proceed to speak in tongues and interpret the message herself. Frustrated with her dance-away mode, I could see that her pains were very deep, and I determined to be patient. Indeed, often her "interpretation" of her tongues supported what I was trying to do and kept me hopeful of her healing. "Listen to what this man is saying," she often interpreted. "He is the one who can bring you to healing. Stay and keep coming. Don't run away." Jane's diversionary chatter often concerned her past spiritual journey, and curiously, she never once mentioned dealing with demons, deliverance, or prayers of protection during her many years of "Holy Ghost ministry." Furthermore, she would cling to her "Holy Ghost experience" as an unassailable defense. "I will have no close personal relationship with anyone who cannot accept my faith as it is," she put it.

I asked if she would come with me to visit a church member housebound by illness, and she declined: "My calling is to prophecy, not to housekeeping chores like feeding others and running errands."

Most disconcerting was her account of having consulted a psychic for guidance at one point in her life. Surprised, I asked how someone of her spiritual maturity didn't know that such activities are channels for demons. "Oh, I'm a Spirit-filled Christian," she scoffed. "I don't have to worry about things like that—I'm protected by the Holy Ghost!"

Meanwhile, several other church members had come to me to express their discomfort with Jane. "She talks too much. . . . She's arrogant, as if nobody else could be as spiritually mature as she is. . . . She's just too quick to grab you and pray with you."

Still, it did not escape my attention that Jane was taking every opportunity to speak up to others in the church about "how wonderful the minister is." She stood up at a congregational meeting and praised me for praying for so many people everywhere I went and for being so "thoughtful and dedicated." Certainly, the criticism I received from others in the church made me especially willing to allow Jane her soapbox on my behalf.

INDEED, AS THE CONGREGATION'S UNEASINESS WITH MY FOCUS ON healing prayer and the Holy Spirit escalated, my desperation for a clear-cut word from God overruled my earlier caution, and I decided to ask Jane to pray for me in my office. I was reassured at our first session, as Jane's messages in tongues and their interpretations showed clear knowledge of my wounded feelings and desire for validation. The second week's session was similar; in fact, every "word from the Lord" that she offered reflected a sense that I had been wronged, treated unfairly, and not acknowledged for my "authority in the Lord."

Much as I longed for an advocate, I was nevertheless puzzled that she never suggested that I had done anything wrong or needed to grow in any way. Her words were strangely too comforting, unlike the truly loving counsel I had been accustomed to from my friends in the prayer group, which was often balanced with honest recognition of my faults.

The Monday after my second prayer session with Jane in my office, I received a phone call from the secretary. "You'd better come over quickly," she said, her voice breaking. "The church was broken into last night and everything's a mess."

And, in fact, it was. The thief not only had entered the office area, but also had taken half of our brand-new handbell set and all of our office equipment, including two typewriters, a phone answering machine, and a copy machine. Desk and file drawers had been randomly tossed about, and papers were strewn everywhere. After calling the police, I called several other church members to come and help us clean up. "I just feel so invaded," one woman sighed after looking around.

Clearly, the enemy was prepared to attack the church in more ways than simply conflict and disunity among the members.

At my next week's prayer session with Jane, it happened. Where before all her words had been comforting and encouraging, this time they were cold and sharp. The Lord, she said, was telling me to separate myself from everyone who opposed me and frustrated my ministry—especially my closest loved ones—because He had a clear and powerful claim on my life. In fact, He wanted to lift me up to a special sort of ministry in the not-too-distant future that would require having close to me only those who would support me in the most devoted way.

I was shocked, shattered, terrified. I couldn't believe the Lord would want me to do that. But weren't all of Jane's other words full of knowledge and truth?

Sensing my upset, Jane quickly offered to pray that the Lord would take from my heart all love for those closest to me so there wouldn't have to be the "terrible sadness" and waste of energy that would be needed instead for my new calling. Of course, she had prayed that way for someone else years ago, and it had worked out just fine.

Reeling, I managed to say no and then told Jane I wanted to be alone.

"I'm so sorry to be the cause of such pain," she said, flustered. "I don't think I've ever given a word quite like that. But don't worry, the Lord did say that He would stand by you and bring others even better for you in the future." Smiling, she patted me on the arm and said she would nevertheless pray that perhaps the Lord would show her "something else that might even make this word all wrong." Then, turning to go, she added, "But I've never received a wrong word before."

Struggling to maintain my composure, I walked her to the door and said good-bye.

Numbed, I turned and walked into the sanctuary and fell on my knees at the altar. As I prayed for help, it occurred to me to call Alice. I did so, and at once she urged me to "find your three witnesses" (2 Cor. 13:1).

I asked if she had any sense about this word for me to sever all close relationships, and she said that on November 10, she had been awakened at night and a word came to her that "Gordon must withdraw from a troubling situation." She had not shared that with me then, pending further confirmation. When I later checked my journal, I saw that November 10 was when I first asked Jane to pray for me. It occurred to me that, ironically, Jane was right. God was indeed calling me to sever a relationship with someone close to me—namely, Jane herself!

I called three pastors I trusted, and to my great relief, all said that this word from Jane sounded suspicious. As one pastor put it, "It just did not ring true."

As I pulled myself together and tried to make sense of what had happened, the thought struck me: *Yes! Thank God I've been saved from the evil in Jane!*

Almost immediately, however, I remembered that in two weeks the new-members class would be received into the church. The whole congregation knew who was in the class, and regardless of a few misgivings, it was accepted that Jane would become a member. What was I to do? Surely, I could not allow this woman to join the church; I could hardly imagine what other seeds of evil she might sow in our already troubled garden!

Few in the church had the spiritual maturity necessary to recognize the genuine evil at work in Jane. The several who were unnerved by her manner would undoubtedly rise to her defense and express compassion toward her—even because I had preached so often on loving others we might not like! If I were to bar Jane from membership, I would be attacked as cruel and un-Christian.

I had caused this dilemma by my own poor judgment. Yet I was responsible to protect my congregation from the danger I had loosed.

The following week, I had an appointment to minister to Jane on Wednesday at 1:30. I also had an appointment just before that, at noon, to pray with Alice and Judy, a particularly gifted and reliable member of our weekly prayer group. When I asked Alice and Judy to pray for my meeting with Jane, Alice had a strong sense that I was not to be alone with Jane again. I certainly agreed to that—and then asked if the two of them would stay and pray with me for Jane. We all sensed a heavy darkness over the whole situation, and though Alice and Judy were understandably reluctant, we prayed for a moment and both had a clear sense that, indeed, they were to stay.

The three of us had hardly closed our prayer when Jane arrived. I asked her if it would be okay for Alice and Judy to join us, and she agreed. We sat at the altar, under the cross, and as soon as I finished an opening prayer asking for protection and guidance, the battle began. Demon after demon identified itself in Jane as Alice, Judy, and I confirmed and called them out—among them "false prophecy," "self-righteousness," and "deception."

Through it all, Jane kept remarkably calm and strangely cheerful. When I asked her to renounce each demon's work in her, she did so dutifully. Occasionally, she would chuckle in amazement as spirits identified themselves, and I was surprised that someone who purported to be so spiritually mature had never experienced such deliverance ministry.

After about an hour, we fell silent and knew the Lord's work for that day was finished. The four of us praised God, sang hymns, and departed. Later, Alice called to say she left feeling "a tremendous sadness, as if the Lord Himself were sad that Jane would not receive His true word." Then Judy called to say she wondered if in fact Jane had ever really received the baptism of the Spirit, in spite of all her speaking in tongues and "Holy Ghost experience."

Two days later, I called Jane to see how she was doing. "Oh, I'm just fine!" she chirped.

"Well," I allowed, puzzled by her apparent lack of concern, "that was a pretty intense prayer time, and I wanted to see how you felt about it all."

"Let me tell you," she shot back, a hardness in her voice that I had not heard before. A heavy darkness began clouding about me. "I've been moving in the Holy Ghost for many years now, much, much longer than you. I am your spiritual mother, in fact!"

"What?" I exclaimed, jerking forward. The telltale knot gripped my solar plexus—by now a familiar sign of the enemy's presence.

"Yes!" Jane declared. "When I told my spiritual daughter what you did, she was furious and said she wanted to come over to your church and give you a piece of her mind. Why, the idea that I might have an evil spirit in me! She confirmed every word I gave you last week, and she said she wouldn't stand for anyone treating me like that!"

Under my breath, I placed the cross between Jane and me and claimed the blood of Jesus to protect me.

"And let me tell you this," she continued; "what you all did was unscriptural."

"What?" I asked. "How do you mean?"

"You search the Scriptures, anywhere you like, and you will never find a single instance of a disciple casting a demon out of another disciple. That just isn't done in Scripture, and you have broken the way of God!"

The words came to me at once: "But you don't see a disciple laying hands on and healing another disciple, either—yet surely, you wouldn't say healing prayer is unscriptural."

"Well . . . er," she huffed. "You read that book in your church library about Kathryn Kuhlman—*she* never had people lay hands on her!"

I recalled Jane's fascination with Kuhlman. "Kathryn's life was just like my own," Jane had said, with more than a hint of pride.

As I listened, I felt the cloud lifting. "What you're saying is that you're not willing to submit to the body at our church, to accept our prayers for you?"

"That's right!" she snapped. "And I won't be back—you can be sure of that!" And she hung up.

I sighed in relief and fell to my knees to thank the Lord for saving both His church and me by removing her. And then a picture of Jane came to mind, terribly alone: cold, lost, cast adrift in the world—and I cried for her.

The next day, Judy called and said she was having a "terribly difficult time praying for Jane," and when she stopped trying to do so, Jane had completely left her mind. Another woman in the Sunday prayer group called and mentioned that she had prayed for Jane a few days ago. Later in our conversation, she said that she'd been "feeling depressed for a couple of days." At that, a light clicked on, and we both connected the depression with her praying for Jane. Whatever was wrong with Jane lay beyond our capacity to handle, and we were simply supposed to stop praying for her and release her to the Lord—which we did.

Later, when our new-members class began without Jane, a disgruntled member of our church called Jane to ask why, and Jane told her I had said I didn't want her in our church. This distortion was spread through the congregation, and at least one family left the church, scolding me for being "so unkind to that nice lady."

Eventually, I called the leader of the Sunday evening group where I'd met Jane some months before to warn of my experience with her. The leader said that Jane had only attended their group the two times I had come, and the others there had discerned during prayer after all visitors had left that, indeed, Jane was a false prophet.

An autopsy was clearly in order. *Okay, Lord,* I sighed in dismay.

*I don't want to waste any of this awful circumstance—teach me whatever I need to learn from it!*

The fact that Jane had come to the original prayer fellowship only when I had come suggested that the enemy was using her to single me out for attack. Obviously, I needed to communicate regularly with the larger body as much as possible for knowledge, wisdom, and protection.

The church burglary, I sensed, was not unrelated to Jane's presence among us. Not that she was involved in it, but that both events were part of a larger enemy invasion. Jane was likely intended to establish a beachhead, and as she gained a foothold in my life, enemy troops soon followed in the form of robbers.

As I praised God for His faithful deliverance and poured out my pain from the experience, I sensed He had allowed my misadventures with Jane in order to train me in His warfare. *How in the world,* I asked the Lord, *could I have allowed myself to be so deceived? Where is the chink in my spiritual armor that left me open to the false spirit in Jane?*

I reread several articles and book chapters in my file on how to discern false prophecy. I could only conclude that Jane had not violated any one of those standards overtly enough to identify her at the outset as a false prophet. None of her actions could be described as harmful; indeed, though pushy at times, she was later spoken of by others as "cheerful . . . friendly . . . optimistic . . . helpful." Though she had visited a psychic, it had only been one time; many of our church members had done that and did not come to renounce it until relatively far along in their faith journey.

Furthermore, Jane did indeed have a spiritual channel of knowledge about my thoughts and feelings. She was convincing. Something was showing her the inner workings of my heart—something that knew my wounds so well that it knew exactly how to capitalize on them, how to manipulate my fears, and how to build on my worst fantasies in my weakest moments.

I realized that I had left a door open to the enemy, insofar as I had made room for those negative fantasies in the first place, before meeting Jane. When she said, "The Lord says you are to leave others who are close to you," I had already given far too much rein to similar thoughts previously, in moments of frustration.

The genesis of sin is pride. When Jane praised me publicly, before my detractors in the church, my wounded pride succumbed to her support.

As I prayed for further understanding, I saw myself as a little boy, longing for a "spiritual mother"—that is, a woman to support and defend me and to lend God's authority to my self-centered flesh that told me, *You are never at fault. You deserve better. You don't have to put up with people who don't give you what you want.* As I offered that boy humbly to the Father, He showed me my adult, manly need—not for a spiritual mother but for a spiritual partner, a woman who could support me and also hold me accountable. I saw how my impatience, my unwillingness to wait for the Lord to provide that partner, had given that wounded little boy inappropriate authority over my life.

Alice was right. I never should have allowed myself to spend such time alone with Jane.

Even now, I'm tempted to excuse myself by saying, "Jane came into my life at an especially difficult time, when I was hurting and personally vulnerable from being under attack. At some other time, when I might have been more fortified and self-assured, I never would have been hooked by her stratagems."

But of course, much of the attack that I suffered *came* from the enemy. Furthermore, the enemy attacks only when and where his chances of success are greatest—namely, when and where you are weakest. And so I immediately sought healing for my mother-wound with a Christian counselor and in several prayer groups.

It's embarrassing to review this season in my life and recall all the women involved locally and not one spiritually mature male leader alongside me at my church. Today, I'm blessed with several men, seasoned spiritual warriors whom I sought out and with whom I pray regularly—and a supportive wife who is a seasoned battle partner.

I came to view the episode with Jane as part of a larger scheme to bring me down, and I can only praise God today for His saving hand when I was unable to save myself. I see it like an inoculation, in which you're injected with an amount of toxin too small to bring you down, but enough to stir your immune system to build up antibodies to fight off future attacks. A big part of the lesson lay in healing the chinks in my armor from childhood wounds, which short-circuited my discernment.

Jesus emphasized in His warning against false prophets, "Be on your guard!" And Peter in turn exhorted the early church, "Be alert, be on watch! Your enemy, the Devil, roams around like a roaring lion, looking for someone to devour" (1 Peter 5:8).

I had learned that such alertness can be sustained only among the fellowship of believers; lone sheep do not escape the attack of a roaring lion. As Peter continued, "Be firm in your faith and resist [the enemy], because you know that other believers in all the world are going through the same kind of sufferings" (v. 9).

Above all, I had learned that the Father is merciful and gracious in training His warriors, that no matter how blind we are, how vicious the battle, or how great the suffering, the victory is His. As John reassured: "But you belong to God, my children, and have defeated the false prophets, because the Spirit who is in you is more powerful than the spirit in those who belong to the world" (1 John 4:4).

# Chapter 12
# SABBATICAL REST— OR BOOT CAMP?

Therefore, since the promise of entering his rest still stands,
let us be careful that none of you be found to have fallen short of it.
For we also had the gospel preached to us, just as they did;
but the message they heard was of no value to them,
because those who heard did not combine it with faith.

—HEBREWS 4:1–2 NIV

E arly in the summer of 1983, beginning the seventh year of my pastorate, I sensed a special need for rest and for perspective on my warrior calling. I requested a three-month sabbatical to begin in January 1984. Fearful that the church might reject my request, I dutifully offered in my proposal that I would take a seminary course in church administration and pursue other opportunities to increase my ministry skills.

The church agreed to the sabbatical—with a sobering one-fourth voting against it.

As the New Year's beginning date approached, I reread the seminary catalog. To my dismay, I realized that the administration course met two days a week at 8:00 a.m. in Pasadena. That meant at least two to three hours on the freeway at rush hour, twice a week! Hopeful that the course work might justify such an effort, I looked again at the syllabus. In a terrifying bolt of truth, I knew that I had absolutely no desire to take that course. Desperately, I asked myself if, in fact, there was any course I wanted to take, and in that moment I knew there was—but it would not be offered in seminary. My spirit cried out the answer, the response to my need for understanding God's purpose in my life: I wanted to study the Norwegian language as the root of my warrior calling and identity.

Hoping that somehow I could manage it among a growing list of other promised sabbatical commitments, I decided to seek out such a course. I recalled an instance perhaps a year earlier, when a Lutheran pastor in our renewal pastors' group had introduced a visitor with a good-natured laugh as "my Norwegian-speaking Lutheran brother." I called that pastor and was referred to Rev. Don Brendtro, then pastoring in Costa Mesa, about an hour's drive south of me.

A third-generation Norwegian American and married to a native Norwegian, Don directed me to a language course at the Sons of Norway hall in San Pedro, about fifteen miles from me. As we chatted in his office, he mentioned "Fredensbolig"—literally "house of peace"—a Spirit-filled retreat center outside Oslo that he and his wife, Astrid, had helped to organize several years earlier. I offhandedly remarked that I would like to go to Norway someday and especially to be with Spirit-filled Norwegian Christians in a place like Fredensbolig. Don told me that the center did not receive visitors except during the summer; in dismay, I explained that my sabbatical was in the winter and my promised schedule would not permit such a visit anyway.

Before leaving, I asked Don to pray for me. As we were about to begin, suddenly his office door opened and a blond, blue-eyed woman stepped in. Noticing me, she hesitated. "Oh, I am so sorry to interrupt," she offered, with a distinct European accent.

Don smiled and introduced me to his wife, Astrid, noting my Norwegian name, Dalbey, and explaining that I wanted to study the language during my sabbatical, which would begin that next week.

"How nice!" she said and then turned to excuse herself. Immediately, Don invited her to stay and pray with us, and I added my encouragement.

With Astrid seated between us, Don offered a brief prayer of thanksgiving for our meeting and then asked God to bless my sabbatical. As I rose to go and shook his hand, Don mentioned to Astrid that he had told me about Fredensbolig.

"Really? That's very strange," she said, knitting her brow.

"What?" Don and I asked in unison.

"As we were praying, I had this sense of Gordon at Fredensbolig. But I wasn't going to say anything about it, because I assumed he knew nothing about it, and they don't accept visitors this time of year."

My heart leaped. What other time in my life would I be able to visit Norway? Could this be a leading of the Lord? In my excitement, I forgot my already filled schedule and turned to Don. Would he allow me to use his name and write the leaders at Fredensbolig to see if they might make an exception to their seasonal restrictions?

He shrugged his shoulders matter-of-factly and smiled. "Why not? The worst they can do is say no!"

The next day—December 28, 1983, three days before the sabbatical was to begin—I wrote a letter to Knute Grønvik, the director at Fredensbolig, telling him the story of my two Norwegian names, Roger and Dalbey, and asking him if I might visit the center during the next three months. I suggested the last three weeks in March—the very last part of my sabbatical. Given my sunny-California conditioning, I wanted the warmest possible weather in Norway!

One other event finally had been added to my calendar: a week-long healing prayer retreat at the Pecos, New Mexico, Benedictine monastery in late February. For the past three years, I had applied for this popular yearly event and been turned down each time. Then "out of the blue," my application for this year was approved.

Apart from the excitement of yet-to-be-revealed plans and the fear of promises too hastily made, my energies during the first weeks of the sabbatical were consumed by anxiety. Seminary registration was not until January 21, and the Pecos retreat not until late February. I had never thought of myself as a person who depended upon external considerations for my sense of self-worth; rather, I considered myself an inner-directed person. When I first looked at all those blank white pages in my desk calendar, however, a wave of numbness swept over me.

Suddenly, with absolutely no immediate obligations, I was thrown back to face no one but myself. I was frankly terrified—not so much by what I might find in me, but by what I might *not* find, namely, inner direction, after all my pretensions to the contrary. Without schedules, plans, meetings, appointments, deadlines, or obligations, I had the sense that all meaning had been drained out of my life. I felt altogether naked and unarmed as a frightening sense of aloneness and emptiness lurked nearby, stalking my very soul.

A sampling of entries in my prayer journal during this time indicates the anxiety I felt:

*Jan 1:* All week I've been nervous about beginning my sabbatical and afraid I won't make the most of it, etc. . . . I want to be redisciplined, intentional in overcoming those hostile voices in me—to praise even in hard times!

*Jan 3:* Up at 6:45. Always the urge to go back to bed "just for a while." After alarm, when I overrule that and just get up and stay up, it goes away and I feel alert and okay. . . . Lord, I feel me still balking a bit at the work, fall to sleep reading a book! Lethargy attack—must be vigilant. I'm afraid I'll blow the sabbatical and get nothing done. Feel guilty—thought of meeting with [irate parishioner], others scoffing at me. Lord, save me! I feel guilty for taking the sabbatical and guilty for not taking or using it fully! Save me!

*Jan 6:* I am frightened by no schedule—fear there is nothing in me to come out—or if there is, it can't be good/right. Fear of myself? . . . I want to get started writing—but not yet? Question: *What am I afraid of?* . . . disapproval of church folks . . .

During the next few days, I met with my monthly pastors' support group and called several other friends to pray for me. One brief entry from January 8 says it all:

"Called [friend]: I'm afraid, lonely." Through the loving compassion, wise counsel, and diligent prayer of these brothers, I came to see that my fear of emptiness was basically a lack of faith. Indeed, in my own human resources, I was empty; I just needed to confess that, to die to my own abilities and humanly devised plans, and to cry out for God to fill me.

"*Jan 10:* After such heaviness—what a release! I felt set free from myself/flesh and really relaxed."

On January 20, the day before seminary registration, my journal entry opens with a brief note of an unusual dream: "*Jan 20:* Dream: I am pregnant." Could this mean the birth of something new in me?

Indeed, several days followed with the promise of new life. As my journal continues, "Letter from Norway—it's okay for me to come!" Knute Grønvik wrote that the residents at Fredensbolig had considered my request prayerfully and decided that they would make an exception to their usual policy in my case.

"Should I call you Roger?" he asked and closed, noting that everyone would look forward to meeting me.

*Amazing!* I thought. First the retreat at Pecos, a Spirit-filled monastery, had opened up at just this time. And now Fredensbolig, another Spirit-filled community in the country where Rogers and Dalbeys come from, was beckoning me! *Could it be,* I wondered, *that the Lord is scheduling my sabbatical Himself?* A flush of joy at such a prospect was checked by fear as I recalled my scheduled commitments to the church.

Praying, I sensed only that God was calling me to the loyalty oath that every soldier must take upon entering basic training, acknowledging the primacy of military orders over an individual's security. As I further reflected on the truly momentous opportunities in Pecos and Norway, the die was cast. Joyfully, fearfully, I wrote to Fredensbolig and accepted their invitation.

I did not register at the seminary the following day.

Needless to say, as my announced schedule began to give way to other, apparently ordained events, the fear of facing the church over this discrepancy invited a host of self-doubts. Even as I knew I didn't want to take a course in church administration, I asked myself what sort of course or training I did, in fact, want for the ministry I sensed growing within me. I had some training in secular psychology and counseling and in recent years had done considerable work in healing prayer. But I sensed a gap, a missing link, as I sought to integrate the counseling and prayer. Nothing in the seminary catalog offered that, and I had been asking fellow pastors to keep an eye out for any workshops or training sessions that might do so.

On January 21, the day after receiving Fredensbolig's invitation and the day I decided not to register for seminary classes, I received a long-distance call from Rev. Vernon Stoop, the director of the Fellowship of Charismatic Christians in the United Church of Christ (FCC/UCC). Through his national connections in the denominational charismatic movement, Bob Whitaker had recommended I contact Vernon for support in my faith journey from a then-fellow UCC pastor, and we had corresponded several times during the past year.

Vernon called from his church in Pennsylvania and told me that he was going to visit California in several weeks and hoped that we might meet each other in person at last. Delighted, I asked where he would be, only to groan in dismay when he said Sacramento. Teasingly, I told Vernon that distances in the West are not so discountable as in the East, that Sacramento is about a five-hour drive from Los Angeles.

We both expressed our disappointment, and the conversation was about to end when I happened to ask Vernon what he would be doing in Sacramento. "I'll be directing a weeklong seminar on prayer counseling," he said.

"What?" I exclaimed. "You mean you'll be leading a program putting counseling and prayer together?" Excitedly, I told him how I had been hoping to find just such an opportunity during my sabbatical. I was about to ask if I could enroll in his prayer counseling seminar when I realized that in effect I had already said the drive would not be worth the effort just to see him personally. How could I say I would come for the course? After some hesitation—and hinting—finally my excitement overruled my sense of shame and I asked Vernon outright if I could get into the seminar.

"Frankly, I'd like to have you with us," Vernon replied with reassuring grace, "but we have to keep these seminars at a strict limit, and it's already filled." He added that similar seminars were being offered at various times around the country; in fact, one was scheduled in April for Phoenix.

I sighed and noted that my sabbatical ended March 31, and after that I would need to stay pretty close to the church for a while. *Lord*, I sighed again, overwhelmed with disappointment, *that sounds exactly like what I've been looking for!*

"Aren't there any more seminars in California?" I pleaded. Thinking immediately of Pecos and Norway, I checked and discounted as outrageous the notion of adding, "before March 8 and not between February 26 and March 3."

"No," Vernon replied. "I don't think there's another seminar in California this year."

"Would you just check the schedule to be sure?" The words were out of my mouth before I knew it. I was about to apologize for being pushy when I heard the rustle of papers on the other end of the line.

"Let's see. . . . Well, actually, yes, there is one more in California this year. I guess I didn't see this one."

"When is it?" I blurted out.

"As a matter of fact, it's only a few weeks off, beginning February 13. I'd have to make some calls immediately to get you in."

"Fantastic!" I exclaimed. "Where?"

"I don't know this town, but maybe you do. It's called Rancho Palos Verdes."

I shook my head in disbelief. *"Rancho Palos Verdes?"* I cried out. "Why, that's the next town over from me, not a mile away!"

Moments later, after we had worked out the details of my attending the prayer counseling seminar and hung up, I sat by my phone in silent awe. Any remaining doubts that God had ordained and scheduled my sabbatical were washed away as the sensation of biblical fear swept over me yet again.

It was time to stop wasting my energies wondering whether or not I should have taken the sabbatical and to begin instead to cooperate with God in His obvious plans for it. On January 24, my prayer journal entry opened with the joyous note: "Began my writing schedule. Up at 7:00, writing by 8:30—praise God!"

WHILE GOD'S HAND WAS BY NOW CLEARLY AT WORK IN MY SABbatical, I still worried about how I was going to explain this to my congregation, whom I had promised a variety of pastoral enhancement activities. On January 26, I wrote in my journal the words of an ancient cry for help: "Be merciful to me, O LORD! See the sufferings my enemies cause me! Rescue me from death, O LORD, that I may stand before the people of Jerusalem and tell them all the things for which I praise you. I will rejoice because you saved me" (Ps. 9:13–14).

The Norwegian class at the Sons of Norway hall would not begin until February 6, but I had been referred for preparatory lessons to a former teacher of the course and had met with her several times. My closing entry for January 26 mentioned that even at that

NO SMALL SNAKES

relatively early stage of my Norwegian experience, resistance was gathering:

> Studied Norwegian—each time I do, I get drowsy attack—enemy very threatened by that! Why? Something powerfully of the Lord in my going to Norway/touching my roots. Last night I jogged, tonight I resisted—sense ancient Norwegian pagan gods?—cast out as best I could—worked fairly well.

Two days later, I had my next Norwegian lesson—and the enemy took a shot at me. That afternoon, I received a call from Jane, whom I hadn't heard from since she had hung up on me angrily months before. Saying that God had sent her to me for support in my time of stress, she cooed, "I just thought that by now all that nasty upset between us would've settled."

"Actually, no," I said, struggling to be civil. "In fact, since we talked last, several others have confirmed that you are not a true prophet."

"Why, I understand," she said, her voice hardening; "you're just angry at me because I brought you such a hard word to hear."

"No," I said again, trembling even as I dug in. "I'm angry at you because you won't look honestly at what you're doing."

Immediately, her voice became light and breezy. "Oh, well, of course I need to know if there's false prophecy in me!" she chirped.

"Are you ready to let others pray with you, and are you willing to accept their discernment?"

She paused. "Well, you know I'm not just a newcomer to this business of the Spirit myself, and—"

"It doesn't sound like you're willing to submit to the body," I interrupted.

"Well," she huffed, "I'm not about to be put down by any group of people." She paused, and again the lighter tone: "Now, if just you and me could get together—"

"I'm sorry," I said firmly. "When you're ready to submit to other Christians, let me know. Until then, I must say good-bye." I hung up and never heard from her again. In my journal, I recapped: "Old enemy trying to get back in—I finally hung up on her—felt good—wish I could've been more 'strong and in charge' and not get ruffled—ah, me! But I did it, halleluia!"

The further I dared to walk in the Lord's plan for the sabbatical, the more the enemy challenged me. Though I had stood my—and, I trust, the Lord's—ground against the demons in Jane, nevertheless my nervousness in doing so convinced me that I would need greater weaponry to face successfully whatever challenges lay ahead.

As usual, the Lord was quick to provide—even that very night.

Chapter 13

# THE WEAPON OF FASTING

Then the Spirit led Jesus into the desert to be tempted
by the Devil. After spending forty days and forthy nights
without food, Jesus was hungry. Then the Devil came to him. . . .

—MATTHEW 4:1–3

For some time before the sabbatical, I had noted that people in the
Bible often fasted when facing some destructive enemy, and God
intervened to save them. As the biblical story became increasingly
real and alive to me, I wondered whether a fast might help me in my
struggles as well.

For example, King Jehoshaphat and the people of Judah are about
to be attacked by the huge combined forces of several enemy tribes
who have already captured one of the king's cities. "Jehoshaphat was
frightened and prayed to the LORD for guidance. Then he gave orders
for a fast to be observed throughout the country" (2 Chron. 20:3).
The king then gathers the people of Jerusalem in the temple courtyard
and prays aloud over them for God's deliverance. "We do not know
what to do," he cries out, "but we look to you for help" (v. 12).

Suddenly, "the spirit of the LORD" comes upon a Levite in the crowd, who prophesies, "Your Majesty and all you people of Judah and Jerusalem, the LORD says that you must not be discouraged or be afraid to face this large army. The battle depends on God, not on you" (vv. 14–15). The people are commanded to attack the enemy the next day, and a strange statement follows: "You will not have to fight this battle. Just take up your positions and wait; you will see the LORD give you victory. People of Judah and Jerusalem, do not hesitate or be afraid. Go out to battle, and the LORD will be with you!" (v. 17).

No commander would send his outmanned army into battle on empty stomachs. And yet, when the people fasted, God sovereignly destroyed the enemy.

*How could that be?* I wondered.

Understanding came as I studied the story of Daniel, when he interceded for the Israelites in Persian captivity: "At that time I was mourning for three weeks. I did not eat any rich food or any meat, drink any wine, or comb my hair until the three weeks were past" (Dan. 10:2–3).

During this fast, Daniel encounters a mighty angel who has been battling "the guardian angel of Persia" on behalf of the Israelites. Physically weak from having no food, Daniel writes:

> I was left there alone, watching this amazing vision. I had no strength left . . . [and] fell to the ground. . . . The angel said to me, "Daniel, God loves you. Stand up and listen carefully to what I am going to say. I have been sent to you." When he had said this, I stood up, still trembling.
>
> Then he said, "Daniel, don't be afraid. God has heard your

prayers ever since the first day you decided to humble yourself in order to gain understanding. I have come in answer to your prayer." (vv. 8–12)

Biblical fasting is therefore a demonstration of humility, an acknowledgment that we "must not depend on bread alone to sustain [us], but on everything that the LORD says" (Deut. 8:3). What more graphic way to confront the futility of human power than to experience in your flesh such weakness? What more appropriate opportunity, in fact, to discover God's strength?

Suddenly, the story of Jesus' victory over Satan's temptation took on a whole new thrust. I had always assumed that Jesus' fasting for forty days left Him at a terrible disadvantage before the tempter, that the story simply demonstrated Jesus' incredible reserve of strength. Now I saw that God led Jesus into the desert to be tempted because only after such a fast could Jesus be so emptied of His own power as to manifest the overcoming power of God required for such a battle.

In beginning to walk as God's warrior, I had soon discovered that I would need every weapon available to me. *Father,* I prayed, *if fasting can help me draw closer to You and mediate more of Your power, I'm open to it.*

In the morning a few days later, I noticed that I was out of milk for my cereal and wrote in my journal, "Should I fast today? Maybe that's why I 'forgot' to buy milk. I could skip lunch to make it 24 hrs. 'til 5:00 p.m. today—I'll try it, use 'lunch hour' for prayer."

Thereafter, I fasted one twenty-four-hour period a week. At first, hunger pangs bothered me, but after several weeks, these became minor irritations easily dispelled with a glass of water. In fact, whereas at first I had been careful to schedule my fast period apart from days of physical exertion, such as playing sports or helping a friend move furniture, in time I found myself able to continue my regular activities without eating that day. One day when I was fasting, my tennis partner unexpectedly called and said he was getting off work early— could we play? I hesitated, decided to give it a try—and played better than ever before!

I soon noticed that on fast days I was clearly more physically alert. More significantly, when I prayed for persons on those days, my spiritual discernment was noticeably quicker and sharper. I decided to make Wednesday my fast day, since on that day we had a noon and an evening prayer group.

As I became comfortable with the one-day fast, others suggested that a longer seven-day, water-only fast would draw me especially close to the Lord and have a significant effect on my life and ministry. Given my work schedule at the church, I discounted the idea as wholly impractical—not without a secret sense of relief!

When the sabbatical first emerged as a possibility, I realized that it might be the ideal time to try the longer fast. But again, when even the sabbatical became so fully scheduled, a seven-day fast seemed impossible.

Throughout my struggle as to whether or not God had indeed ordained the sabbatical, I couldn't shake the vision of an extended fast. As the sense grew within me that the Lord was overruling my agreed-upon schedule, it occurred to me that I might no longer have any excuse for not doing it. At the same time, I was not anxious to take on what promised to be a very unusual ordeal and shelved the idea as something to be considered "later, maybe."

On the evening of January 27—a week after the prayer counseling retreat had convinced me that God was scheduling my sabbatical, and the day my shaky stand against Jane's return convinced me I would need greater weaponry for His plans ahead—something very strange happened. As I got into bed and pulled up the covers, I realized to my surprise that I hadn't eaten dinner! After the day's considerable stress, I decided I was more tired than hungry and would simply wait for breakfast the next morning.

When I awoke, I did my daily devotions and went to my desk to continue working on a book I had recently decided to write. When I next looked at the clock, it was almost noon. *Maybe time to take my lunch break,* I thought—and then sat bolt upright in amazement. I had forgotten breakfast!

Puzzled and dismayed at my apparent forgetfulness, I determined to make up for my lost meals with an especially big lunch. As I considered a variety of sandwiches and such—maybe going out for a pizza, even?—nothing at all sounded very good. In fact, and this struck me as truly weird, I still was not really hungry.

After what must have seemed to God an interminable bumbling about on my part, it finally occurred to me: Could the Lord now be inviting me to the longer fast and, in fact, reassuring me that it would be easier than I had anticipated? I fell on my knees, and before I could open my mouth to pray, I heard a voice in my heart saying, "This is the time. Trust Me."

Another week divinely scheduled!

The next evening, I had tickets to hear a speaker on the subject of psychology and religion. During the break time, I happened to wander outside. Off to one side, I was surprised to spot the speaker leaning up against a wall, cigarette in hand, shaking noticeably. Instinctively, my heart went out to him, but I found myself too intimidated by such a personality to approach him.

Quickly I prayed for guidance, and an unexpected picture came to mind: a young boy with wings, flying upward, then plunging to the ground. I asked the Lord for understanding and at once remembered the Greek myth of Icarus, the boy whose father fashioned wax wings for him with which to reach the heavens; as he approached the sun, however, his wings melted, and he plummeted to his death. Icarus could be seen as a pagan example of the prototype Adam, who aspired to be like God and fell into sin—and therefore death—by eating the forbidden fruit.

I decided to bind a spirit of pride over the speaker, then pray for humility within and protection without. A few years later, I read a newspaper interview in which that speaker discussed circumstances under which it might be "helpful" for a therapist to have sex with a client.

Today, I would be more likely to continue praying for him, and if that same word of danger through pride persisted, I would make an effort to contact him, simply to pass on the warning as I had received it, allowing him to draw his own conclusions. That night, however, I was aware only of a special alertness in my spirit and a sense of power as I prayed for the speaker.

After I had finished praying for the anxious speaker, I felt as if I had done such a good job that I wanted to celebrate and even reward myself. The others with me at the event were going for pizza afterward, and I prayed, *What about it, Lord?* The only sense I received was, "Good job, My son! Enjoy!" And so I did, having several slices.

The next day, before approaching breakfast, I reflected on my experience. Doing without food had been absolutely no trouble, and the payoff in terms of being able to minister powerfully had been significant. On the one hand, I felt no fear that to eat now would be a sin; on the other hand, I was drawn to what might unfold if I chose to go further with the fast. God was not sitting in heaven with a club ready to punish me for not fasting, but rather was promising me an exciting adventure in His power if I would.

I decided to go for it and wrote:

Fasting: yesterday I approached it differently. Now it's not "Is it Your will for me to fast now?" but a decision on my part. "I give this fast to You, Lord—do with it/me as You want." Felt no desire for food, and Lord used me with [the speaker], essentially saying, "Okay, Gordon, if you're giving this to Me, I'll for sure use it— and what's more, I'll tell you when it's over."

With the pizza "celebration," God had reassured me that the fast was not about some religious duty but about a Father-son relationship. I needn't worry about when to end the fast; He would let me know.

To my pleasant surprise, a friend in the pastors' group phoned me the next day to tell me that Delores Winder was back in Los Angeles that week and gave me her schedule. I drove to the church where she was ministering that night and afterward asked her to pray for me in my struggle at the church. "Pray that you might see others as Jesus sees them and feel toward them as He feels," she said. Driving home, I realized that in my own hurt, I often am so busy defending myself that I don't see the other person's brokenness, which may be fueling his or her hurtful actions.

"Still fasting," I wrote the next morning in my journal. "It was hard for a while but did some good writing." I also wrote that a close friend had told me that "fasting is bad for you." After considerable experience now years later, I have learned to expect others to express such concern and even try to discourage me from fasting. (Of course, those with medical restrictions, such as diabetes or pregnancy, should consult their doctor before fasting.) Now when I sense a call to fast, I pray and seek confirmation with my prayer partners, and if I get a green light, I'm discerning about whom I tell. To any who caution me, I simply say, "Thank you for your genuine concern for me. I ask you to accept that this is something I need to be doing for myself right now."

I went to Delores's ministry again that night and "felt not much into it all" at first. Disappointed, I tried to shrug it off but eventually became so piqued by it that I cried out quietly in prayer, *Lord, how come I feel so "flat" tonight?* I waited and moments later had the sense that God was showing me in a very graphic manner the resistance to His healing ministry of many persons there that night so that I would pray against it.

I puzzled over that sense for a while and began to understand as I observed Delores. She always opened the time of healing ministry by praying for the Holy Spirit to be present and thanking Him for His ministry among God's people. Then she would "call out" healings according to where she felt pain in her own body. For example, if her right elbow began to ache, she would say, "Someone here has a right elbow that needs healing."

Often, the person is too embarrassed to come forward for healing, and once, after Delores had waited several minutes for the needy person to speak up, she declared half-jokingly, "Please come forward soon—my elbow is killing me!" At that, a friend whom I had brought to the service leaned toward me and whispered, "My elbow has been whacked-out lately." I gave him a firm but friendly elbow in his side, and finally he got up sheepishly and went forward. When Delores prayed for his arm, the pain left his elbow—and hers as well.

The Christian intercessor must bear people's pain to God, even as Jesus on the cross. If you willingly offer yourself to God for that ministry, you'll be "touched," even literally, by the other's broken-ness—not to bear it yourself, but deeply enough to be acutely aware of it and bear it to God for His healing. When placed in His hands, as it were, the "touch of brokenness" appropriately passes to Him from the broken one and from the intercessor. This process models the Crucifixion, in which Jesus bore the heaviest touch of human brokenness to the Father on our behalf.

I REALIZED THAT GOD'S PURPOSES AMONG US THAT NIGHT WERE being threatened by resistance in persons present, and God had cho-sen me to "feel" that resistance long enough to recognize where it was coming from and bear it to Him. I asked the Lord what, if any, enemy spirits might be binding people that night. Sensing disbelief and skep-ticism among the congregation—and God's calling to act—I bound and cast those spirits from the event. I then asked the Holy Spirit to replace them with His works of humility, faith, and trust. I continued praying that the hearts and minds of those present would be open to receive the fullness of the Holy Spirit at work in their lives.

As I write this, I see how the word of compassion that Delores had given me the night before was becoming operational. God was teaching me not only how to see others as He sees them, but also to suffer with them—graphically showing me their brokenness by caus-ing me to feel "flat" myself so I would bear it to Him.

That night, I learned an important lesson in spiritual warfare:

God will sometimes allow the workings of the enemy to touch warriors just enough to get their attention and call them into action. He inoculates you, injecting you with just enough evil to stir your defenses and produce sufficient antibodies to overcome its full onslaught.

After carrying out God's orders by praying over the assembly, I was then freed in my own spirit to participate actively in the evening's worship and ministry. Delores asked me to help minister to those who were lined up for prayer, and I was surprised at how readily I sensed what God was doing in each person and how to pray in each case.


AFTERWARD, DELORES MINISTERED TO ME AGAIN. AS MY JOURNAL notes, she began:

> "I rebuke you, Satan, for harassing Gordon. You will not have this man, Satan. He belongs to Jesus!" Then she addressed me: "You've been walking a tightrope, but the Lord's going to open the path for you. He knows all the hurts and longings within you. Let them out so He can bless you with His joy."

Encouraged and elated, I prayed quietly, *Lord, what about Norway?* But God—as I have experienced often since then—has His own mind, and the word Delores offered after that simply reassured me that something important was to come: "Rest in Me. Don't rush, and I will unfold great things."

I was beginning to experience the most basic truth about the spiritual discipline of fasting. As Richard Foster affirmed in his classic *Celebration of Discipline*:

More than any other single Discipline, fasting reveals the things that control us. . . . Anger, bitterness, jealousy, strife, fear—if they are within us, they will surface during fasting. At first we will rationalize that our anger is due to our hunger; then we know that we are angry because the spirit of anger is within us. We can rejoice in this knowledge because we know that healing is available through the power of Christ.

I confessed my impatience to Jesus and asked for renewed trust in Him and His promises regarding Norway.

ON DAY FIVE OF THE FAST, I RECEIVED A CALL FROM ALICE, MY best ally in the church's Wednesday afternoon prayer group, telling me that she felt it was important that I pray with Judy and her as soon as possible, that Judy was having recurrent problems and only I was able to discern the spiritual situation and pray effectively. Since I had not planned to minister to any church members during the sabbatical, I hesitated, but as I prayed quickly, I sensed that indeed Alice was right. I told her that I would meet Judy and her at the church that afternoon. We prayed together for perhaps an hour, with significant results. Physically weak, I nevertheless found a surprising strength and authority in my prayers.

I could not discern any one significant focus to my prayers during the fast and wrote that evening, "What is this fast for, Lord? I don't see any clear and direct purpose—but I'll go with it. I love You, Lord. Already it's helped Judy."

The next day, Alice called, her voice ecstatic. "You remember the brief prayer you offered for the three of us, to cleanse us from narcissism?" I hesitated, as most of my recollection focused on our prayers for Judy. "Well, when we talked about what that was, I knew I'd been bound by it most of my life—and today, I'm free! In fact, I asked the Lord, 'Why didn't I see this before?' and He answered, 'This can only be handled through prayer and fasting!'"

Greatly encouraged, I resolved in that moment to keep fasting whether or not I received any clear sense of its larger purpose. Before Alice hung up, she mentioned that she had been to a revival that week at the local community college, led by British pastor David Watson. Praying later, I felt that I was to attend on day seven of the fast and to break the fast afterward.

The next morning, I prayed about the revival service that night and sensed, "The fast will end with this, but go. There is still work for us to do tonight."

After seven days on water only, I moved slower than usual and was late that evening. Loud and joyous singing was already filling the air as I stepped carefully down the college auditorium aisle. To my delight, I spotted two Lutheran ministers from the renewal pastors' group and eased my way into a seat next to them.

Almost as soon as I had greeted my friends and settled into my seat, an overwhelming sense of alertness, openness, and brightness came upon me. A warmth flushed through my body, and before I could sing a note, I began to cry. A moment later, the crying eased— and then came again stronger, deeper, as in waves. As I sat there sobbing—hoping my friends were too busy singing to notice—a voice seemed to speak in my heart, "Have I not loved you, My son?"

Within moments, I felt strength within me akin to anger, but before I could begin to worry what was wrong with me, I sensed something amiss in the atmosphere. *What's wrong here, Lord?* I asked.

Immediately, the word *self-righteousness* came to mind; I bound that spirit over the gathering and, sensing the authority, cast it out. As the singing continued, I waited, alert for any further leading from God.

When the song ended, the worship leader began to speak with great enthusiasm about the power of God, and I found myself amazed to hear such unbridled excitement in a British accent. *Lord*, I thought, *why am I so struck by that? I must have a real prejudice against the British.* As the next song began, I sang out in praise to God, and I noticed the leader lifting his hands in joyful abandon.

*Poor, uptight England!* I thought. *Imagine the joy they've missed by not letting go and praising God like that fellow!* I stopped singing, shook my head, and sighed in dismay.

Suddenly, I heard a voice within me: "Pray for England."

*What?* I almost blurted out loud, sitting bolt upright. I waited and "heard" nothing more, but the presence and power of those words remained electric within me. "Me?" I asked under my breath. "You want me to pray for England?" I felt as if I had been listening to a symphony and the conductor's arms were now raised, awaiting the musicians. Sure, I'd prayed before for individuals, meetings, even churches. But for a whole nation?

*Well . . . okay, Lord,* I thought uneasily. I closed my eyes, and a map or picture of England came to mind. I prayed that the blood of Jesus would cleanse the entire island, and I saw great dark clouds pouring out of it. Emboldened, but careful not to go beyond my annointing, I asked God to identify particular enemy spirits working against Him in England. As the names of their activity came to mind, I asked God to pour out His Spirit on England in specific ways to counter those demons.

In that moment, I recalled the teachings on territorial spirits by

Australian John Dawson, which I had received in the pastors' group. I thought also of my guitar and tape deck, stolen after I had rushed to pray against territorial spirits over Los Angeles. Instinctively, I hesitated. Was I rashly exposing myself again to further counter-attack and destruction in my life? Yes, I was fasting and expected greater power to overcome the enemy—but could such prayer for entire nations be overstretching proper caution?

I realized that the most compelling argument for my staying open and continuing to pray this way was simply that I had not sought this ministry of warfare, nor had I in any sense set out with a prayer agenda for England. In the past, I had, for example, focused on Los Angeles out of my own impetus. Now, however, the thrust seemed to be coming from outside of myself. *Okay, Lord,* I prayed, *if You're calling me in this moment to pray for particular nations, lead on—but I will not pray any further unless You show me.*

I sat quietly waiting. Moments later, an outline map of Australia came to mind. I waited longer, and the map remained. *All right, Lord, if this is from You, show me the spirits over Australia You want me to pray against.* Once again, names of demonic activity came to mind, and I yielded and prayed. Within a half hour, I was led to pray as well for Japan, Nigeria, and Russia. (Later, between 1995 and 2008, I ministered in England on nine visits and in Australia on four.)

When at last a sense of victory and peace settled over me, I sat quietly awhile—and then decided to wait for one particular country. I waited. And waited. But no more countries came to mind, just a sense of victory and peace. *Lord,* I finally prayed, *I'm awed by what You've been doing and don't want to sound disappointed . . . but what about Norway?*

I waited and sensed that tonight was a beginning and that more would be shown me when I arrived in Norway. I felt a smile come to my lips, as if the Lord were smiling at my impatience, and recalled the "Don't rush" word that had come through Delores Winder earlier in the week. In my journal that night, I wrote:

Praise God! What a week!
11:00 p.m.—broke fast with vegetable juice—tasted fantastic!
Thank you, Lord.
Bed midnight.

## Chapter 14
# NORWEGIAN BIVOUAC: OF HERITAGE AND DESTINY

I am coming to gather the people of all the nations.
When they come together, they will see what my power can do.
—Isaiah 66:18

March 7, 1984, I flew into Oslo, where a resident of Fredensbolig guided me along snow-covered sidewalks to a bus that took us to a small hamlet about ten miles outside the city. We were met there by another resident in an old Volkswagen van and driven up an icy forest road five miles farther to the retreat center. I stumbled along in my freshly learned Norwegian and was duly embarrassed by the excellent English of the others, who greeted me with warm hospitality and enthusiasm.

*This is Norway!* I kept saying to myself excitedly. *The home of Roger and the Dalbeys!*

That night, ministry director Knute Grønvik told me that he would be driving into the city the next day and asked if I might like a ride there to do some sightseeing. I had poured over several tourist pamphlets back home and had felt particularly drawn to the Homefront Museum, which commemorated the underground resistance during the Nazi occupation. Knute loaned me a map and said he would be glad to drop me off.

The next morning, packed into as many layers of clothing as might permit movement, I braved whistling, stinging chill winds. *(If this is March, what must January be like?)* When Knute dropped me off, I quickly jogged the short distance to the museum. Inside, as the heavy door whooshed shut behind me, I took off my ski cap. Alone in the sudden hush, I thought of a man taking off his hat upon entering a church sanctuary. A sense of ultimate seriousness, commanding reverence, struck me at once, and I paused quietly to gather myself.

Easing into the first room, I was immediately seized by a picture on the wall of Nazi troops goose-stepping down the main street of Oslo—the very same street I had jogged just moments before! Continuing among exhibits of old wireless spy radios, makeshift handguns, Nazi documents, and other memorabilia, I came to a letter written by the Norwegian underground leaders declaring their determination to stand firm against Nazism—and at once a flood of tears came to my eyes. Another statement, reminding fellow Norwegians of their Christian heritage as a rallying impetus for the Resistance, touched me as deeply, and I wept quietly in the otherwise deserted room.

Before long, an all-too-familiar drowsiness came upon me, and I struggled to shake myself awake as I stood among the exhibits. I realized the enemy did not want me to experience what God was revealing there, and I battled to remain alert and open.

Only as I write this some years later have I come to see what was happening there at the Homefront Museum. In a very real sense, as I was soon to discover, Norway was even then an occupied territory, from which the enemy of God had not yet been fully dispelled. And in that spiritual battle, I had been sent to encourage the resistance among God's people as an officer in God's forces.

As C. S. Lewis asserted in *Mere Christianity*:

> Enemy occupied territory—that is what this world is. Christianity is the story of how the rightful king has landed, you might say in disguise, and is calling us all to take part in a great campaign of sabotage. When you go to church you are really listening-in to the secret wireless from our friends: that is why the enemy is so anxious to prevent us from going.[1]

After returning to the retreat center that afternoon, I decided to hike up the snow-packed road beyond where it banked to the left and disappeared into the woods. Strolling along, I marveled at the hushed beauty of the snow-blanketed trees about me. Moments later, I paused before a large white expanse of meadow, interrupted occasionally by huge boulders and an apparent stream channeling under the snow. Then, suddenly, the stillness of the moment was jarred as in my mind's eye I saw a strange-looking figure dressed as an old horn-helmeted Viking, standing near the center of the field.

Startled, I drew up in the wind, which in that moment felt distinctly sharp and merciless. In a flash, I wondered, *Could this signal the beginning of the battle I came to fight?* I prayed for wisdom and sensed a number of demonic principalities over the retreat center property—apparently ancient Viking spirits. By virtue of having been invited there, I sensed also the authority to send them away in the name of Jesus. "Unmerciful" seemed to lead the pack, which included condemnation, rigidness, legalism, and many other related spirits.

At one point, I was surprised to "see," perched on a large boulder, a figure not unlike the troll characters of Norse mythology. It disappeared quickly, and in that moment, I had little sense of how—or, indeed, whether—to pray against it. When the parade of Viking spirits ceased, I tightened my parka about me and headed gratefully for the warm lodge, shaking my head in amazement. *Father, was that for real?*

Excited as I was about what I had experienced essentially in the retreat center's backyard, I decided not to tell anyone about it yet. I had only just arrived at the center, and although I knew everyone there was Spirit-filled, I was not yet ready to step out in what might be fantasy kindled by my expectations. It had seemed no less real than my prayers for various nations at the end of the fast. But it seemed prudent to wait until we became better acquainted before broaching with my hosts the subject of pagan spirits over the retreat center grounds and, indeed, over the nation itself.

The next day, Knute invited me to take a hike with him in the afternoon. Hoping to get better acquainted, I readily accepted. As we trekked along a snow-crusted path and chatted, I asked him about the history of the area itself, mentioning that I had seen what appeared to be an old stone marker along the road bearing a date in the 1500s.

"This road," he noted, "is called 'Kongeveien,' or 'King's Highway,' and has been used since the very old days. This area itself is well known in Norway for its history." He paused to kick a pack of snow off his boot. "In fact, many of the most famous fairy tales of Norway are told about the woods in this area."

"Fairy tales?" I exclaimed, startling Knute. "You mean, like stories about trolls and Vikings and such?"

"Well, yes," he replied tentatively, guarded before my sudden outburst.

"Listen," I said, "I don't know how this is going to sound to you, but yesterday I was taking a walk around here, and some pretty wild things happened." I told Knute what I had seen in my mind's eye and asked if he thought it might have any basis in reality.

Hesitating, he knit his brow. "I don't know," he offered finally, lifting his eyebrows. "It's possible."

By midafternoon the next day, I found myself sagging under more lethargy attacks. I decided to go to my room and pray to overcome them. My journal notes a confusing assortment of perhaps a half dozen disjointed visions and ideas, followed by a blank line.

I must have become disgusted with the lack of focus in my prayers, and in that moment of determination and grace, God pulled back the veil—for I then wrote, "Apparently all this lethargy was a diversionary tactic of the enemy; I was being called to battle major spirits over Norway."

Again cautious to stay within my anointing, I sensed these spirits: apathy, religion, self-righteousness, alienation/separation from each other, formality/tradition, pride, and regulation. I set the cross between me and my Norweigan ancestors and bound and cast these spirits out of myself. I then asked, "Jesus, how are You praying for Norway?" and recorded this answer: "For a spirit of unity, love, freedom in the Holy Spirit." I added a further sense that "national spirits undealt with are more evident here [at the retreat center], shown forth in bold relief against the Christian background."

Some confirmation of the spirits I had discerned followed soon. Knute had told me when I arrived that the year-round residents consisted of three married couples, their children, and a total of five single adults. After four days of sharing meals and rubbing shoulders, however, I realized with some dismay that I could not tell who was married to whom—not because affection was indiscriminately displayed, but because it seemed not to be displayed at all. Throughout all our comings and goings, I had not seen any man and woman hold hands, kiss, hug, or express any gesture of physical affection that might indicate their relationship.

Anxious to avoid a faux pas, in desperation I shared my confusion with Knute, who smiled genially. "Here in Norway, we are not so open with our affections, such as you Americans." Indeed, I affirmed that in California it's just the opposite, as people rush to hug and kiss without even knowing each other. In any case, other Norwegian American friends of mine have confirmed spirits of alienation and isolation as part of that culture.

I hasten to add here that no culture—certainly not our American culture—is without its principalities or cultural demons. Norwegian culture is no more—or less—infected with evil than any other. I trust my reader here to extrapolate to your own cultural heritage and seek appropriate deliverance.

The next evening, a physical sensation of homesickness stirred in me after being in a new culture for several days—reminding me of my boyhood in Karachi, Pakistan, where my father had been stationed in the navy, and later, my two-year Peace Corps tour in Nigeria. I wrote in my journal, "I'm feeling a little sick—like Karachi. I know now I am far from home. Also like Nigeria."

In fact, after traveling so much of my life, I had begun to despair of ever finding a place to settle down and call my own. Though I had not told anyone, I had come to this, the country of my Dalbey ancestors, hoping perhaps to discover my "place in the world" at last. If I already was feeling "far from home" in Norway, that final hope was lost. But the Lord was just preparing me for the profound truth He was about to reveal.

Soon, I began to see His wisdom in scheduling the sequence of my sabbatical activities. I had talked with many of the retreat center residents about my recent "Dreams and Inner Healing" retreat in New Mexico, and one young mother asked if I would pray for her with her husband about a frightening recurrent dream. She had often dreamed it years before, but it had stopped for some time; suddenly, it had recurred that week. I agreed, assuming by faith that God had stirred the dream at that time because I was prepared to deal with it.


THE THREE OF US GATHERED IN THEIR MODEST FLAT, AND SHE shared the details of her dream: An older woman and a girl are riding in an open carriage past a house, when from inside the house a child's scream is heard. The girl is terrified and cries out, "The child is dying!" Whereupon the older woman turns a dark and sinister look upon her and says, "Oh, it's nothing—we'll just ride on past!" The girl desperately cries out, "No! We must go back and help! No!" But the carriage passes by the screaming child, and the dream ends.

"I'm so afraid," the young mother worried, "that this dream means something terrible is going to happen to my child!"

I had learned at the retreat that the characters in a dream can represent aspects of the dreamer, and I suggested that we pray and ask the Lord if that was true in her dream. As we did so, I sensed that the girl in the carriage represented the young woman sitting in front of me, the older woman was her mother, and the child screaming was the woman as a young child crying out for her mother's love. I shared that interpretation, and the woman balked. "Did your mother demonstrate much affection for you?" I asked.

"Oh no," she replied immediately. "She was so cold and distant, always acting as if feelings didn't matter at all."

I pointed out that this characteristic perfectly fit the older woman in the dream and that without loving touch, a child can literally die— as the girl in the dream feared for the screaming child in the house.

A light broke across her face. "Yes," she said, nodding, "I think that's true. I always wanted so badly for my mother just to hold me and hug me!" She paused, knitting her brow. "But why the evil look on the older woman's face? Was my mother evil?"

I assured her that her mother was not evil but that she had very likely borne enemy spirits of punishment, shame, and abandonment, which led her to insist on ignoring even cries for love and life. The dream was demonstrating the enemy at work in and through her mother.

We prayed, and I asked the Holy Spirit to bring to this young mother's mind a time from her childhood when she had especially longed for her mother's affection. I then prayed quietly in tongues. In a moment, she recalled having fallen and hurt herself; when she ran into the house crying, her mother scolded her and told her not to make "such a fuss."

"As you hold that memory," I said, "can you ask Jesus to enter the scene with you and your mother?"

She hesitated, then said, "Yes, He's there with us."

"Lord," I prayed, "show us whatever You've been wanting my sister to know for all these years since that happened." Praying quietly in tongues, I waited.

"Oh!" the woman exclaimed. "He's taking my mother's hand, and all the coldness is passing out of her. She looks at me. Oh, I can't believe it—she's saying she really wanted to pick me up and hold me but was so afraid to, because she had never experienced that kind of caring herself as a girl and just didn't know how to give it."

She paused, and I waited, continuing my prayer quietly. "Mother says she's sorry she didn't give me the affection I needed. Oh, Mother! I forgive you!" she cried out, breaking into tears. "Yes, I forgive you!"

Moments later, when the tears had subsided, I placed the cross between the woman and her mother, and between mother and grandmother, then bound spirits of mercilessness and abandonment, then cast them out of the generations—even as a week earlier I had done over the territory. I prayed that God would heal and fulfill all the longing for affection from her mother, then read Psalm 131:2: "I am content and at peace. As a weaned child lies quietly in its mother's arms, so my heart lies quiet within me." I asked God to pour out His mercy upon the woman and to reassure her that He heard her cries for love and would provide for all her emotional needs according to His will.

The woman smiled broadly as I finished the prayer. "I see now that the dream was not about my own child, but about me as a child," she said.

"Yes, I think so," I said. "But just to be sure, let's also pray for your family's protection and well-being."

Afterward, I embraced the woman and her husband. "I feel so free!" she exclaimed. Quietly, I praised God for the tools He had given me at my sabbatical healing class just weeks earlier.

KNUTE HAD ASKED ME TO TEACH THAT NIGHT AT THEIR REGULAR Monday evening worship. After praying, I decided to teach on Romans 12:1–2, in which Paul urged the believers to offer themselves as a "living sacrifice" to God. I shared how the Lord had been leading me to let go and give to Him my church, my family, and all that comprised "me," and pointed to Jesus' humbly riding the donkey into Jerusalem unto death as the ultimate model for doing so. Whoever would lose these things to the Lord, I paraphrased, would gain them, but whoever would cling to them would lose them— render them useless to serve God's purposes.

When I had finished teaching and invited questions and response, one woman who had driven up from town for the program said in an awed voice that she had been thinking about Romans 12:1 all that day.

Two days later, Knute asked if I would teach again the following week. I accepted readily and said I was glad he appreciated my teaching.

"It is not only your teaching," Knute said. "I want you to know that we now trust you. Many Americans we have met, and what we read in your news, frighten us. You want so many nuclear weapons and talk so big against the Russians. But Norway borders Russia on our north, and we cannot afford or respect this attitude." He paused. "You may have noticed that we opened this issue in our early conversations with you."

I remembered mentioning to Knute that I was uncomfortable with our president's focus on the arms race instead of negotiations. "Actually, I didn't realize you were being intentional about it at the time," I remarked. "I just gave you my honest opinions."

Knute smiled. "I can only say that we were pleased that you understand our position. Also, we have noticed that you are humble and want to learn our language and customs, instead of assuming English and your American culture are better. That is why we invited you to teach again."

As I write this years later, I realize that the Lord was leading me months earlier, after the church meeting on where to place the flag during worship, to face and renounce the national idolatry within me—in order to open my heart to Norway and prepare me to bring His teaching to believers there.

I had also humbly asked my Norwegian friends to pray for my needs. Indeed, I was delighted to discover that a monthly agape-meal evening, which included a special prayer time, would fall during my stay, shortly before my second teaching night.

That evening, we enjoyed a delicious meal topped off with fresh fruit imported from Israel, a rare and expensive luxury in Norway during the winter months. Afterward, we gathered to pray for one another, and when my turn came, I said that I still was uncertain about the Lord's full purposes for me in Norway and would like prayer that I would receive all He intended while I was there.

I hesitated and added cautiously that I was wondering if perhaps the Lord might want me to stay in Norway for some length of time.

The group gathered around and laid hands on me. For several moments, everyone prayed in silence, and as I waited, I heard a gentle voice in my spirit: "You have found your home." I sat bolt upright. Could this mean what I hoped it meant? *Lord,* I thought, *do You want me to move to Norway and settle here?*

Excitedly, I began to think about moving to Norway. Then again, I heard the words "You have found your home"—and after that, with equal clarity, I heard, "Your home is not in Norway but in

Me. You have found your home in this world—not in Norway, but among others who love and serve Me. Wherever in the world you may go, there you shall be at home."

The next morning, I wrote:

> If that's true, I could never have heard it before coming here. I'd always have been holding out on the Lord to see if maybe, just maybe, my *real* home were in Norway, where the Dalbeys came from, or in some other city. Maybe the Lord has freed me at last from my deep *hjemlengsel* (homelonging), restless seeking for a home in this world? What a peace, if so!

For several moments, I basked in that peace. Then I prayed aloud, "I don't want to cling to my earthly roots, but to You, Lord." Remembering that "God will root out any remnants of place idols," I recalled the list of faithful saints in Hebrews 11:13–16:

> It was in faith that all these persons died. They did not receive the things God had promised, but from a long way off they saw them and welcomed them, and admitted openly that they were foreigners and refugees on earth. Those who say such things make it clear that they are looking for a country of their own.
>
> They did not keep thinking about the country they had left; if they had, they would have had the chance to return. Instead, it was a better country they longed for, the heavenly country. And so God is not ashamed for them to call him their God, because he has prepared a city for them.

After reading this, I cast out of myself a spirit of "homelonging," declaring, "In the name of Jesus, I release any claim I might have on any place in this world as my own."

And at last, I prayed, "Forgive me all my searching when You've been there all along, Jesus, just waiting for me to stop and turn to You."

Later, I prayed about what to teach at the next evening's worship and sensed that I was to affirm the need to be bold in faith and, indeed, to be warriors. For a while, I worried about how to tie this theme in with my previous lesson, and then it struck me: humility before God is precisely the prerequisite to boldness before human beings. Jesus' willingness to empty Himself before God on Good Friday made Him able to receive God's power and battle victoriously in His resurrection power (Eph. 1:15–20).

That evening, I emphasized that although humility is essential to faith, it is not the end of faith but rather, the beginning. I urged the residents to recognize that God had poured out the power of His Spirit on them, and they were responsible to exercise it boldly for His purposes. "God has called you to be warriors," I said. "Your retreat center is not just a hospital where you receive the Father's healing, but also a barracks, a training ground where you are to learn how to use the sword of the Spirit."

I quoted Paul's letter to his young prodigy Timothy: "For the Spirit that God has given us does not make us timid; instead, his Spirit fills us with power, love, and self-control" (2 Tim. 1:7). In conclusion, I declared that only those who dare humbly to ride the donkey into the old Jerusalem are qualified boldly to ride the warhorse into the New Jerusalem. (See my concluding chapter, "From Jackass to Warhorse," in *Fight Like a Man*.)

Before I could ask for questions, excited comments began filling the room, and to my delight, we spent the next two hours discussing what it means to be God's warrior. I realized that this call to boldness was challenging cultural spirits of passivity and religion.

After my first week, I knew that I wanted to see more of the country and decided to leave the center after the second week. Before leaving the United States, I had been given the names of two Norwegian pastors who had visited my friend's Lutheran church in San Pedro. Once in Norway, I realized that the two lived on opposite sides of the country, and I could not visit both in my one remaining week. I wrote each a letter shortly after arriving to ask if I might visit, hoping that at least one would reply.

By day thirteen, I had received no reply, so I began planning a scenic railroad trip out of Oslo the next day. That night, however, one of the pastors did call and invite me to visit him. In fact, he said, before hearing from me, he had already invited the other pastor to visit him then! He would be delighted to have us both for the weekend, and longer if I desired.

ONCE AGAIN, GOD'S SCHEDULING WAS PERFECT AND MY NEW HOST immediately made me feel part of his family, graciously tolerating my broken Norwegian. The day after arriving, I hiked into the town and stopped by a souvenir shop, which featured a variety of local Norwegian crafts. As I looked over a beautiful assortment of hand-hewn woodwork, I was surprised and amused to find a display of troll dolls, each of which bore a distinctly negative appearance with facial expression to match. One had two faces, another had only one eye, another simply drooped pathetically from eyes to knees, while another looked patently stupid.

As I admired the fine craftsmanship, suddenly the negative aspect of their "personalities" arrested my attention. *What sort of imagination would conjure up things like this?* I wondered. I could see nothing redeeming in any of the images projected by the various dolls and shuddered to think of how a child playing with them might internalize those images.

After a moment, I decided simply to forget the troll dolls and concentrate instead on the beautiful *rosemal,* or painted wood dishes and cups. I selected some of these and several tree-bark jewelry boxes for gifts and had turned toward the cash register when my eye again was seized by the troll dolls nearby. I was about to shake my head in a final gesture of dismay when all at once I recalled the troll-like figure that had come to mind two weeks earlier while I was praying against Norwegian territorial spirits in the fabled woods near the retreat center.

Momentarily transfixed, I stepped aside as another customer moved toward the cash register. *Could it be* I wondered, *that the explicitly negative personality or character trait that each of these dolls projects reflects a territorial pagan spirit of the enemy that remains unbound over Norway?*

At once, my gaze fixed on the "droopy" troll, and I recalled one of Garrison Keillor's many satires on "Norwegian bachelor farmers" during his *Prairie Home Companion* radio show. Only a snippet came to mind, in which he spoke of men whose necks were bent over from always looking at their shoes out of shyness—just like the expression on one troll doll.

*Could it be?*

Amid the ring of the cash register and the chatter of customers,

I prayed, *Lord, show me if this is true, if these dolls indicate territorial spirits.* In a moment, each doll became associated with the name of an enemy spirit:

Two faces: "double-mindedness," which would keep people half-committed to the ways of the world and half committed to the ways of God.

One eye: "tunnel vision," which would keep people ingrown and unable to see God's larger perspective.

Droopy: "shame" or "self-denigration," which would keep people saddled with guilt.

Stupid buffoon: "inadequacy" or "failure," which would keep people from boldness.

In considering my hypothesis, I reflected on the fact that Norwegians seem to be regarded by other Europeans as unsophisticated, old-fashioned in morals, and outside the mainstream of modern European culture. In no way do I wish to impugn the Norwegian national character, which I can testify is as admirable as that of any other nation. I am proud of my Norwegian ancestry. But in fact, I often see myself—like my father—as uncultured, saddled with a sense of social inadequacy, and removed from the popular mainstream.

These perceived character traits in Norwegians are eminently redeemable by Christian spirituality, which most certainly requires a separation from the world's values. The enemy would undermine and co-opt such traits by portraying them in doll caricatures as utter foolishness. Before leaving the souvenir store, I made a note of every troll doll "personality," and later that afternoon, I prayed against each in myself, asking God to replace it with an appropriate aspect of His personality.

I HAD LOOKED FORWARD ESPECIALLY TO WORSHIPPING IN A Norwegian church on Sunday, if only to experience a state-church service. My pastor host told me that his parish included nearly seven thousand members, so I anticipated a large congregation for worship. We visited the sanctuary before Sunday, and I noticed with some confusion that although it was no more than five years old, it seated hardly four hundred. Trusting that pastors in Norway are as apt to be defensive about attendance statistics as pastors anywhere else, I said nothing.

I knew the service would be in Norwegian, including the sermon, and I hoped my on-site practice would help me translate. I had learned many Norwegian praise songs at the retreat center, and my favorite was "*For Stor Ting Har Han Gjort Mot Meg*," literally, "For the Great Thing He Has Done for Me," based on Mary's prayer following the Annunciation.

On Sunday morning the pastor and I went early to the church, and I sat up front in order to hear as clearly as possible. Only a handful of others were there, but I attributed that to our early arrival. Not until several minutes into the service, when we stood for the first hymn, did I turn around; to my shock, no more than fifty persons were present. *What in the world does this mean?* Later, I was surprised and delighted to discover that the sermon for the day was titled "*For Stor Ting Har Han Gjort Mot Meg*," right out of the Annunciation text!

After the service, my pastor host invited me to stay for a baptism. Two parents, a grandmother, and two older children came with the tiny infant. The mother and older daughter were dressed in traditional Norwegian garb, but neither they nor any of the family had attended worship earlier. Such casual lack of church participation, I discovered, is widespread in Norway, as in most of Western Europe. Ironically, only a generation earlier, this nation had risked their lives in the explicit name of their Christian heritage to meet secretly and resist the occupying Nazi enemy. Today, materially comfortable and spiritually unaware, like most Americans, they ignore the church and its "great campaign of sabotage," recalling C. S. Lewis's words, against the true spiritual enemy—who yet remains, long after all flesh-and-blood Nazis have been overcome.

That afternoon, I prayed for the city, and I sensed a spirit of self-satisfaction that was keeping people out of church by making them feel "quite good enough without God." I prayed for the Holy Spirit to convict the people of their pride, and for those who preach the truth of our brokenness and God's saving power in Jesus to find an increasing audience.

As we three pastors chatted after dinner, the other two began to share openly their deep concern for the state of the church in Norway and the widespread lack of interest in spiritual matters. Each was committed to Christ and had received the baptism of the Holy Spirit, but both were frustrated in their attempts to proclaim that faith and power in such an unreceptive spiritual climate.

At the other pastor's church, in fact, some newly Spirit-filled believers had a few years earlier attempted deliverance prayer without proper discernment, and the person prayed for became angry and went to the newspapers. The media had held the church up to public ridicule, and even years later the wounds remained, making everyone afraid to entertain any workings of the Holy Spirit.

As our host put it, "You must try so hard to hold on to the few active members you have, and most of these would be upset if I talked too much about the real work and power of the Spirit."

I sighed deeply, thinking of Peter's words, "Be firm in your faith and resist [the devil], because you know that your fellow believers in all the world are going through the same kind of sufferings" (1 Peter 5:9). I reassured my fellow pastors that they were not alone, that in my own church in California, I was experiencing almost exactly the same problems. Before going to bed, we decided to pray together at the church the following day. For almost an hour the next afternoon, we took turns laying hands on one another before the altar and praying for strength and courage.

AFTER ENJOYING THE GRACIOUS HOSPITALITY OF MY PASTOR HOST for four days, I decided to spend my last two days in Norway with a young teacher and his family, whose name had been given to me by my Lutheran pastor friend in San Pedro. After a scenic train and bus ride through the snow-covered countryside, I reached the school and was humbled again by the warm welcome that I had come to appreciate so much among Norwegians.

The school, a post-secondary residential institution, occupied a large estate, and my host soon took me on a tour. The administrative offices occupied a large converted mansion, and as we entered the front door, I noticed a huge tree adjacent, which I imagined would provide wonderful shade when covered with leaves in the summertime. Inside, I noticed several pictures on the wall, and one, near a window overlooking the front yard, caught my attention. Grayed with age and slightly blurred from enlarging, the picture showed a group of soldiers at attention, in front of the building in which I stood.

I asked my host about the picture, and he noted matter-of-factly that during the German occupation, the Nazis had taken over the estate as a regional headquarters. Drawing closer to the picture, my eyes widened in amazement as I recognized the Nazi uniforms from old movies. But I was not looking at actors. A chill of fear startled me as I noticed how terribly unremarkable the soldiers appeared, except for Nazi insignias on their collars. No pitchfork, no horns—just blond, blue-eyed, scrubbed and clean faces—even like my own.

Stunned, I turned to gaze out the window and drew up in amazement to realize that right there, just forty years earlier, those Nazi soldiers had stood on the very ground I had walked across a minute before! I turned back to the picture in disbelief, and a small detail caught my eye. It was summertime, grassy under clear skies, and there, off to the side of the front column of soldiers, no more than an inch from being cut out of the picture, stood a skinny sapling with three or four leaves on it—a "baby picture" of the huge shade tree now towering in somber witness outside!

That evening after their two small boys were in bed, my hosts shared their conversion to Jesus and the ministry of His Holy Spirit several years before through an international mission. They told me how much they had missed the fellowship of believers since coming to the school two years earlier.

I encouraged them to start a prayer group at the school, no matter how small, and we spent some time discussing how to identify and approach other staff members who might share their need. Their enthusiastic response to my encouragement led me to ask if I might pray for their family in any way, and immediately they poured out their concern for their four-year-old—whom I had noticed seemed unusually volatile. As we talked, the mother used the word *skrikerunge*—literally, "shrieking youngster"—and explained that the term is a common colloquialism in Norway.

The boy's birth had included complications, so I suggested we go to his bed and pray over him. There I asked God to heal the boy's emotions with reassuring love, especially in his memory of his birth. As I prayed, I sensed the possibility of a *skrikerunge* spirit over the country itself, which I quietly bound and cast out of the boy. Later, I thought about the screaming child in the woman's dream at the retreat center and its connection to the "merciless" spirit of the old Vikings, who were known to offer child sacrifices. Indeed, could the famous Norwegian modern-art painting *The Scream* have its root in this spirit?

Returning to the living room, I prayed for the couple, especially that they would soon find a fellowship of believers. "Good prayer time," I wrote in my journal:

> They have been out of Spirit-filled fellowship for two years— tonight was a real release for them! Thank You, Lord! What a privilege, to bear power to set free and heal. There has been a lid on the Spirit in Norway—time for Spirit to move is soon. New wave of revival is coming here. I might be one of the go-ahead intercessors sent to break strongholds, prepare the way—thank You, Lord!

The last night before leaving Norway, I asked my hosts to pray for me, that I might retain everything the Lord had taught me there. To my surprise, an image of a spaceship came to mind, and with it a sensation of fear. I prayed for understanding and recalled a basic fear that had come to me at some point during the Star Wars / Star Trek genre films: Once they get out there in the vast universe like that, how do they ever find their way back home again?

I often had frustrating dreams in which, after setting out on a journey, I sought to return—only to discover that the original "path" had changed and led elsewhere. But now, through my Norwegian journey, a new freedom and courage had been revealed. As my journal records:

> Jesus has taught me in Norway that [fear] is unnecessary. My food for the journey is on the way [in the process]—not at some fixed spot. You don't have to fear being "lost" because there really is nowhere (no place in this world) to go home to. But that is a blessing, not a curse: God is on the journey, ready to feed His people with manna at various "stations"—*I don't have to fear getting lost!* [i.e., getting cut off from the source of life/love/warmth/caring].

And so I went to Norway to discover that my home is nowhere in this world—except where others gather in the name of Jesus. That's where He promises to show up. And there in His fellowship—with the Commander in Chief presiding—the warrior finds rest, refreshment, focus, and renewal.

I came home knowing I would need it.

# Chapter 15
# TIGHTENING THE BELT OF TRUTH

You will know the truth, and the truth will set you free.
—JOHN 8:32

My sabbatical had been no getaway vacation from warfare at home, for I had every reason to believe that I was returning to face a battle even fiercer than before. Indeed, the enemy often had tried to use my worries about my failing marriage and the church situation—from nightmares to anxiety attacks—to divert my attention and energy away from God's sabbatical agenda.

As I flew back to Los Angeles on March 28, the fact that several days remained before I returned to the church was little comfort to me. When I entered my apartment and set my suitcase and packages on the living room floor, a heavy sense of loneliness fell over me like a dark, oppressive cloud. For a moment, I stood struggling to remind myself that I was quite alive and well with the Lord there beside me—wholly prepared to suspend indefinitely any productive activity and simply hang on until the heaviness passed.

And yet I sank to my knees on the carpet in utter despair. "Lord!" I cried out loud. "I'm fed up with this gloomy depression and loneliness!"

I knelt there, whimpering and seething, and waited. Utter silence in my heart, in my spirit, in my mind. Darkness, emptiness beckoned.

Momentarily, my gaze fell upon my carry-on travel bag beside me, and in a fierce burst, I seized a small cross from it that I had taken with me to Norway. Jumping to my feet with my fist clenched around the cross, I held it high and furiously shook it at God. "Father, I'm tired of this happening to me, and it's got to stop!" I cried. "You're Lord of heaven and earth and I've given my life to You, so come on! Save me from this and set me free!" Raging, I shook both of my fists at the Lord, as if pounding on His chest, and continued doing so for several minutes. Finally, I stood there panting, sweating, waiting.

Gently at first, and then as a shower of cleansing, a flush of strength and assurance swept over me. No words can explain it, but from that moment, I knew I would never again have to yield my attention and energies to that dark loneliness. The battle ahead was not over, but I knew that the war had been won, that a new power had been poured out upon me to wage it victoriously. Later, it occurred to me that in my holy fisticuffs, God had confirmed my Roger-warrior identity in a virtual reenactment of my very first sermon about Jacob's wrestling with God: "Your name will no longer be Jacob. You have struggled with God and with men, and you have won; so your name will be Israel" (Gen. 32:28).

The opening salvo in the church battle ahead was fired on the Friday before I was to begin preaching again. I was informed that no fewer than six families in our seventy-member congregation had decided to leave the church. The next day, the church held a "Saturday Talent Night" at which I was to be welcomed back. Three of the six "leaving" families came, and two of them performed major acts in the show. None of the six attended worship the next morning.

At my apartment later that night, all the old fears and angers assaulted me with a vengeance and, as the week progressed, became increasingly resistant to my counterattack. Within several days, I had discovered that virtually every leader who had supported me before the sabbatical was considering leaving the church. Desperately, I grasped after memories of God's assurances, but even the sabbatical signs and wonders seemed a dim uncertainty. Within a week back at the office after my sabbatical rest, I was agitated and exhausted.

Adding considerably to the pressure were all the necessary preparations for Easter, which lay just two Sundays ahead. On Palm Sunday, I preached on the need to overcome our self-centered human nature through honest repentance, and for the first time in my ministry, I mentioned the enemy in a sermon. If there is an enemy of God, I said, certainly we allow him full rein when we turn away from God in pride. For a closing hymn, I had chosen "Onward, Christian Soldiers," trusting that some might be moved by the reality of its words, and those who might be offended would allow it merely as an accommodation to the old-timers among us.

A time had been scheduled after worship for me to share highlights of the sabbatical with the congregation, and about twenty persons stayed. Their response was surprisingly positive, and when afterward several people asked if we could reconvene our post-worship prayer group at that time, I agreed enthusiastically.

As perhaps a half dozen of us gathered chairs together around the altar, I was delighted to see Alice, who had been so helpful months earlier in removing the false prophet Jane from our midst, then dismayed to see Liz, who had done more than anyone to sow dissension and division in the church.

*Oh well,* I thought, *at least it's great to be back with the prayer group again!*

When one or two had shared their needs and been prayed for, Liz—who had guardedly never asked for prayer—turned to Beth, a woman who had been dealing with some particularly traumatic experiences. "Can we pray for you, Beth?" Liz asked.

I was about to check the all-too-familiar resentment rising in me toward Liz when, to my shock, Beth suddenly jerked forward from her chair and fell unconscious onto the floor before us.

Immediately, Alice knelt down and laid hands on Beth and began praying in the Spirit while the others looked on in amazement. I knelt down by Beth also, and as I prayed for her, I sensed a spirit of death had quite literally lashed out at her. After some moments of prayer, Beth regained consciousness and sat back up in her chair.

None of the others had seen either such a dramatic attack of the enemy or such powerful deliverance prayers, and everyone expressed an honest desire to know what had happened—except Liz, who sat quietly watching. I did my best to offer an on-the-spot teaching on deliverance ministry, and after praying for several others, we closed the group for that day.

When everyone had finally left, I flopped down on the front pew. Shaken, exasperated, I tried to gather my thoughts. Had I stirred the enemy by referring to him in my sermon and having us sing "Onward, Christian Soldiers"? It seemed likely. It could then be no coincidence that Liz, through whom the enemy was already working in the church, was the one who sparked his display in Beth.

Was I premature in broaching the issue even so slightly? Confused, I sighed and shook my head in dismay.

Certainly, I knew the enemy would seek to capitalize on this event through Liz, who no doubt was on the phone already, reporting the unsettling event in our prayer group. The next morning, I called Bob Whitaker for advice.

"There must be something unhealed in Beth—maybe an inner emotional wound—that's allowing the enemy to attack her so viciously like that," Bob said. "You and Alice need to meet with her regularly, just the three of you, to pray for her healing. She may well need outside counseling too. But meanwhile, until she's healed of that, you need to ask her not to come to open prayer groups where such disturbances can cause unnecessary upset in the church."

That night was my first church council meeting since returning from the sabbatical. Emotionally drained, I struggled to participate in what seemed to be an endless debate over trifles. When the time came for my pastor's report, I summarized again the highlights of the sabbatical and thanked them and the church for such an opportunity. I then said that I would like to have a second day off that week, reminding them that I had never taken more than one day off a week during the previous six years.

The atmosphere darkened immediately, and the others wanted to know why I was so tired after three months off. Wasn't the point of the sabbatical to give me rest and renewal? Fighting to maintain my composure, I explained that everyone knew the tensions at the church, most of which seemed focused on me, and I needed to gather myself to find ways to overcome them. Nobody seemed convinced, and eventually I simply insisted that I must have a second day off. They agreed to my request, but it was no victory to savor. My journal tells the story: "I've forgotten Norway so fast it scares me. Council meeting long and drawn out. I'm dragging, frazzled, exhausted."

At the next day's noon prayer group, I shared my need for the second day off, and one person said bluntly, "You have let them push you to lose authority. Don't ask for a day off when you need it; tell them you're taking it!" The others nodded.

Chagrined, I thought about what they had said. All along I had essentially been angry, even resentful, toward the church leaders for not giving me more authority. Could it be that I was asking them for something that was not theirs to give but indeed something that God had already given me as their pastor? If so, the question was not whether they would give me their authority, but whether I would dare to exercise God's authority among them.

I could hardly avoid recognizing the parent-child dimension of the conflict between the church and me. Clearly, I had often responded as an adolescent: still demanding from my earthly "parents" something that only God can give—and, indeed, more comfortable doing that than accepting responsibility for what God was giving. An adolescent, after all, is primarily in search of identity, and the battle with parents is an effort to establish the authority of that identity apart from theirs.

Yet in confirming me as "Roger," God had essentially declared to me, "It's time to grow up. I, who have created you and called you by name, have given you your true identity and its authority. Accept it. Walk in it. Grow in it. And as you do, others will recognize it." I remembered how at first I had considered legally changing my name to Roger but, after praying with several others, had sensed that God was more concerned with my accepting what the name meant for my life than with any outward label.

In a very real sense, the church, too, was acting as an adolescent with respect to Father God—proudly resisting His call to accept His saving forgiveness through Jesus and His healing, delivering power through the Holy Spirit. But two adolescents do not bring each other into maturity by accusing each other of immaturity. Clearly, it was up to me first, as pastor—literally, "shepherd"—to opt out of the adolescent game and focus my energies instead on modeling authentic maturity, by accepting the Father's authority over my own life and through me in others' lives.

Alice called the next day. "I've been praying about Beth and what happened Sunday after church," she said. "I believe that she's being used by the enemy to attack the church; and you, Gordon, seem to be the focus of the attack."

I believed that, too, and even the response of the church leaders seemed to confirm it. Often in discussing those in the church who were upset with me, one of the leaders would say, in effect, "Everyone says they're leaving 'because of Gordon,' but so far we really haven't gotten to any specific reason or thing that you've done." Their desire to get to the root of the upset was making them try harder and harder to find something that I had done wrong. Indeed, I was and am not perfect, so they were prepared to seize upon any shortcoming of mine to justify their response.

Meanwhile, not one member of the church—with the ironic exception of Beth—would understand if I told them, "Though I have made my share of mistakes, the root of the upset among us is not anything I've done but what the enemy of God is doing. His aim is to destroy the work of God among us by sowing division. He has used my shortcomings to do that, and he has used yours as well.

"You and I are fellow victims in this conflict, not enemies, and until we unite against our true and common enemy, we won't see God's victory here at the church." And so, indeed, since I was the only one who could recognize him, the enemy was focusing his attack on me.

At that time, the sabbatical was an ever-present target, and I felt myself laboring against a sense among the entire congregation that I had done something shamefully wrong in taking it. Even my supporters seemed to be saying, in effect, "We support you because we love you—no matter how wrong you were." A voice within me often felt like crying out from the pulpit, "Okay, I give up! It's true! I lied to you all. I just took the sabbatical for myself and a free vacation!" But in my heart, I knew that was not true.

By Holy Week, I was still "dragging, frazzled, and exhausted." On Maundy Thursday morning, I entered in my journal a dream from the night before, in which one of my most persistent detractors had put a huge face up close to mine and said, "I saw what you did to [woman's name], and she was so devastated when she came to me, from what you did to her!" That morning, I decided I would fast— the entire weekend if necessary—until I found release from the oppressive sense of shame and guilt I felt chained about me.

Preparing my meditation and sermon for the Tenebrae service that night had been increasingly frustrating, and eventually I decided to talk on communion without notes. I focused on preparing for the sacrament by confessing our sins, and before moving to the table, I led the congregation in an open-ended prayer of confession. "Lord, forgive me for ways I've hurt my family," I began, then paused a minute to allow people to recall how they might have hurt their family. I repeated the invitation, adding "my friends," "my church," "people where I work," and other relationship categories, and then I ministered the sacrament.

Everyone left the sanctuary in darkness after the Tenebrae service, and as I chatted with people outside, I sensed a refreshing peace, a clearing amid the storm. *There's power in the blood!* I thought and realized that the Lord had struck out against the enemy through the sacrament that night.

When everyone had left, I decided to go up to the altar to pray. After I had knelt there for some moments, I could think of nothing to say—then it occurred to me that perhaps it was better to listen. I waited, and after a while, I sensed a voice within me say, "Get up, turn around, and look out at the sanctuary. Then tell me what you see."

I stood and turned around, and in my mind's eye, I saw a host of people fighting and scuffling with each other as if in a barroom brawl. "I see people fighting each other," I said aloud.

"Take up the sword!" I heard.

I walked down the aisle without hesitation and began angrily casting out spirits of division, conflict, and disunity. When I had walked the full length of the church, I turned and walked back to the altar.

"Go to the pulpit."

I turned and stepped up into the pulpit, even as I had done hundreds of times before. But this time, something startling happened.

"Look now again, and tell Me what you see."

A vision arose in my mind's eye. "I see people on their knees crying, reaching out their hands, like starving people."

"Gordon," I heard, "feed My sheep."

As I drove home that night, it struck me that a shepherd must have a staff, or sword, to fight off the enemy wolf, even as he must feed his sheep. *Lord,* I prayed, *give me everything I need to fight off the enemy at the church and nurture Your people there.*

The next day, I received a call from Liz. "One leader who has been resenting you came to me in the parking lot last night after the service and said, 'My heart is changed. Anything Gordon needs, he has my support.' I thought you'd like to know that."

Amazing, that God should change someone's heart like that—even Liz's, making her willing to share those words with me! I thanked her for passing that on to me, wishing she had told the person to call me but knowing she relished her position as go-between power broker.

Encouraged, I knew nevertheless that the oppressive guilt had not lifted from me. Before going to bed, I was as distraught as ever and finally seized my cross again and knelt on the carpet.

"Why is all this happening, Lord?" I cried out. "Was the sabbatical really just my own selfish desire, as everyone's been accusing? I'll apologize and make it up to the church if that's true—but just tell me!" Furiously, I raised my fisted cross and shook it. "This has got to stop, Lord! What's going on?"

Quiet. No voice, no sense, no image. Dismayed, I fell on my face, holding the cross before me. And then, almost at once, I heard a gentle voice within me say, "You didn't stand up for Me."

"What?" I exclaimed, looking up. "What do you mean, I didn't stand up for You?" I waited, and moments later, I began to see at last. The Lord had indeed called me to the sabbatical and even scheduled it for His purposes. But in the face of criticism from others, I became fearful they would not approve it—and therefore I became defensive in a way that drew distrust. *My fear of others trumped my trust in Him.*

In that moment, I sensed that the Lord had wanted me to stand up before the church and say, "I feel God is calling me to this sabbatical, which is in accord with denominational practice. Our polity requires you either to confirm or to deny this by your vote. I will therefore abide by your vote. But I trust the Lord to use the three months for His purposes, and therefore I will not promise you anything regarding my use of that time, except that I will do my best to discern and carry out His purposes." That would've been clean, straightforward—giving the situation to God in trust and respecting the people enough to make the right choice.

Even as the truth dawned upon me, I felt my fear of the others and their judgment. In that fear, I was convicted of the sin of idolatry, of attributing saving power to people's approval of me rather than solely to God. As I confessed the sin of letting my fear of human rejection turn me from God's call, I knew at once that I did indeed need to apologize to the church—not for taking the sabbatical, not for using the time for activities besides those I had promised in order to placate them, but for not modeling for them at the outset a pastor who stands firm in his trust of the Lord and his respect for them.

In fact, as I sat there in the quiet of that Good Friday evening, I saw how my fear of others had prompted even my original plan for members to pray and ask God whether or not the sabbatical was His will. Few in the congregation were that mature in their relationship with the Lord, and I knew it. They simply were not capable of releasing their own human feelings and seeking instead God's heart. In even suggesting they do it, I was making them feel inadequate and frustrated, thus contributing to the spirit of distrust—as if to say, "We don't understand this strange way our pastor says we should know what to do, so he must be trying to pull the wool over our eyes just to get what he wants."

A firm faith in the Lord would have allowed me to meet the congregation directly on their terms and trust the Lord to work His will through them as they were, instead of fearing they would not vote as He wanted and compromising my schedule to preclude even the Lord's plans. In not trusting God to accomplish His purposes, I had sought to please human beings and not God—and had paid the consequences in loss of respect (Rom. 2:28–29).

When by late evening I finally rose from the floor, I felt an overwhelming sense of freedom, relief, and renewed determination. I was learning that the truth does in fact set you free—just as Jesus said—and is a major weapon against the enemy. It had indeed been a Good Friday.

My ego, certainly, had been nailed to the cross. On Easter Sunday, therefore, the prospect of victory shone ahead brilliantly. Before the Easter lilies had been spirited from the sanctuary to shut-ins, I knew that as soon as possible, I needed to contact each of the families that had left the church. I felt equipped to listen at last, and prepared, if not anxious, to confess the liberating truth I had been shown. Still, I was as uneasy as anyone might be at placing myself in so vulnerable a position before those who had rejected me.

Early in the week, I called Pastor Don Brendtro, who had told me about Norway, and he graciously reminded me that Jesus had modeled that same position.


I CALLED THE FIRST COUPLE; THE WIFE HAD COMPLAINED TO church leaders about the way I had handled Jane, the false prophet. The husband answered the phone, and I told him what the leaders had told me about their leaving because of me, and then I said I wanted to hear from him directly. To my surprise, he said that while his wife had been concerned, the basic issue was that they wanted a church "more interested in saving souls for Christ" and the leaders didn't seem to understand or appreciate that.

When I explained that, indeed, that was why I had withheld the spiritual dimension of Jane's problem from the leaders, he said, "Well, I had to ask myself, *Why does Gordon stay at that church if they are so resistant to Christ?*" I replied that I felt called by the Lord to stay and be used in some further way to open people there to Him. Though he declined my invitation to give the church another try, I felt a genuine sense of reconciliation and affirmation when I hung up.

The wife, however, had not been home, and when I called later and talked with her, my efforts to reconcile the Jane issue with her proved futile, and we hung up without any sense of resolution. In fact, as I contacted the four other families that had left, in each case the wife was clearly the driving source of discontent; two husbands told me outright that they preferred to stay at the church but had decided to follow their wife's decision in order that the family might continue to worship together. What that implied for the man's voice in his family was so profound that I realized at once my broaching that issue in a farewell conversation could only deepen the wound. So I simply affirmed our friendship, expressed my disappointment at their leaving, and blessed their future church experience.

One surprising outcome of these visits was that two of the wives asked me to minister to them afterward, one of whom had been my most vehement opponent. The other I visited at home with her husband one evening, and the living room was thick with tension as I entered. When we sat down, I looked at each and invited them to tell me as openly as they liked how they felt about me and about my ministry at the church. The woman began immediately scolding that I had taken a sabbatical when her husband worked so hard at his job without any such thing. In fact, she did not expect a man of the faith to be "pushing for things like that." Lastly, she felt I had not been honest with the congregation by not taking the courses I had agreed upon, and in general had not been up front with everyone about the sabbatical.

I listened as graciously as possible, then turned to her husband, a man with whom I had developed a reasonably good rapport through persistent efforts at one-on-one lunches and church workdays. "I want to respond to Marge, but first I want to hear how you feel, Bill."

"Well," Bill said hesitantly, glancing at Marge. A moment's pause, then: "I agree with Marge."

*Oh, Lord!* I cried out in my heart. *What's happened to the men?* I took a deep breath and nodded.

Shifting in my chair, I plunged ahead. I said that I, too, wished Bill could get a sabbatical, as he certainly worked as hard at his job as anyone I knew and deserved one. The sabbatical, however, was not a vacation or diversion from my holy calling, but rather a direct expression of it. I then told them about several clearly ordained events during the sabbatical that confirmed that. Finally, I agreed that I had not been as up front with everyone as I should have been—not because I had anything to hide, but because I did not trust the Lord enough to confirm His decision for the sabbatical. After explaining that I had asked His forgiveness for that, I then asked their forgiveness.

"That's as honest and direct as I can be," I said, leaning back into my chair.

Marge sat silent, expressionless. Bill, however, raised his eyebrows. "That puts it all in a different light," he allowed.

The darkness had clearly lifted amid the light of my truth-telling, and I proceeded to share more highlights of the sabbatical. When I mentioned the seminar "Dreams and Inner Healing," to my surprise Marge began to tell me about an unsettling dream that had troubled her for years. After we talked, I offered to pray for her, and she accepted. When I left that night, we shook hands warmly and genuinely. Still, I never saw them again.

Outside in my car alone, I praised God for the courage He had given me to be so bold and direct with people who had rejected me and simply savored the new strength I felt rising within me. As I turned the corner and headed home, I clenched my fist in victory—then suddenly found myself crying. "Lord," I said aloud, "we need You so desperately—but our hearts are so closed!"

I knew that the Lord had not led me to contact those five families in order to vindicate Rev. Gordon Dalbey but rather Himself—that is, as a last-ditch effort to keep them open to His healing, reconciling power. True, as a rabbi friend and confidant assured, after that week I could look myself in the mirror and see a *mensch*, perhaps for the first time in my life. As I looked out on their empty pew-spaces on Sunday morning, however, I saw only the haunting image of souls lost from the family, even as they hungered for the fellowship of God's healing presence.

In the weeks that followed, I took every opportunity to express to others in the church what I had told those who had left about my lack of faith in presenting the sabbatical at the outset. As the issue of the sabbatical began to lose its effectiveness toward dividing and destroying the church, my opponents began to dust off the old issue of the "direction of the church" and wield it again.

This time, however, I was not caught either so unarmed or so surprised as before, and I was quick to mobilize all the resources of spiritual warfare that I had learned from the past year's battling. Above all, I had learned that the number-one weapon in spiritual warfare is truth, as the early church understood, closely followed by righteousness. "So stand ready, with truth as a belt tight around your waist, with righteousness as your breastplate" (Eph. 6:14).

This meant that I needed at all times to examine myself as truthfully as possible in order to discover my shortcomings. For a perfectionist like myself, this is to invite self-condemnation. The only safeguard would be taking those revealed shortcomings to the Lord, trusting in His saving mercy. I came to treasure David's ancient prayer as he railed against evil in others: "Examine me, O God, and know my mind; test me, and discover my thoughts. Find out if there is any evil in me and guide me in the everlasting way" (Ps. 139:23–24).

Similarly, it occurred to me that when ancient Israel sought greater firepower against its enemies, God reminded the people that their strength lay not in their physical weapons but in their willingness to draw close to God, who alone was their defender. "I am the high and holy God, who lives forever. I live in a high and holy place, but I also live with people who are humble and repentant, so that I can restore their confidence and hope" (Isa. 57:15).

The most dramatic reinforcement of this need for constant self-examination came to me when one of my critics had accused me of being judgmental in a particular situation. Immediately, I stiffened and became defensive, and the encounter ended in a tense standoff. Later, as I offered it to the Lord in prayer, I knew in my heart the terrible truth, that this person who had channeled so much of the enemy's destruction into the church was nevertheless altogether correct. I had indeed been judgmental.

Anguished, I asked the Lord's forgiveness and called the person to acknowledge my wrong attitude. I tried to forget it, but the sense of being humiliated by such a perceived enemy kept grinding away at me, and again I grasped my cross and fell to my knees. *Lord,* I asked, *how can I avoid that kind of thing in the future—please?*

His reply came quickly and simply: "Come to Me first, My son."

As I chewed on those words, I began to digest and assimilate their impact: *The Lord wants me armed with His strength in battle. I cannot receive His strength as long as I am turned away from Him in sin. He wants very much, therefore, to show me my sin so I will bring it to Him and be cleansed. The easiest way for that to happen is to go to Him each day and ask Him to show me my sin. Surely, if my heart is sincere, He will. And if my faith is sure, I will offer it to Him expecting His mercy.*

If you're real, God can make you right.

But if you're right, the enemy will make you real.

If I do not go to God asking for His truth, He must find other ways to communicate it to me. Perhaps He may first try friends. But if I have not cultivated honest friendships or if I am too proud to listen, as a final resort He can only unleash the enemy to drive me into the Father's saving hands.

By that point, the snowball is pretty far down the hill, and to continue resisting is to invite dire consequences. As Jesus urged, "Come to terms quickly with your accuser while you are on the way to court with him, or your accuser may hand you over to the judge, and the judge to the guard, and you will be thrown into prison. Truly I tell you, you will never get out until you have paid the last penny" (Matt. 5:25–26 NRSV).

"The accuser," of course, is Satan's name. The first thing to do when accused is to ask God for His word of truth. If the accusation is true, agree quickly and make amends, for the more you try to defend yourself, the deeper the lie drags you down, like struggling in quicksand. To agree with the accuser is often the most effective way of disarming him, if he's accurate in his accusation. "Thank you for showing me my sin, Satan!" you can say. "I'll take it right to Jesus and be freed from it."

While false accusations can, of course, be harmful, often they simply can be proven false and thus defused. The enemy is far more likely to fire accusations that are true, banking on our proud human inclination to defend ourselves far more quickly than to agree—and thus bind ourselves over to him.

I learned to apply this truth not only to accusations from other persons, but also to the voice of the accuser in me. For example, the enemy would often whisper to me as I was about to preach: "You can't preach! You're not a good enough person to do anything at all like this. What right do you think you have to get up there like that and talk to people?"

Immediately, I would become defensive. "Oh yes, I can preach! I'm ordained by my denomination, and these people hired me, and I know pretty well how to do it!" But in my heart, I knew the accuser had a point, and the more he persisted, the weaker my defense became—or the more rigid—either one adversely affecting my preaching. If by no other means, the enemy would win such a battle simply by engaging and consuming my good energy, which should have gone into my preaching.

Through the experiences of those several months of combat, however, I learned not to bite the accuser's bait and justify myself, but rather to agree with him and say, "You're right. I can't preach and I'm not a good enough person to do this. In fact, I can't do anything without Jesus doing it through me [John 15:5]. Thanks for reminding me. But though I'm unworthy, by His death Jesus has saved me from my sin and by His grace has made me worthy to do this, His work. And I will not allow His grace and sacrifice on my behalf to go for nothing. So I'm getting up there, and I'll preach with all the power He gives me." With that, the enemy was disarmed. My mind was freed to concentrate on opening my heart to the Holy Spirit and preaching as I sensed God's leading.

Perhaps most significantly, through my recent spiritual combat, I had begun to learn a new strength and courage by trusting in God's mercy even as in His power. This was confirmed later that year in a strange and marvelous prayer.

At the Charismatic Pastors' Fellowship, one man had spoken out especially convincingly on the need for Christian spiritual warriors to learn a new boldness. I decided to call and ask him to pray for me. He invited me to his church, and when several days later we settled in his office, he remarked that sometimes his prayers were more like "running images," which he would just "speak out loud" as he "saw" them.

As we began, he sensed that God wanted to heal me from my very beginnings as an infant, and he lifted up an image of me as a tiny baby coming out of my mother's womb, with Jesus standing there to receive me, arms outstretched.

"I can see Jesus take you into His arms. He's strong and muscular, very manly, and He goes to draw you up to His chest. But it looks like you're very angry. In fact, you're fighting mad about something—I don't know what. But as Jesus draws you to Him, you make fists and you're pounding Jesus on His muscular chest. You're just furious, beating on Him with a rage!"

At that, I sat up tensely in my chair. *What in the world is this all about? And what would Jesus do to me if I beat on Him like that?*

"But the funny thing is," my friend continued, "Jesus is smiling. He's not angry back at you. In fact, He's just beaming at you. And it's not as if He's spaced out or anything, unaware of what you're doing. In fact, He's smiling because you're pounding on Him. 'That's My man!' He's saying. 'Yes, that's My man!'"

*Amazing!* I thought, sighing and leaning back in my chair. Obviously, Jesus not only tolerated my fighting spirit, but was in fact encouraging it. I was not damaging anything or hurting anyone— it's not as if I could destroy Jesus! And I sensed a genuine strength in the image. It occurred to me later that a "Roger-warrior" would necessarily have a fighting spirit; that without it, I could hardly be an effective warrior. Of course, to be God's warrior, I would need to submit that fighting spirit to God at all times, even focus it on Him when I saw no other choice but to suppress or squelch it altogether. Better to pound on Jesus than to withdraw from the battle—or to pound on another person!

Then it struck me that my friend was "seeing" in his prayer precisely my pounding on Jesus after returning from Norway, depressed and alone in my apartment, and how that had set me free! As I prayed further, I remembered my mother's telling me of stressful events she suffered during her pregnancy with me during World War II that had come to focus negatively on "the baby on the way." No wonder I came out of the womb with such anger!

Being *ex-pressed* safely with Jesus released me from being *de-pressed* alone.

That angry image begs comparison to my pounding pillows when I was in psychotherapy years earlier. But through this prayer image of graphically giving my anger to Jesus, as it were, I saw at last that to pound pillows and scream anger at the other person who has hurt you—while initially helpful in identifying the focus of your feelings—eventually indulges a spirit of anger from the enemy, thereby giving him an even deeper hold on your life. No wonder I never experienced the peace I sought from such therapy!

I had campaigned vigorously against TV and movie violence, rejecting the notion that such images provide a helpful catharsis to release or "work off" violent impulses. My growing experience in spiritual warfare had now allowed me to realize that images of violence against another person, whether in the media or in our own psychological fantasies, only foster the enemy's spirit of destruction among us.

In the cross, God said essentially, "The buck stops here. I can't bear to see My children destroying each other any longer! If you must retaliate, don't strike the other person; strike Me instead, and let Me bear your brokenness!

"And maybe if you stop avenging one another long enough, you can at last recognize the enemy laughing as you have harmed and destroyed one another, and will turn to Me to save you."

Still, my natural heart of flesh worried, *If I stop pushing the church, can God's plan move ahead among us?*

But my submitted heart knew God had not sent me there to push His plan but to open hearts to know Him and receive it. The church was His, and He loved it far more than I could ever love it with my broken, sinful heart. My job at that point was, in fact, to stop pushing, let go, and surrender the church and my destiny to Him.

I called Bob Whitaker for advice. "For your own sake and for the sake of the church," he said, "at some point—and likely soon—

you're going to have to tell your church, 'This is where I believe God is leading me. If you want to go with me, then let's go. If not, I'm not the one to be pastoring you.' In all honesty, it doesn't sound like they want to go, which means you may need to leave the church."

Bob's advice made absolute sense, but his conclusion frightened me. "Without followers, you're not a leader," he said. "A leader takes people someplace they otherwise might want to go, but can't by themselves. If the people don't want to go, they won't follow—and then by definition, you're not their leader."

At the next council meeting, one member said matter-of-factly, "Gordon, you're not the pastor we hired." I was about to defend myself when by grace I paused—and listened. It was true. To defend myself on that point would be to deny all that God had taught me, to waste all the suffering I'd been through to learn it.

The recent understanding garnered by my truth-telling and asking forgiveness had brought us to a plateau. The congregation and I now held each other in respect—a necessary, but not sufficient, condition for growing together. The storm had subsided and the ship had been righted, but in my heart I knew I was not its captain any longer. It was time for new leadership at the church and a new focus for my life.

I was soon single and unemployed. Much grief and healing work lay ahead. But never in my life had I felt closer to my Father, nor more secure in my calling and confident in His provision to fulfill it.

From what you've read here, you can be sure that God worked His many "holy coincidences" to confirm this. Someday, perhaps in another book, I'll tell the whole marvelous story.

But now, it's time for the explorer to come home.

# Part III

## THE RETURN: SHARING THE LESSONS

"The LORD, Your God, is in your midst,
a warrior who gives victory."
—ZEPHANIAH 3:17

## Chapter 16

# HOW DEMONS ENTER– AND LEAVE

E nemy spirits, I have discovered, enter human beings by at least five basic avenues.

## Generational Ties / Familiar Spirits

Demons most commonly enter by piggy-backing down the generations. Often these are called "familiar spirits," insofar as the word *familiar* shares its root with *family*. You may have a biological ancestor, that is, who harbored a particular spirit as spiritually defective DNA, which continues to manifest in later generations. These spirits make the most rational sense, insofar as they are often clearly reflected in a parent's behavior.

Generational spirits can be the easiest to overcome once identified and renounced. At the same time, they can be easily overlooked, simply because they're not associated with any memorable event; you never did anything wrong, nor was anything wrong done to you, to bring them into your life.

Every child experiences his or her own family behaviors as normative, and family dysfunctions are often whitewashed by denial. "That's not a demon," you may scoff. "That was just the way we did it in our family." As you surrender to Jesus, however, His Spirit of truth can discern for you the difference between mere quirky behavior and the ongoing generational work of demons.

When any points of entry bring demons into your life, those spirits often pass down to your children. Parents who want to protect their children not only pray against external attack, but also go to Jesus for deliverance from such family spirits in themselves, passed down from their parents and ancestors.

Father God honors heartfelt desire for deliverance. My experience suggests that once parents have surrendered their hearts to Jesus and invited His Holy Spirit into their lives, demons often do not pass down to their children even when they may remain hidden in the parents.

Nevertheless, parents' demons that are not appropriately identified and cast out can cause damage within the family. Responsible Christian fathers and mothers seek deliverance ministry for themselves so that they and their children might be as cleansed as possible for the work of God's Spirit.

During the Exodus, God said that He would "not fail to punish children and grandchildren to the third and fourth generation for the sins of their parents" (Ex. 34:7)—a curse later lifted in Ezekiel 18:1–4. I interpret this to mean that all powers that have conspired to trap us in demonic generational patterns have been overcome.

But because God respects our will, we need to exercise the authority we have in Jesus to name and cast out these demons.

A man came to me distraught and harried. He could not rest, even when he took a vacation. I asked if either of his parents suffered similarly. "Oh yes!" he exclaimed immediately. "That's Mom. She was always on the go, a regular human whirlwind." We prayed, and I sensed a "driving" spirit. He set the cross between himself and his mother, renounced the demon, and cast it out. He then claimed the blood of Jesus to cleanse his natural family bloodline of this evil and asked for a spirit of rest from the Holy Spirit to replace it (Heb. 4:1–11).

Evicting a familiar spirit usually follows this general pattern:

- Identify the spirit and confirm by recognizing how it acted out in your parent.
- Set the cross between you and your children, between you and your parent, and as far back between the generations as you can discern is necessary.
- In the name of Jesus, cast the demon out of you and send it into the hands of Jesus.
- Ask that the blood of Jesus cleanse your family bloodline of this evil, both in you and in your children.
- Ask the Holy Spirit to come and show you with what work of His own He would replace it, and ask for that to replace the enemy's work.

## Shattered Emotional Defenses

Germs are everywhere, even on the surface of your skin, but can enter the body only where the skin has been broken or cut. Similarly, the shock and trauma of deeply painful and fearful events cut through our natural human defenses, and the resulting wound in the human spirit creates an opening for the enemy.

Consider the electric wiring in a house. Current comes into the house from an outside source that is not perfectly consistent. American homes are wired to function on 220 volts of current. A power surge in excess of that voltage would overload the circuit, heat up the inside wires, destroy appliances, and set the house on fire. Houses, therefore, have a protective fuse box, through which all outside current must pass before entering the home circuitry. The fuses are calibrated to trip at more than 220 volts incoming.

When that happens, the good news is that the wiring and appliances are not destroyed, and the house does not burn down but remains. The bad news, however, is that no electricity comes in and the house is without power or light. (The body remains, but the spirit shuts down.)

God has created human beings with an internal "fuse box" to protect us from an overload of our pain circuits. After World War II, psychologists called this "post-traumatic shock" when many soldiers shut down emotionally after participating in unspeakable violence. Their emotional fuse had blown. In extreme cases, amnesia set in.

While this has become widely recognized amid adult trauma such as war or sever illness or accident, it has often gone unnoticed in children who suffer proportionately similar trauma from painful emotional experiences. An eight-year-old child's nervous system, for example, is not yet fully developed. Let's say it can only handle 100 "volts of pain." Suppose the pet goldfish dies. That hurts—call it 50 volts of pain—but doesn't overload the child's capacity. The child cries; the parent comforts the child, puts the dead goldfish in a matchbox, buries it out in the yard, talks about how much you liked the fish, says good-bye, then buys another one. The child is happy again. The incoming pain (voltage) passes the fuse box into and through the body (house), leaving it wholly functioning.

But now suppose a teacher or other adult authority shames you in front of others. Or Mommy and Daddy get into a violent, terrifying argument and threaten to divorce. That's 250 volts of pain. Or Mom gets drunk and beats you; Dad leaves home and never returns—400 volts.

This is a circuit overload for an eight-year-old's nervous system. Your defenses are shattered. Fear and panic grip your heart. You're all alone, at the mercy of overwhelmingly painful events with no one to comfort or defend you. This is more pain than a child's nervous-system wiring is capable of processing without burning up. And so the internal emotional-shock "fuse" trips.

The good news is that the child does not die but often continues to function and perform basic life tasks.

The bad news, however, is that a circuit blows in your heart, and the lights go out. You shut down emotionally and function less brightly, as the overwhelming pain in that memory requires increasing energy to be numbed and shoved down below consciousness.

With enough struggle and effort, you grow up to be a functioning, performing adult but may find yourself incapable of healthy, caring relationships.

Because the child's natural system can neither process nor suppress that much pain, *super*natural power is required to overcome its effects. Your heart cries out for help. If you don't know Jesus, your cry echoes in the darkness.

Enter the Prince of Darkness. The awful pain in that memory

threatens to surface and overwhelm you; without Jesus, your only hope is to keep a heavy lid on it. Here the enemy is well equipped to assist. He may offer you a defensive spirit, or perhaps vengeance, stoicism, passivity, even addiction—whichever of his agents would most readily make you trust him instead of God to deliver you from the pain.

In your heart, the enemy strikes a bargain. "You just can't live with all that pain, and no one around you has any power to help you. But I can help. We don't need to take away your pain. All you need to do is let me put one of my agents in you who will make sure you don't feel it anymore." The enemy can only stay with your permission, and he gets it by seducing you. It may not have been an open, articulated transaction. But the deal went through. The evidence is your shut-down heart later as an adult—and the dysfunctional relationships you engender.

If you're not covered spiritually by parents or someone else who moves in the full power of the Holy Spirit to deliver and heal, numbness is an attractive option. Your heart closes the deal subliminally, and you walk away "forgetting" the pain but oppressed by an enemy spirit.

Because your pain and fear have not been processed but only buried, all that suppressed "negative voltage" will stir later if the two frayed ends of the fuse wires ever threaten to reconnect. A movie in which parents yell at each other or threaten divorce, for example, or a sad song, or news of a similar tragedy in another's life—or when you think about moving ahead with your life in ways that you associate with that pain, as in getting married yourself—will trigger the deep pain from your original trauma.

In your heart, the sirens shout now as then, "Don't let those wires touch again! You'll get electrocuted! No one will be there to save you. Don't dare feel all that pain; keep it hidden, or it will flood in and overwhelm you!" Panic attacks, addiction relapse, irrational fear, and overwhelming anger often emerge here.

Jesus, meanwhile, has come into the world to save us from the effects of such crippling pain and demonic sabotage so that we can be whole and active agents for His coming kingdom. In fact, God wants to use every wound, every painful experience in you to shape you for His calling. As the apostle Paul declared:

> Let us give thanks to the God and Father of our Lord Jesus Christ, the merciful Father, the God from whom all help comes! He helps us in all our troubles, so that we are able to help others who have all kinds of troubles, using the same help that we ourselves have received from God. (2 Cor. 1:3–4)

Jesus alone can receive and process any excess "pain voltage," not only without being burned up by it, but indeed to manifest His glory through it in you.

That means you can invite Jesus into the traumatic memory, let Him take the broken wires in each hand and absorb the otherwise-lethal current into His body. With that security, you can express freely the feelings you've suppressed, release all your energy bound up in hiding the truth, and spend it by walking confidently into your created destiny.

Often Jesus shows you that the ones who hurt you were badly wounded and acted out of their own brokenness. This understanding allows you to forgive them. The enemy's hook is thereby removed. You can let go of your perpetrators and stop wasting your energy focusing on the enemy's "payback" agenda. You can name and cast out the lying, destructive spirit and get on with your destiny.

As an adult, for example, I always had an abiding fear of being abandoned. When I asked the Father to show me the root of this, I remembered a time when I was about six years old, several weeks after my navy-officer father had left for sea duty. I was playing in a friend's backyard and decided to climb a bunch of thin logs leaning up against a tree trunk lengthwise, in tepee-like formation.

The sapling logs, however, were not secured in any way, and halfway up I lost my balance and fell to the ground flat on my back, knocking the wind out of me. Startled and frightened, unable to breathe for a moment, in a flash I realized that my father was far away—and a bolt of terror struck me.

Ideally, if I had cried out for Jesus to protect me as I fell from those shifting logs, or if a spiritually mature adult had prayed over me, I still would have experienced the physical effects of pain and breathlessness, but the enemy could not have entered me. The child, of course, sees his earthly father as God, and when my father was not present to rescue me, I blamed him for causing my fear. In reality, my initial sensation of fear as a six-year-old was simply a natural human reaction to a present physical danger, which the enemy seized upon to enter me.

As long as I childishly blamed my father instead of the enemy, the enemy got off scot-free and continued to wield his deathly fear against God's purposes in me, with no threat of being either recognized or cast out. A major key to overcoming demons that prey on shattered emotional defenses lies in seeing the perceived "shatterer," or wounder, in a spirit of truth and forgiveness.

To prepare my heart for deliverance, I brought this original memory to mind in prayer and then asked Jesus to be present with me as I fell from the logs—as I might ideally have done years before. Without conjuring any image of my own, I waited quietly, praying in my prayer language. Eventually, in my mind's eye, I saw Jesus come into the backyard scene, hold me, and comfort me. Then He brought my father to me, and in Jesus' presence, speaking out loud, I told my father how much I had missed him and how much it hurt me that he hadn't been there to pick me up and comfort me.

I began to cry, and my father then said how much he loved me, that he wanted very much to have been there for me, but circumstances he could not control kept him from being there. He asked if I would forgive him—and in the presence of Jesus, I did.

The enemy was brought clearly into the open as the true perpetrator, and in the name of Jesus, I cast the spirit of "abandonment" out of myself. Without that resolution of my childish resentment of my father, I could have cast out the demon, but it would have been able to reenter me through that gap in my spirit, which remained uncovered by Jesus and His forgiving love. Paul wrote, "For when I forgive . . . I do it in Christ's presence because of you, in order to keep Satan from getting the upper hand over us; for we know what his plans are" (2 Cor. 2:10–11).

Certainly, not all wounding comes out of the perpetrator's own wounds. Sometimes, the person chooses to hurt you out of natural, human self-centeredness. This is harder to overcome, but the way through and out lies in deciding to forgive the person by calling Jesus into the scene and saying out loud what harm you are forgiving, laying down before Jesus all your right to revenge, praying for the person, and leaving him or her in His hands. Then you are free to name and cast out the demon. This does not, of course, rule out taking action to protect yourself against future harm, but frees your heart to discern God's purposes.

Once the territory in my heart occupied by the enemy had been cleared, I asked the Holy Spirit to come and rule there instead. I remembered and proclaimed Psalm 27:10: "My father and mother may abandon me, but the LORD will take care of me." Finally, I asked specifically for a godly spirit of sonship (Rom. 8:14–16) to replace the demon of abandonment, and for a clearer vision of God's purposes in my life and a deeper trust in Him to fulfill them.

The issue becomes not "I can do it with Your help," but rather "You can do it with my cooperation." That is, "How can I cooperate with You, Father, in bringing about Your plan for my life?" Thus, as the Holy Spirit of God begins to retake that territory in your heart, the tripped fuse is restored and His light reenters your house. Your energies refocus away from the enemy's work and back to the Father's call.

## Sinful Habits Indulged

Spilled glue, if wiped up immediately, is easily disposed. If allowed to sit, however, it bonds so firmly to the object that a tool is required to remove it. Similarly, if you persist in yielding yourself to behavior contrary to God's purposes, the enemy of God will take over your willpower and you can no longer simply choose to stop. Even as you can jump into a pit deeper than you're capable of climbing out, you can easily continue a harmful habit until your natural will is no longer strong enough to counteract it.

As John put it, "Whoever continues to sin belongs to the Devil, because the Devil has sinned from the very beginning. The Son of God appeared for this very reason, to destroy what the Devil had done" (1 John 3:8).

At one period, while going through my divorce and struggles at the church, instead of pressing after the Father, I tried to avoid facing my pain and fear by watching TV late-night shows and sleeping late in the morning. Eventually, my willpower was simply not strong enough to pull me out of this destructive pattern. Some mornings, I would literally lie half asleep in bed, aware that I wanted to get up but feeling as if a heavy weight were pushing me back into the mattress. If I gave up and fell asleep again, I would be assaulted with frantic, bizarre, run-on dreams that left me exhausted when I finally awoke.

I sinned in turning away from God and not taking my need to Him. My indulgent habit therefore beckoned the enemy, who obliged with spirits of lethargy and narcolepsy. To counter these demons, I first renounced my habit of sleeping late and confessed it to God as a sin—not because it's somehow immoral or lazy to sleep late, but because doing so in this instance was separating me from Him. It missed His mark for me in trusting Him to walk with me through a difficult day, plus it kept me from fully doing the work He had called me to do that day.

Asking forgiveness, I then confessed that no power of my own could set me free from the bondage I had brought on myself. *Give me Your power to break this habit, Lord,* I prayed—and in the name of Jesus, I cast out from me the spirits of lethargy and narcolepsy.

This did not complete the work of deliverance, however. Because actions of my own choosing had given the enemy this hold on me, I needed to commit myself to new action counter to the old habit by going to bed at a decent hour and getting up earlier. After the deliverance, when my early alarm went off, no external heaviness pushed me back into the mattress—but the lazy impulses of my human nature still stirred. The difference now was that I had regained my original ability to choose to get up.

If I chose not to, and instead chose to further indulge the sinful habit, the enemy would have swept back into me. I know that because, almost like a child testing a parent, I once hit my alarm button and thought to roll over again "just for a minute." Almost immediately, the old heaviness began creeping over me, and I saw myself standing, as it were, on the brink of more agitating roller-coaster dreams.

I opened my eyes with a start and sat up. A quick prayer of confession and I jumped out of bed! "Wake up, sleeper, and rise from death," as Paul said, "and Christ will shine on you" (Eph. 5:14).

Still, this was no easy habit to break. As the impulse to oversleep intensified and the enemy determinedly sought to reclaim territory in my life, I knew I would need additional help to resist. After desperately praying, I decided to call a friend across town for help, and we agreed to phone each other every morning at six o'clock and pray together. For perhaps a month, we prayed on the phone in the morning darkness. Looking forward to my friend's support gave me a foothold, and I was able to gain considerable strength to break the habit of sleeping late and thus to walk in the deliverance that God had provided.

Still, the enemy did not give up. When it became clear he could no longer bind me by making me sleep late, he intensified the attacks at the "other end of the candle" to keep me awake at night. I had to renounce late-night movies on TV, and even then found myself drawn to read magazines, eat snacks, write letters, and do a host of other diversionary activities. When one evening at midnight I began rereading my *Doonesbury* comic collection for the third time, I knew I had to draw the line and get into bed earlier.

The enemy persisted. I would get into bed drowsy at eleven or earlier—and lie there wide awake, struggling with a headache or worrying about something. I would bind the enemy in the name of Jesus, recite Scriptures, sing songs of praise, call out to God, and then finally fall asleep—anywhere from a minute to hours after getting into bed. Of course, the longer I was kept from going to sleep, the harder it was to hold the line in getting up early the next morning.

But I was learning to fight.

Some years later, when I began writing this book, I prayed and sensed the Lord was telling me to get up at 6:00 a.m. I did, even if I had gone to bed as late as midnight the night before, and found myself surprisingly refreshed on awakening and energetic during the day. When the main body of the book had been written, I began the more tedious, far less engaging task of polishing—and decided that I had earned a letup. For several days, I hit the snooze button on my alarm. To my chagrin, as soon as I would go back to sleep, a host of ugly, terrifying dreams would ensue. Furthermore, the rest of the day, I was subjected to lethargy attacks.

Finally, I realized that the enemy had seduced me. In rolling over after the alarm, I thought I was rewarding myself with more rest and, hence, more vitality for the day. In fact, however, I was turning away from God's instruction and was merely inviting the enemy to steal both my rest and my vitality.

I learned a simple and essential lesson for spiritual warfare: God had told me when it was best for me to arise. When I disregarded His instruction, He allowed the enemy rein to attack. The next morning, I was out of bed at six o'clock sharp, jogged five miles in the afternoon, and had a full day's writing and ministry—and felt great. Of course, the enemy may attack even when you're following God's plan. But when it seems as if the enemy is gaining unusual power over me, I now pray immediately: *Lord, am I disregarding some instruction of Yours?*

A friend described it this way: The enemy has vicious dogs

chained alongside the path God has set for you, and their chains are only long enough to allow them to the edge of the path. As long as you stay on God's path, they can bark—but cannot touch you.

This is not to say that 6:00 a.m. is God's time to get up, and if you don't, you're in sin, but simply that at this time in my life, the Father spoke that specific instruction to me when it was necessary to break the power of a particular sin over my life. It's not about performance at the right time, but about relationship with the real Father.

VICTORY OVER HABITUALLY ENTRENCHED DEMONS USUALLY REQUIRES ongoing, vigilant discipline of the flesh. Lethargy and narcolepsy, for example, still nip at me once in a while, and when that happens, I remind myself and those demons that I have the victory in Jesus and in His name command them to go. If they resist, I sing praises to Jesus, use my prayer language, and turn my energies instead to Him.

Sometimes the oppression lifts only as I cooperate with Jesus in securing the territory now reclaimed for His purposes in my life. For example, I refuse to lie in bed any longer but instead schedule early breakfast appointments with battle partners or do something else during that time that enhances God's purposes. And sometimes I simply need to pray, *Jesus, I turn that bad thought over to You*, and go my way.

The spiritual and physical dimensions of the battle complement each other. My natural, human desire to please myself instead of God cuts me off from God and draws me blindly into the enemy's hands. Hence, the diabolic aspect of my habits became clear. Each had presented itself to me as self-affirming, as "Go ahead and sleep in; you don't have to do anything you don't want to!"

Yet each habit was ultimately unmasked as self-destructive; for example, sleeping in destroyed my ability to grow into the life God had planned for me, even in that morning.

> Don't think that there is no truth in the scripture that says, "The spirit that God placed in us is filled with fierce desires." But the grace that God gives is even stronger. As the scripture says, "God resists the proud, but gives grace to the humble."
>
> So then, submit yourselves to God. *Resist the Devil,* and he will run away from you. *Come near to God,* and he will come near to you. (James 4:5–8, italics mine)

My personal experience suggests that this powerful text has often been misinterpreted to imply, "All you have to do is say no, grit your teeth, and dig in, and the enemy will stop bothering you." While an underlying perseverance is often necessary for victory, it may not be sufficient. Those Europeans who lived in Nazi-occupied countries during World War II and participated in the Resistance, for example, exercised a wide variety of creative, proactive tactics. They did not passively withdraw, nor did they stand out on the street and shout no to the Nazi troops—which would have been suicidal—but instead continued working underground.

Spiritual warfare is not simply a call to say no to the enemy, but must include a more primary, conscious yes to God. Once the enemy has been expelled, you must commit to a plan to get rid of the chinks in your armor and train for victory. You need to refurnish the newly cleaned house with God's furniture, as it were, so the enemy no longer feels at home in you. God has not only a house to clean out, but also a home to build. As Jesus warned:

When an evil spirit comes out of a man, it goes through arid places seeking rest and does not find it. Then it says, "I will return to the house I left." When it arrives, it finds the house swept clean and put in order. Then it goes and takes seven other spirits more wicked than itself, and they go in and live there. And the final condition of that man is worse than the first. (Luke 11:24–26 NIV)

Similarly, alcoholism and other compulsive-addictive behaviors—often embraced to avoid pain and born out of a distrust in God's ability to save you—frequently require a commitment to cooperate with God's purpose beyond healing wounds and casting out demons; hence the twelve-step programs, which are tailored to a variety of addictions, from sexuality (Homosexuals Anonymous) to overeating (Overeaters Anonymous) and shame-based religion (Fundamentalists Anonymous).

I discovered that an effective habit of the Spirit with which to replace habits of the flesh is regular reading and memorizing of Scripture. The psalmist said, "Your word is a lamp to my feet and a light for my path" (Ps. 119:105 NIV). Lamplight dispels darkness. The word of God in the Bible, therefore, is a primary weapon against the enemy and his rule of darkness. When Jesus battled the enemy for forty days in the wilderness before beginning His ministry, He struck back victoriously against each of the three temptations by declaring, "The scripture says . . ." (Matt. 4:4, 7, 10).

OFTEN WE DON'T KNOW WHAT GOD'S WILL IS IN PARTICULAR circumstances and need to struggle with Him for discernment. But where He has already declared His heart and will in Scripture, we need not waste time and energy and instead can readily speak out His promises.

And so I spent time each morning reading the Bible and chose one portion a day to memorize, typing it on a three-by-five-inch card and carrying it with me to pull out and review when necessary. Some of the most helpful to me were—and continue to be: Deuteronomy 8:2–3; Joshua 1:9; 2 Chronicles 20:15, 17; Psalms 57:6–11; 91:1–4; Proverbs 3:5–8; Isaiah 30:19–22; 43:1–3; 1 Corinthians 10:13; 2 Corinthians 4:7–10; 10:3–5; Galatians 2:19–20; Ephesians 3:16–21; 1 Peter 1:6–7; 5:8–11.

As ongoing measures to overcome sinful habits, I urge regular prayer with other believers (see my chapter "The Wolf Loves the Lone Sheep" in *Sons of the Father*), physical exercise, praise and worship, and prayer in your special prayer language.

## Invitation

This point of demonic entry may be difficult at first to imagine. Who would willingly *invite* evil into their lives? The enemy, however, is a deceiver, and people often do not realize it when they are literally asking demons to enter themselves.

To seek spiritual knowledge or power besides that of the Holy Spirit released through Jesus is to invite demons. Occult practices, such as fortune-telling, astrology, séances, Ouija boards, ESP, and the host of New Age spiritual practices, are common avenues of entry. The Bible is very clear about such psychic or metaphysical activities: they are idolatrous and therefore to be strictly avoided by faithful believers (Deut. 18:10, 11).

Any Christian who has battled to keep the enemy out can

appreciate how delighted he is simply to be invited in. The very first of the Ten Commandments proclaims, "Worship no god but me" (Ex. 20:3). The God revealed through Jesus is the only spiritual power to be sought or heeded, the supreme authority over our lives.

In the verse preceding the Ten Commandments, God said, "I am the LORD your God, who brought you out of Egypt, out of the land of slavery" (v. 2 NIV). We heed God's commandments not because they are cold, impersonal, and arbitrary moral standards, but because they are warnings and promises from the God who has our very best interest at heart, who loves and cares for us, even rescues us from the snares of this broken and seductive world for His eternal purposes. We do what God says not because it's morally right, but because it's best for us.

We respond to the Father's instructions, therefore, out of humble, heartfelt thanksgiving. The answers we seek for our lives follow upon the questions, What is God doing in my life? and How can I best cooperate with Him?

We know that God doesn't hide from us but has come out openly in the flesh-and-blood Jesus to reveal Himself. What's more, Jesus is alive and present today in His Holy Spirit, to guide us in all our decisions. As Paul taught:

> The Spirit gives one person a message full of wisdom, while to another person the same Spirit gives a message full of knowledge. One and the same Spirit gives faith to one person, while to another person he gives the power to heal. The Spirit gives one person the power to work miracles; to another, the gift of speaking God's message; and to yet another, the ability to tell the difference between gifts that come from the Spirit and those that do not. To

one person he gives the ability to speak in strange tongues, and to another he gives the ability to explain what is said. But it is one and the same Spirit who does all this; as he wishes, he gives a different gift to each person. (1 Cor. 12:8–11)

God *does* communicate with faithful believers through His Holy Spirit. Those who cry out to Him with "ears to hear" will hear from Him. *We don't need to seek any other source of healing or knowledge besides the Spirit of God revealed in Jesus.* When we invite His Spirit and not demons, we realize that He first invited us and has equipped us for His calling.

Jesus is the living Law, the only spiritual power Christians need turn to for authority and guidance. In Jesus, God has provided everything we need to become who He has created us to be, and to look elsewhere is not only unnecessary, but manifestly dangerous. All other spiritual sources of knowledge besides Jesus and the Holy Spirit separate us from God, and the Bible records God's strong opposition to them:

> But people will tell you to ask for messages from fortunetellers and mediums, who chirp and mutter. They will say, "After all, people should ask for messages from the spirits and consult the dead on behalf of the living."
>
> You are to answer them, "Listen to *what the LORD is teaching you!*" (Isa. 8:19, italics mine; see also Deut. 18:14)

The true Spirit of God is no magic wand, no formula for gaining your own desires. The Holy Spirit is a Person, the revelation of God in this present era, and the One who draws us out of our self-centeredness into full dependence upon God—and thus into the fulfillment of His purposes:

> The Lord said, "Now, mortal man, look at the women among your people who make up predictions. Denounce them and tell them *what the Sovereign LORD* is saying to them: You women are doomed! You sew magic wristbands for everyone and make magic scarves for everyone to wear on their heads, so that they can have power over other people's lives. You want to possess the power of life and death over my people and to use it for your own benefit." (Eze. 13:17–18, italics mine)

Again in Acts 16:16, Paul encounters a slave girl who has an evil spirit that enables her to predict the future and commands the demon of divination to come out of her.

Astrology is a similar idolatry, saying that not God but rather the positions of the stars dictate human destiny. That's quite different from saying, "God is master of the heavens and can use a star or other celestial phenomenon as a sign of His activity," as with the Christmas magi—who were not astrologers in today's sense, but simply those who believed that God would send a special star as a sign for them. That star was merely a sign of God's activity; it changed no human life by itself. Christians do not worship creation but rather the Creator.

"I make fools of fortunetellers," God said, "and frustrate the predictions of astrologers. . . . But . . . *when I send* a messenger to reveal *my* plans, *I make* those plans and predictions come true" (Isa. 44:25, italics mine). The so-called "power of the stars" is counterfeit, based on human idolatry (47:10–15).

A living, loving Father God is even now reaching out to save His children for their created purpose; Jesus has died on the cross that His Spirit might be loosed in and among us. Why, then, are we anxiously searching astrology forecasts and flocking to see movies and read books on occult practices—from witchcraft to telepathy?

While the enemy of God rejoices at deceiving a mentally intelligent but spiritually ignorant people, he reserves his most seductive attacks for the most vulnerable among us, namely children. For example, in the immensely popular Harry Potter books and films, battles are fought not between good and evil—as a helpful exercise in discernment—but rather between varying kinds of evil. All spiritual forces portrayed in these books center on sorcery—a patent evil explicitly denounced in the Bible and forbidden to believers, because it seduces people away from God.

In families in which Jesus is not experienced as real and present, children are easily drawn to the charismatic Harry and his manifest powers, and to his demon-ruled spiritual worldview. They naturally seek to emulate their heroic Harry, often practicing sorcery themselves and thereby inviting demonic power into their lives.

Such counterfeit spirituality thrives among us, stealing a generation of youth from God, because we as the body of Christ have abdicated our calling to proclaim true supernatural reality and the God revealed in Jesus who rules over it. Children would not be feeding from Harry Potter's occult trough if Christians had clearly presented the Father's banquet of authentic spirituality, described by Jesus in the Bible and revealed today in the Holy Spirit and His powerful gifts.

We are spiritual creatures of the God who must be worshipped "in spirit and in truth" (John 4:23 NIV). When we deny our spiritual nature by relying totally on our rational minds and believing that only material things are real, we refuse to let God nurture our spiritual selves and draw us to Him through Jesus. And so we turn instead to false and dark spirituality for stimulation and satisfaction.

Because we are created by the God revealed in Jesus and born again into our created destiny by the power of His Spirit (John 3:1–8), all human beings hunger to experience the reality of His supernatural presence. Like abandoned children, our spirits cry out in the darkness for spiritual revelation and saving power. When the church either ignores that cry or, worse, scoffs at it, the Prince of Darkness welcomes it with evil delight and wastes no time responding. When truth is denied us, we're readily suckered into lies.

In fact, we become so accustomed to the enemy's deceptive substitutes that we begin to believe the counterfeit is real—even that pig slop tastes good. Thus, young readers are excited to replicate Harry Potter's dark spiritual powers themselves. I often hear even Christian parents defend such books, saying, "But they're so engaging and inspire my child to read more." Yet the same could be said of pornography.

The truth that our materialistic Western culture conspires to suppress, because it's an affront to our pride of control, is this: We human beings are spiritual at the core of our beings, created by the God-who-is-Spirit. We long to be restored to our spiritual home in the God revealed in Jesus. In the absence of authentic spirituality, the seductive New Age practices—in reality, ancient demons newly attired—fascinate, excite, and draw us away from God as spiritual pornography.

The authentic Holy Spirit for whom humanity yearns is present in, and properly animates, the body of Christ—if it's alive (James 2:26). He's therefore readily available today in every church that proclaims Jesus as Lord and Savior and welcomes His active presence and power. When Christians withdraw from this spiritual reality behind manageable religion, it is properly called a crime against humanity.

The Bible, in fact, is a handbook for life in the spiritual world and reveals how that affects life in this natural, material world. In portraying authentic spirituality through Jesus, the Scriptures are a loving Father's reality check for children seduced by the enemy's counterfeit power into a destructive, demonic charade. The Scriptures both warn and promise that true spiritual life is found only through surrender to the God revealed in Jesus.

Those who read horoscopes, look to fortune-tellers, or seek knowledge through any other psychic or occult medium—such as Ouija boards, pendulums, tarot cards, ESP, astral projections, spirit guides, Masonic oaths, and the like—have been deceived into thinking that this God revealed in Jesus is neither real nor sufficient. In turning to other spiritual powers besides Him, they violate the very first commandment. The ancient prophets called this adultery, for it meant breaking the eternal covenant between God and His beloved people (Jer. 3:6–10).

Cleansing from having invited enemy spirits requires confessing the sin of seeking spiritual power from a source other than God—that is, idolatry. You must then renounce any such future activity and ask the Holy Spirit instead to provide you with whatever you sought through the false, counterfeit spirit.

Then identify the particular demon associated with the occult activity you engaged in, such as divination or numerology, and cast it out. Receive the baptism of the Holy Spirit, asking for an infilling of the Spirit along with His biblically certified spiritual gifts

(1 Corinthians 12). Finally, rededicate yourself to worshipping only the God revealed in Jesus and present today in His Holy Spirit.

## Sexual / "One-Flesh" Union

As the Bible clearly records, for millennia people have worshipped sex, that is, looked to sexual desire for saving power. The ancient Canaanites, among whom the early Israelites settled, sacrificed to the god Baal and goddess Astarte before altars festooned respectively with male and female genitalia. The Greeks of Corinth, to whom the apostle Paul wrote two epistles, worshipped Aphrodite, the goddess of lust, complete with a hundred-foot-tall naked statue at the harbor entrance and a temple with one thousand male and female prostitutes.

The Old Testament prophets and the apostle Paul denounced these pagan practices—not primarily because they violated some arbitrary religious standard of morality, but because they were animated by manifestly real, harmful, and ultimately destructive spiritual entities that diverted God's beloved children from their created purpose.

Most people today would agree that such worship of sex gods and goddesses was grossly misfocused. Our materialistic worldview, however, does not know where to refocus sexual desire. In fact, those ancient peoples were far more spiritually realistic and more honest than our modern society, which bows before the Hollywood sex queen and hunk without a nod to the dark spiritual forces that proclaim them. The truth, which the ancient pagans affirmed but which remains steadfastly obscured by our proud materialistic worldview today, is that *sexual desire is a spiritual phenomenon.*

Typing this sentence, for example, is a physical act. I touch the keyboard and the keys move. But when a man and woman see each other a hundred yards apart, without touching and with nothing but air between them, something can stir in their hearts and in their bodies.

With no natural explanation, a mere mustard grain of humility would lead us to confess that sexual attraction is a *super*natural force—in fact, a spiritual phenomenon, which originates not in our bodies but in the spirit realm. As such, it can't be understood apart from surrender to the God who created it and rules over both material and spiritual reality—who, in fact, made us "male and female" in His image (Gen. 1:27).

"There are four things that are too mysterious for me to understand," the father wrote to his son in Proverbs, "an eagle flying in the sky, a snake moving on a rock, a ship finding its way over the sea, and a man and a woman falling in love" (30:18–19). Our modern scientific culture exults in aeronautical engineering, zoological research, and GPS (Global Positioning System technology). We're puffed up with knowledge.

The power that stirs between a man and a woman, however, remains a mystery that no computer or laboratory experiment has yet explained.

In the realm of the spirit, all time blends with eternity; a thousand years in human history is as but a day in God's eyes (2 Peter 3:8). Because sexuality is spiritual at its root, sexual relations cause a spiritual bond between the partners that lasts, as the traditional marriage ceremony affirms, "for better or worse, 'til death do us part."

This is not morality; it's reality. Any honest person knows it. It's why a person can think of an earlier sexual partner long after that relationship has ended. It's why a loving Father God does not want His children to have sexual relations apart from marriage—because acts that bear eternal consequences are not designed for temporary relationships. As the apostle Paul warned:

> There's more to sex than mere skin on skin. Sex is as much spiritual mystery as physical fact. As written in Scripture, "The two become one." Since we want to become spiritually one with the Master, we must not pursue the kind of sex that avoids commitment and intimacy, leaving us more lonely than ever—the kind of sex that can never "become one." (1 Cor. 6:16–17 MSG)

When the two become one flesh (Gen. 2:24), both partners connect spiritually. Even as when two space modules connect, the inhabitants of each module have access to the other, so in sexual union all spiritual entities in one partner now have access to the other, and vice versa. This holds true for same-sex partners as well as heterosexual and takes place even in two-dimensional pornographic experiences.

In God's plan, sexual union is designed for a man and a woman who have surrendered their lives to Him forever. Moreover, it requires first that each has taken time to seek His plan for his or her life and thereby chosen a "suitable companion" (Gen. 2:18) with whom to fulfill it. Among other requirements, this means one who has been delivered of demons and filled instead with His Holy Spirit.

After the man and woman have together confessed the Father's call and their common destiny before wedding witnesses and submitted to His purposes, the appropriate spiritual bond can be consummated in the flesh. In that physical union, the fullness of His

Spirit that God gives to the man flows into the woman, and the fullness of His Spirit that He gives to the woman flows into the man. Thus, the partners complement and appropriately draw through each other God's provision for their created destiny together.

Among a people blinded by materialism, however, this divine plan is rarely seen and even less often walked out. The culture, in fact, is not only wholly incapable of portraying it, but because it requires surrender to a God manifestly more powerful than us, is hell-bent to distort it. From adultery and gender confusion to pornography and prostitution, we pay the awful price of our pride and enforced spiritual ignorance.

Meanwhile, when couples unite sexually without God's covering and deliverance, every demon that the man has accumulated in his heart now has access to the woman, and vice versa.

For example, suppose a woman was molested as a girl by a man, and in a desperate effort not to open her heart to a man again and risk such wounding, she allows a man-hating spirit to enter and harden her heart. She now carries that demon as a spiritual disease, and it can enter her male sexual partner and begin to attack and diminish his manhood.

Of course, insofar as he now carries the demon, the infected man in turn can pass the man-hating demon on to other sexual partners. The implications of this spiritual contagion are much more vast than the worst of physically contracted sexual diseases, because the symptoms often remain hidden in the partner's heart and unrecognized even in his or her destructive behavior. In that very real sense, the clinical term *STD* for "sexually transmitted diseases" can just as authentically mean "spiritually transmitted diseases."

Consider, on the other hand, a man who rapes a woman. As researchers have discovered, rape is more a crime of anger than sex, often rooted in a mother-wound. The rapist often bears a demon of woman-hating, abuse, and/or vengeance. After a rape, those demons may pass into the woman, and she may find herself belittling or punishing herself, feeling disrespected by men, even feeling taken advantage of by salesmen in business transactions. Often she is raped again.

In desperation, to repel men and thereby avoid the associated pain, she commonly makes herself as unfeminine and unattractive as possible, often by gaining excessive weight, and can turn sexually to other women for comfort.

While sexual intercourse always results in a spiritually vulnerable connection, because of the strong emotional and spiritual engagement in sexual desire, sexual intercourse is not wholly necessary for an exchange of demons between partners. A sufficient surrender to the other and opening of your heart—some term it a *soul tie*—can clear the path.

If you're in doubt whether a particular relationship has produced such a bond, ask God. He's not playing hide-and-seek; He wants you to know and come to Him for healing.

To find freedom from demons entering through these "one-flesh unions," the following process is helpful:

- If you have had sexual relations without being married to your partner, confess the sin of fornication. Ask your Father to forgive you—not for breaking some abstract law, but for not trusting your Father enough to wait for His leading and design for your life.
- Declare yourself on your Father's side by renouncing all spiritual and emotional bonds between you and that partner. Of course, if you were married, that was not fornication, but

you still have a mutual bond that the enemy can use to access you. Tell your Father that you don't want any more connection or access spiritually between you and that person or those persons. "We have renounced secret and shameful ways," Paul affirmed; "we do not use deception, nor do we distort the word of God" (2 Cor. 4:2 NIV).

- Take authority to break those bonds. Pray, *In the name of Jesus, I take the sword of the Spirit and I cut those bonds between me and [name of partner].* If you need to name names, do so; if you're not sure, ask your Father. It's important that you speak with authority and not simply ask Jesus to do this for you, in order to fortify your confidence to stand firmly in the face of future temptations.

- Release the partner or partners to God. Let go of them, putting them out of your mind and into His hands. You can pray, *In the name of Jesus, I release [name of partner] at the cross and put him or her in Your hands.*

- Ask for the blood of Jesus to cleanse you from all effects of that unholy union.

- Ask the Holy Spirit to reveal any demons that entered you through it, take authority over them in the name of Jesus, and cast them out.

- Put yourself in God's hands. Declare a "Manufacturer's recall" for your body. Lay your sexual desire on the altar and give it back to Him—who created it in the first place—for His restoration according to His purposes. "Therefore, I urge you, brothers," Paul exhorted the Romans, "in view of God's mercy, to offer your bodies as living sacrifices, holy and pleasing to God—this is your spiritual act of worship. Do not conform any longer to the pattern of this world, but be transformed by the renewing of your mind" (Rom. 12:1–2 NIV).

This sexual fasting, Paul said, is wholly appropriate for married couples. "Do not deprive each other except by mutual consent and for a time, so that you may devote yourselves to prayer" (1 Cor. 7:5 NIV).

## Other Possible Entry Points

The following list of avenues for demonic entry is not exhaustive. For some it may seem too narrow, judgmental, or exclusive, insofar as it implies that any spiritual activity apart from Jesus beckons evil. A larger perspective here may be helpful.

God was around long before religion. When God eventually decided to reveal Himself to humankind, He did not establish a religion but a people to identify with Himself—as a Father-son relationship. He chose Abraham and raised up the Jewish people to be His "light to the nations" (Isa. 42:6). To ensure the light of that revelation, He sent His Son, Jesus, from among His chosen people to bring all humankind, both Jew and Gentile, into His Father-heart for us.

Demons like darkness and do not want the heart of the Father to be revealed. So the primary work of demons is to deny, obscure, or otherwise distort the Person Jesus. Other religions and spiritual perspectives may contain measures of truth—and often do, if only to seduce people away from the Father's protection and purposes. But Jesus alone has come to "destroy the devil's work" (1 John 3:8 NIV). When the chips are down and the battle is raging, victory in spiritual warfare is neither about theological truth and moral judgments nor about religious tolerance and ideological correctness. It's about the power of evil to destroy life and the overcoming power of God in Jesus to rescue His beloved children and deliver them into His destiny.

In addition to the five categories listed above, you can expose yourself to demons in other ways, including the following:

- Being baptized or otherwise consecrated into spiritual organizations that pray to and/or dedicate members to persons other than Jesus
- Participating in religious organizations that either
  1. promote saving relationship with God through measuring up to behavior and performance standards or
  2. deny sinful human nature and the need for saving relationship with God
- Joining an organization or fellowship that includes secret initiation or advancement ceremonies that require spiritual vows or oaths
- Living in an area where the predominant culture fosters harmful and ungodly practices, which become demonic "principalities"—such as racism or hedonism
- Receiving spiritual "medical" treatment from modalities that claim a healing source other than God revealed in Jesus
- Being hypnotized or otherwise placed in a passive spiritual state and subjected to suggested behaviors or responses

Above all, remember this encouragement from Paul:

For though we live in the world, we do not wage war as the world does. The weapons we fight with are not the weapons of the world. On the contrary, they have divine power to demolish strongholds.

We demolish arguments and every pretension that sets itself up against the knowledge of God, and we take captive every thought to make it obedient to Christ. (2 Cor. 10:3–5 NIV)

## General Considerations

• Having a demon in you does not mean you are "possessed"—a very rare condition implying wholesale control of your entire personality and being. Rather, it means that you, like other human beings, are "oppressed," insofar as an evil spirit has entered you and influenced your thoughts and behavior.

Christians are by no means excluded from demonic oppression. Surrendering your heart to Jesus does not automatically remove every demon from you any more than it heals your body in every aspect. It means that now the weapons are available—downloaded into your spiritual hard drive, as it were—to identify and expel those demons from your life.

When Jesus set his face toward Jerusalem and the cross, the apostle Peter protested, "Never, Lord!" whereupon Jesus declared, "Get behind me, Satan!" speaking to the voice of evil then manifesting in Peter. If so emminent a follower of Jesus as Peter can be oppressed by an evil spirit, certainly you and I can too.

• A helpful way to reveal demonic activity in a person's life is to ask these questions:

1. With what pattern in your life or behavior are you fed up? Have you done all you can do to change it, including con-

fessing your sin, exercising self-discipline, and sincerely forgiving those who have sinned against you?

2. Are you ready and willing to ask Jesus to come here now and do whatever is necessary to overcome that pattern in your life—to show you what you need to see, to take you where you need to go, to tell you what you need to hear, no matter how painful, fearful, or shameful?

• Before ministering deliverance, I pray a prayer as follows. Please note that this is no formula, but rather, a personal attempt to center myself in a trusting relationship with my Father in this critical, yet often confusing arena. Sense the spirit of my prayer, and then pray as you feel led.

"Father God, we give up. Not to the enemy or circumstances, but to You. Come now by the power of Your Spirit and rule and reign over us in this time and place. [Here, it's helpful to offer specific prayers of thanksgiving to remind yourself of God's goodness and care for you.] Above all, I thank You, Jesus, that You came to destroy the works of the devil [1 John 3:8b], and that You who are in us are greater than he who is in the world [1 John 4:4]. In the name of Jesus, I set the cross over us all here. Let the blood of Jesus cover, cleanse, and protect us. In Your name, Jesus, I ask for warrior angels to come into this place and take up positions to protect us. We want everything You died to give us, Jesus—every healing, every deliverance, every promise of new life.

"So pour out the fullness of Your Holy Spirit on us here and now. Give us Your supernatural knowledge, wisdom, discernment, healing, and every gift we need to walk in Your victory. Come now and lead us as we surrender to You: mighty Jesus, victorious Lord Jesus, King of kings and Lord of lords.

"Thank You, Jesus, that You're already 'at the right side of the Father, pleading with Him on our behalf' [Rom. 8:34]. Show us how You're praying here so we can take Your prayer to the Father and experience His healing and deliverance."

• Whenever possible, it's best to minister with a team, in which a variety of the Spirit's gifts can manifest—in which one person may be gifted with knowledge, another with wisdom, another with discernment, and another with healing.

• Others may ask you to pray a demon out of someone else, such as a distraught family member. Be very cautious about this and seek the Spirit's wisdom before doing so, considering the oppressed person's spiritual walk and resources. If a person is willfully engaging in sinful practices or otherwise rejecting God, he or she will have no spiritual strength to resist when that demon returns with several others (Luke 11:24–26)—leaving him or her in a worse condition.

On the other hand, when a Gentile mother asked Jesus to cast a demon out of her daughter (Matt. 15:22–28), Jesus honored the mother's faith and did so, without seeking the daughter's agreement.

Discerning the Father's direction is essential, and the Holy Spirit will guide you in that process. Above all, remember: God is the creator; the enemy is a destroyer. God initiates; the devil reacts. The immense evil in our time—from the Holocaust to child abuse and terrorism—has erupted not because Satan suddenly decided to go on a spree, but because God has increased the tempo of His coming kingdom.

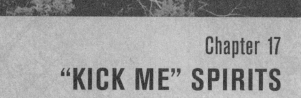

# "KICK ME" SPIRITS

Years ago on my elementary school playground, a particularly creative bully had a favorite trick for tormenting smaller kids like me. The bully would write "KICK ME" in large bold letters on a paper and attach a piece of rolled-up tape on the back. Hiding it behind him, he would saunter up casually from the side and slap you on the back in feigned friendship, so that the sign stuck to the back of your shirt. After he walked away, other kids nearby would come up to you snickering and kick you in the legs. As one of his first puzzled victims, I shouted, "Stop that! Why are all of you kicking me?"

"We're just doing what you're telling us to do!" they all laughed—until a friend of mine came over to take the sign off my back and show it to me.

Bullies often carry deep shame and anger from having been abused themselves by a parent. That's why they pick on smaller kids, who represent the weak part of themselves that they scorn and want to be rid of. So they play the familiar dominant parent who first bullied them and try to displace their brokenness onto weaker kids, who testify to their own shameful weakness.

Beating up on weaker kids does not relieve bullies of their brokenness. It only propagates it—because its spiritual root has not been named, cast out, and thereby uprooted. That is, *the perpetrator infects the victim with the demons that animate his or her destructive behavior.*

The enemy of God is a spiritual bully who often deceives us similarly by planting demons in us that call out and beckon specific negative reaction from others. Remember, this is war. The enemy is a saboteur who seeks to establish a secret place inside your own territory from which to broadcast your weakness and thereby call down strikes against you.

This vulnerability can be perceived by those who are themselves given over to evil. I once read a newspaper interview with a reformed mugger who said that he could identify an easy target among a crowd on the street. He watched how people walked, how they carried themselves. He avoided a confident person striding along; someone slouched or walking with an uncertain or hesitant gait, he saw as fearful and weak, and thus, an easy mark.

Those who are not sufficiently surrendered to Jesus to recognize spiritual evil will be similarly drawn by the evil in others. I hasten to say that this urging of the enemy does not excuse someone for complying with the demon's harmful beckoning in another. "The devil made me do it"—even the work of the devil in the other person—may bear some truth, but it is not sufficient defense for a responsible person. In fact, not every kid on the playground who saw the bully's sign on my back kicked me. Those who did can justly be held accountable for doing so.

From God's view, rightful accountability is useful to convict you of complicity with the enemy and lead you to fall humbly before God for forgiveness and deliverance. In a spiritually blind culture such as ours, however, mere accountability and even conviction may lead you to a courtroom or jail—but does not stop the enemy from working in and through you.

Prisons, police, and the containment of worldly authority are necessary in this as-yet unredeemed world. But no amount of bricks, mortar, and vigilant enforcement agents can exorcise a demon. In fact, mere punishment without spiritual awareness often simply draws other demons, such as resentment, bitterness, rebellion, and revenge. Thus, prisons can become "schools for crime," where inmates learn and plot newer crimes—and the recidivism rate soars. Whether in society or within families, punishment may stop immediate behavior, but it cannot heal the spiritual and emotional brokenness that fuels it.

In the "kick me" process, meanwhile, the enemy is like a spy enclave broadcasting from within Allied territory. Those who get hooked and begin kicking are often predisposed to succumb to the ruse—in this case, kids who had likely been scorned, abused, or otherwise "kicked" themselves.

Years ago, as a college undergraduate who attended church regularly but was blind to spiritual reality, I volunteered for a YMCA social service project in a local orphanage. After the required sensitivity training on what to expect from orphans, the leader of the project mentioned several children who especially drew the volunteers' attention and compassion. One seven-year-old boy they nicknamed "Droopy," because his eyelids and other features seemed to hang low on his face.

When I entered the orphanage playground, a saggy-faced but smiling boy ran up to me whom I immediately recognized as Droopy. As I stepped forward to receive his friendly greeting, a strange and frightening impulse stirred in me to kick and throw him aside. Startled and ashamed, I managed a smile and quickly called another volunteer over to step in and play with Droopy as I withdrew. I visited the orphanage often after that but could not allow myself to get close to this particular boy because of the frightening reaction he stirred in me.

Many years after I became initiated in spiritual warfare, I understood. Children in an orphanage have all been abandoned, some even kicked out by their blood parents. Spirits of abandonment, abuse, worthlessness, and alienation frequent orphans. My malevolent urge to kick Droopy was in reality a response to those spirits calling out from within him.

I wondered, *Why did Droopy's demons hook me but not the other orphanage volunteers, who could freely hug and enjoy him?* Very likely because those spirits of abandonment and alienation in him were also in me but not in the other volunteers. As a schoolboy and navy brat, I had changed schools often and skipped two grades, leaving me smaller and an easy mark for bullies—and for those same demons. By the grace of God, I did not act out against Droopy, but only withdrew from him. Thus, I hearkened to the demon of abandonment in us both. In my natural ability, I could only choose literally the lesser of evils—because I did not know Jesus, the best of all good.

Even though I did not physically kick him aside, nevertheless this unholy spiritual alliance kept me from ministering the Father's love to a child who needed it terribly—even as I needed it. That's why it's so important to seek deliverance for yourself first, before attempting to pray demons out of others. Otherwise, you risk being drawn into the very evil you seek to cast out of someone else.

"Kick me" spirits can often emerge to sabotage loving relationships. It's the responsibility—and mark—of the more mature partner not to react to the enemy's call but instead to respond to the Spirit's call for healing love. For example, a husband or wife may say, "For some reason, I feel like I want to condemn, abandon, crush, or otherwise hurt my spouse." In such instances, you can check your impulse, go to Jesus, and ask Him if it's coming from some brokenness in you or if your spouse is carrying a demon that calls it forth. If the former, go to your prayer partners and deal with it; if the latter, name, bind, and cast the demon out of your spouse and pray to heal its source.

In a more graphic example, during my years of pastoral ministry, I've seen many women who were sexually abused as girls. Often the women have reported that after the abusive incident, they felt at the mercy of powers that seemed to draw harmful men to them again and again. In fact, other men do begin to take advantage of them—and not just sexually. One abused woman said she was afraid to buy anything from salesmen, who often cheated her because she could not speak up against their high-pressure sales tactics.

In my ministry, I've walked through this awful valley of pain and degradation with many women. I'm not saying that it's the woman's fault for being raped. I'm saying that rape bears spiritual consequences that must be recognized and addressed if the victim is to be free of its long-range effects. Demonic spirits of abuse, degradation, humiliation, shame, and even rape itself can enter her. Thus ensconced, they call out for others to repeat the harm.

One of the most common demons that enters abused women is a "woman-hating" spirit, which leads them to hate their femininity and its appropriate expressions.

The enemy gains credibility by telling her that being unattractive will turn men away from her and protect her from being hurt again. But being so wholly focused and defended against abuse hardens her heart so that she cannot receive and even suppresses unto forgetfulness what she longs for in her feminine soul: a man to love, respect, and desire her.

For example, lesbian desires are often driven by a woman-hating spirit, which may come not only from abuse by a male who carries it, but also from hatred toward her distant, complicit, or abusive mother. In any case, if either of her parents carries this spirit out of his or her own wounded background, it will lurk in her and even beckon abuse not only in men but in other gender-confused women.

A similar "kick me" spirit was evident in Joe (not his real name), who came to me afraid that he was homosexual because gay men would "hit" on him. Joe's father had hated his own father, and that man-hating spirit, which fuels homosexuality, had simply been passed down to Joe.

Shame is a widespread "kick me" demon. Bob, a married bank clerk with two children, told me that he had been verbally abused by his father as a boy. "Dad was always putting me down," he said. "I felt like a worm around him." Bob donated large sums of money to his church and worked hard on committees, trying desperately to obey and please his pastor. One day, the pastor and his wife came to visit Bob at home. "I welcomed them," Bob said, "until they began telling me all the bad things they saw in me and how I was a poor influence on others at church." Utterly shamed, too shocked to respond, he sat quietly until the pastor and his wife left.

When I prayed with Bob, the Spirit led us to a demon of shame from his father's bloodline. We prayed it out and asked for the Father's spirit of sonship and dignity to retake its rightful place in his heart (Romans 8:14–16). With the demon expelled and no longer drawing others to shame him, healthy and affirming relationships became possible for Bob. Two days later, in fact, he e-mailed me that his pastor and wife had come back and apologized for the way they had berated him and asked his forgiveness.

Shame is a gnawing, gut sense that says, "I don't measure up, and if others find out, they'll reject and cast me into outer darkness." In fact, not one of us is capable of measuring up to God's standard. If we could do it ourselves, why would Jesus have needed to come and die on the cross for us? The net effect of our not-measuring-up-ness is shame, and the spiritual contest is framed by how we deal with it.

The enemy likes to distort truth and mislead you to a false conclusion with destructive consequences, even as the serpent misled Adam and Eve: "You don't measure up to God's standard because God doesn't want you ruling up there with Him [Gen. 3:5]. Your only hope is to hide your shame.

"Your shame, however, is so deep, so intrinsic, that you can't keep it from cropping up. So let my agent cover it up for you with money, guns, heavy makeup, sex, alcohol, positions of power. Or dump it on others, as in racism or sexism. That way, even if you don't look good, you'll look better than those others and no one else will find out how bad you are."

Jesus, however, says, "You don't measure up to God's standard because the sin in you keeps sabotaging your best efforts. You don't need to hide from your shame. I bore your sin and covered it on the cross. Come to Me, cry out your inadequacy to Me, and I will release My Spirit in you to empower and fulfill your destiny."

That is, "I will give you a new heart and put a new spirit in you; I will remove from you your heart of stone and give you a heart of flesh. And I will put my Spirit in you and move you to follow my decrees and be careful to keep my laws" (Ezek. 36:26–27 NIV).

The world's antidote to shame is pride; the Father's antidote is humility, whereby we become able to receive His grace and adoption (Rom. 8:15–16). The latter bears unmerited acceptance that allows us to face squarely our human sin and inadequacy, seek the Father's forgiveness, and receive His blessings, which overwhelm our sinful impulses.

Demons try to intimidate us into rash decisions. The demon of shame says, "You're no good. Get back, cover it up." Jesus says, "You can't be good. Come to Me, and I will make you good enough even to enter the Father's throne room."

When people come to me struggling with the sense, "People always seem to treat me that way," I ask the Holy Spirit if there might be a demon broadcasting, as it were, from within the person, calling forth precisely that mistreatment from others. This does not excuse the mistreatment, but victory in the spiritual battle begins when avenging the mistreatment is not as important as getting rid of the demon in you that draws it. The goal is not to change what's in others—although legal restraints may be necessary at times—but to let God change what's in you so that it doesn't trigger what's in others.

Most people in our materialistic society are simply not spiritu-ally mature or alert enough to recognize demonic impulses and may react to the demon's call in and from you. You can't realistically expect the world to stop reacting to spiritual "kick me" signs in you, simply because the brokenness of the world is in us all and intrinsic to human nature. You may need to tell the principal, call the police, or sue people—but the only way to stop this kind of abuse is to evict the evil spirit in you that beckons it.

The Father, after all, does not want His children abused by demons. When you stand against "kick me" spirits, you can trust that the power of the almighty God stands with you. Once you've been delivered, most often people do stop treating you that way. At the same time, demons tend to return, as Jesus said, to check if you've not only cleaned house but also refurnished it with things of God. So others may try to mistreat you similarly in the future, but you don't have to give in or lash back.

Because this time you'll have a choice. You can call out to Jesus, ask Him to show you how to act with truth and grace, and redefine the relationship accordingly. You don't have to play the enemy's game any longer. When he leads someone to deal you a hand of cards, you can either grit your teeth and vow to win or just fold your hand and leave the table.

You can stop letting the enemy broadcast from within you. You can pray as King David prayed: "Examine me, O God, and know my mind; test me, and discover my thoughts. Find out if there is any evil in me and guide me in the everlasting way" (Ps. 139:23–24).

Casting out an evil spirit does not remove the power of sin in your heart. Sin is not a demon to be cast out but an innate condition to be overcome by walking with Jesus throughout your life in this fallen world. Demons take advantage of our sinful condition precisely insofar as we do not walk with Jesus.

The powers of evil seek to bind and take away God-given free will, which is essential to the loving relationship that sustains that walk. Deliverance thereby releases you at last to make God-oriented choices. Being delivered from a spirit of lust, for example, doesn't mean you'll never again have a lustful impulse. It means that when you do, you'll be free to say no, turn away from it, and focus rather on the Holy Spirit's agenda.

After deliverance, you're free to choose evil again and let the demons return. In sending Jesus, however, the Father has banked His very heart on winning our hearts and thereby stirring us to choose Him now and always.

## Chapter 18

# LETTERS FROM A
# SPIRITUAL WARRIOR

**M**uch confusion reigns over the church and world about the dangers of spiritual ignorance, because not all churches today recognize and teach spiritual truth. Before encountering the reality of Jesus and the power of the Holy Spirit, I shared in that confusion— so I am bound not to judge those who still seek clarity as I did. Yet I feel equally bound to speak the truth as I have experienced it.

Following are several letters of mine that address the most common misunderstandings—hopefully with the balance of truth and grace that helped me eventually see the issues from a larger spiritual perspective.

## LETTER 1

### To a Young Seminary Graduate Desiring to Serve
### a Spiritually Responsive Church

Dear ———:

I appreciate your good letter—and your wanting to serve a spiritually responsive church as you begin your ministry.

I'm glad my article about the recent healing program at our church inspired you to want that for the church you will serve. Delores Winder (who led the ministry) will be pleased to hear it. I realize that this openness to the Holy Spirit is not common in churches today, but after Easter, anything is possible, right?

At the same time, I must tell you that my article was limited by space and did not mention the spiritual battle going on here at my church, even amid—and very likely because of—such victories as our evening of healing. As Delores told me: "I've been ministering all over the world for years and have never seen pastors under attack like I see now. They're dropping all over the place—through burnout, immorality, church splits—anything the enemy can throw at them."

I recently returned from a three-month sabbatical to find that six families had left the church: one because there was no altar call or other outward sign of commitment to Jesus, and another because I talked too much about Jesus and His healing power. Most had been dedicated, hardworking members for years. False rumors have been circulated accusing me of "kicking people out of the church" even after I have visited with them to seek reconciliation and tell them how much it hurts to see them leave.

Not long ago, an elderly woman with a deceptively bright smile came to our worship and announced that the Lord had sent her to support and pray for me. When I had nearly fallen into bondage with her for want of encouragement, I learned from another pastor that she was a false prophet who tried to capture pastors as her "spiritual sons." The first and only person to receive the baptism of the Spirit here was used by the enemy to discredit the Holy Spirit by falling to the floor and fainting at one of our after-church prayer groups.

During the past two months, the church offices have been burglarized twice, and several hypervigilant false alarms have discredited our church to the police chief. My car has been broken into twice—each time on a day when I was meeting with the Los Angeles Charismatic Pastors' Fellowship. The thieves took not only my tape deck, but also my three-hundred-dollar guitar, which I played in worship and with which I was beginning to write music to various psalms.

I could continue detailing the attacks, but these are enough to let you know that stepping out with the Holy Spirit marks you clearly as a threat to the enemy and puts you in the thick of battle at once. I have asked God to send me to a spiritually responsive church, but I simply don't know of any in this area.

I've learned to be cautious even of asking. "There's no such thing as a Spirit-filled church without a crucified pastor," as one friend of mine put it.

My brother, I honor you for wanting to see the full presence of Jesus at work in His church. But if you intend to welcome Him in your church, you'll need to count the cost. Forgive me if this sounds overweening. But as I read your letter, I felt moved to ask you to think seriously about whether you are ready to "drink this cup." I say this only out of genuine concern for you and any church you might serve. I used to be a Peace Corps volunteer in Nigeria; if you asked me about the prospects of living in that area and I failed to warn you to take a mosquito net, I'd be guilty of neglect and in some measure responsible if you contracted malaria.

At our church, we have a few very small prayer groups, and I'm always amazed at the power and grace of the Father's healing among us. We've seen some mighty workings of the Spirit. It's an exciting adventure. But the more Jesus begins to take back His church, the more it becomes a battleground—and you, as pastor, become the enemy's major target.

I'm delighted to hear from you as another member of our fellowship who's a brother in the Spirit. I want very much for the Lord's call in you to be fulfilled. So if you're really serious about seeking a Spirit-filled church, I suggest you begin asking Him to get you ready for it. Then look out, because He will take you into His boot camp.

First, He'll begin allowing your weak spots to be revealed, bringing them out into His light to be healed. That means your ego will get nailed to the cross, along with every other human pride, strength, ability, talent, or plan that you've got. The Father loves you so much that He won't send you into battle with big chinks in your armor—so He must deal decisively with your most persistent shortcomings.

You cannot fight this enemy with your own power, so the Father must strip you with a brutal mercy of every human strength you're tempted to claim. When I came out of seminary, I was naturally unsure of my abilities, so I worked hard to highlight my "strengths." But I did not have the security of faith to let the Father examine my weaknesses— which soon became revealed as chinks in my armor and hooks for the enemy. I hope you and others can learn from my early mistakes.

Toward that end, how diligent are you at seeking out your weak spots and getting help to heal them? The enemy's best shot at bringing you down is by attacking them. The brokenness you don't face up to, therefore, will be a red carpet to him. For example, do you feel threatened when a credible friend says, "You could use some counseling and prayer" for some aspect of your life? Can you praise God for such caring honesty and schedule and pay for the counseling?

Again, how willing are you to share your heart and soul with fellow ministers, revealing your brokenness openly and asking them to pray for you and your deepest needs? Are you ashamed to show them your weaknesses, or do you know that Jesus has already borne your shame on the cross—so you can now risk the rejection in order to discover God's grace? I honestly don't think you can survive ministering in the Spirit without a close, intimate support group of fellow pastors; the enemy picks off lone sheep with relish!

And last but certainly not least: How strong is your marriage? As a reflection of Jesus' relationship with His church, your relationship with your wife is a major focus of the Father's support and renewal. As such, the enemy will attack it ruthlessly, relentlessly.

If you allow the Father to use this as an opportunity for each of you to root out your sin, cast out your demons, and heal your wounds, the Spirit will transform the enemy into a diagnostic tool for divine healing. If you balk, he'll become the destroyer of your marriage and ministry.

In that process, the Father will teach you by His fierce grace and truth to minister not by your education, rhetorical and administrative skill, official authority, or moral uprightness—but by the power of His Spirit alone. As someone has said, "You don't know that Jesus is all you need until Jesus is all you have." He's a refining fire.

Like any surgery, it's not pleasant. But it is healing. In fact, as you begin to pass the Father's boot camp, you become His true son and thereby a real man. When you begin to taste that, there's no man on earth you'd rather be. You'll find a strength within you that will make the world's macho antics look like child's play.

In a word, you'll be the Father's warrior: outfitted for battle, one of His chosen ranks. You'll praise God for every person you're privileged to serve in His name. No life at all is worth comparing to it—and that, of course, is why the price tag on it is so high. You have to take everything you claim as your own and lay it down at the cross: your ministry, your marriage, your family, your money, your health, your peace of mind, your racial and ethnic heritage. Terrifying and painful as it is, you have to give up yourself, as Jesus did on Good Friday, and trust the Father's resurrection power to reshape and restore you as He wants.

To put it another way, you have to ride the lowly donkey into the Old Jerusalem before you can ride the warhorse into the New Jerusalem. You've got to be crucified before you can be resurrected as a vessel fit to bear the Father's Spirit to a world drunk on its own spirit. But that's where the battle is going on, and I'd welcome you as a brother in it anytime.

In answer (at last) to your question: No, I don't know of any other congregation in our regional fellowship that's wholly open to the Holy Spirit, or any that would welcome you if you said you were. Why? Likely because not enough pastors in our fellowship have been willing yet to pay the price. May I pray that the Father might honor you by asking you to do so?

Shalom,

Your brother and fellow warrior in the Lord,

Gordon

# LETTER 2

## To a Church Member Who Asked, "What Does the Bible Say About Psychic or Occult Practices?"

Dear ———:

Great question. No doubt you've seen plenty of this going on these days, and it can all be pretty confusing.

The Bible, however, is very clear about these practices: They draw upon real and ultimately destructive power from the spirit realm. They're not mere parlor games to be scoffed at, but seductive diversions away from God, and as such, they are to be strictly avoided by faithful believers.

"Worship no god but Me" is the first of the Ten Commandments, given not by a harsh Judge to punish sinners, but by a loving Father to protect His children from deception and harm. Christians honor this God revealed in Israel and, later, in Jesus as the only trustworthy spiritual power.

Two thousand years ago, Jesus rose from the dead. He's alive and active even today in the Holy Spirit, who animated Him then as now. In this lost and broken world, He hears our deepest cries for deliverance and healing. He's not an absentee Father, but a very present help in time of need. The answers we seek for our lives come as we ask, not as the popular slogan would have it, What would Jesus do? but rather What is Jesus doing?

Faith, therefore, means trusting that Jesus is already here and acting on our behalf. It's not about speculating what Jesus *would* do *if* He were here, but discerning what He's *already* doing by the power of the Holy Spirit. Of course, our natural human vision can't see this. God has therefore poured out His Holy Spirit so that we can have His *super*natural vision and see life as He sees it. Such divine knowledge, wisdom, discernment, and prophetic vision—among other spiritual gifts—are explicitly promised to us in 1 Corinthians 12.

The Bible reassures us that God's "divine power has given us everything we need for life and godliness" (2 Peter 1:3 NIV), and we need look nowhere else. Jesus is the only spiritual force Christians turn to for help. All other spiritual sources of power separate us from God, and the Bible records His strong opposition to them.

Astrology provides a clear example in saying that human destiny is determined by the positions of the stars and not by God. Certainly as the Creator and Master of the universe, God can use a star or other celestial phenomenon as a sign—as to the wise men, who were not occult astrologers in today's sense, but men who simply sensed that God would send a special star as a sign to confirm the coming of Jesus. The star of Bethlehem was a tool of God and by itself changed no human life.

And so God said, "I make fools of fortunetellers and frustrate the predictions of astrologers. . . . But . . . when I send a messenger to reveal My plans, I make those plans and predictions come true" (Isa. 44:25). The so-called "power of the stars" to dictate your destiny is counterfeit, based on human idolatry (47:10–15). We worship not creation but the Creator; your destiny is in God's hands, not in the stars.

The Holy Spirit is present today to provide us with all supernatural knowledge necessary for God to complete His purposes in us. "But people will tell you," God said, "to ask for messages from mediums and fortunetellers, who chirp and mutter. They will say, 'After all, people should ask for messages from the spirits and consult the dead on behalf of the living.' You are to answer them, 'Listen to what *the LORD* is teaching you!'" (Isa. 8:19, italics mine; see also Deut. 18:14).

And again: "Look at the women among your people who make up predictions. Denounce them and tell them what *the Sovereign LORD* is saying" (Ezek. 13:17–18, italics mine).

Significantly, God's case against these occult practices is not that they simply use bogus, sleight-of-hand magic or stir naive superstition. Rather, they mediate genuine power from real spiritual beings—which therefore compete with Him for the attention of His beloved sons and daughters, to seduce them away from His purposes and protection. We thwart these beings and their destructive schemes, not by rolling sophisticated eyes and scoffing, but by facing and countering their power with the greater power of God.

As Paul told the story: "One day as we were going to the place of prayer, we were met by a slave girl who had an evil spirit that enabled her to predict the future. She earned a lot of money for her owners by telling fortunes" (Acts 16:16). This girl was clearly mediating genuine power; folks would not have been paying good money for false information or the fantasies of a lowly slave girl's imagination. Paul did not discount or mock her unholy ministry. Instead, he confronted this fortune-telling slave girl and commanded the demon providing her with supernatural knowledge of the future to come out and leave her. And, indeed, "the spirit went out of her that very moment" (v. 18).

Clearly something palpably real and powerful had disappeared, because after this confrontation, "her owners realized that their chance of making money was gone" (v. 19).

The fortune-telling demon of divination was—and sadly often is today—competing with God. It's natural to want to know what's going to happen, especially amid troubling times, when the stakes are high. What if I marry this person? Invest this money here? Take that job? The pressing questions of life are often as many as its moments.

The pain and fear on those occasions open you to reach beyond your natural comfort zone to seek guidance and help. God, meanwhile, has what we need and is ready to give it generously. But we are not slaves or robots; as a good lover, He has given us free will to choose Him and not another. I tend to think God allows uncertainty and upset for just that reason, to draw us humbly to Him so we can learn to know and trust Him. "Perhaps in their suffering they will try to find me" (Hos. 5:15).

But the enemy of God also sees this golden opportunity in our suffering. In an effort to turn people away from God, he offers the quick-and-easy counterfeit, with all the spiritual nutrition of cotton candy. "Trying to find God is dicey," he urges. "It's safer for you to stay in charge. Come to me, listen to my fortune-teller, and I'll tell you all you need to know without all the messy worry and doubt that go with trusting God."

Because today God has been revealing Himself powerfully through the work of His Spirit, the enemy has been working overtime to stage such a counterfeit revival. Fascinated by spiritual power and psychic phenomena, people have been flocking to movies dealing with dark occult powers, from *The Exorcist* to Harry Potter. This signals that the body of Christ has abandoned its calling to reveal true and authentic spirituality.

The truth—so well hidden by our many material comforts—is that this physical, material world is not our home. We do not originate here, nor do we end up here. On earth, we're just "sojourners," as the psalmist wrote (Ps. 119:19 NRSV), or "foreigners and refugees" (Heb. 11:13). So "as long as we are at home in the body we are away from the Lord's home" (2 Cor. 5:6). We're creatures of a God who "is Spirit," as John wrote, "and only by the power of his Spirit can people worship him as he really is" (John 4:24).

As creatures of a spiritual God, we are primarily not bodies who occasionally enter or glimpse the world of the spirit. First and foremost, we're spirits who have been commissioned out of the spirit realm to take on bodies. Because we are fundamentally spiritual creatures, spiritual power will always be attractive, engaging, even fascinating to us, because it reminds us of our true home beyond this world. We're all homesick for God. Our hearts long to reconnect with our authentic spiritual home in Him (2 Cor. 5:1–7).

The good news of our faith is that Jesus has come—and is still here—to provide that connection and draw us back to God and our true selves at home with Him. Jesus said, "I am the way, the truth, and the life; no one goes to the Father except by me" (John 14:6). When we refuse to recognize Jesus as the way back home to the Father, our basic inborn need to connect with our spiritual Source through Him will turn elsewhere for satisfaction.

The enemy, meanwhile, has spread his smorgasbord with a host of tempting, tasty spiritualities. Those who eat from the enemy's occult table will soon believe that his counterfeit is real—and discount Jesus. Their vision becomes upside down—like the city child who visited a lemon and lime orchard for the first time, tasted real juice, and exclaimed, "Hey, that tastes like 7UP!"

We in the church have for so long abandoned our true spiritual nature and calling that we have forgotten from where—indeed, from whom—we really come. We forget that we are agents of a spiritual Creator designed to bring His power and rule on earth as they are in heaven.

The Bible is our Creator God's letter to us, reminding us of where we come from and where we're designed to go. In the Bible, He assures us of His power to get us there. Scripture reveals spiritual reality to creatures blinded by the material world (that's us) and shows how that spiritual reality affects us in our natural, material lives.

Those who read horoscopes, visit fortune-tellers, consult psychics, attend séances, "play" Ouija boards, engage spirit guides, read tarot cards, and practice ESP and other occult activities have been deceived into thinking God is not real and present and powerful and loving. They have turned away from the God revealed in Jesus and sought saving power from other spiritual sources. They are playing with a force that for millennia has subtly but surely led men and women away from God's protection unto destruction.

The final word here must, of course, be the Father's grace. Those who have dabbled or indulged in such practices at any time have invited the enemy of God into their hearts and lives. To be free of its destructive effects, you can renounce and confess your sin of not trusting Him to be enough, then take authority over the demons that have entered and cast them out. Having evicted the unholy spirits, ask the Father to fill you instead with His Holy Spirit, and rededicate yourself to trusting Jesus and Him alone.

Shalom,

(Rev.) Gordon Dalbey


# LETTER 3

## To a Pastor Indignant That I Have Warned Him Against Astrology

I had mailed a flyer to more than two hundred pastors offering my teaching services and had included "Astrology as Idolatry" among the topics. A pastor responded in a letter that he was planning to try a "healing service" after worship on an upcoming Sunday, and he asked if I would assist him. I was already booked for that date, but I called him to establish contact. During our phone conversation, he mentioned my astrology topic with indignation. "You can't judge such things outright!" he declared. "Have you tried it yourself and had your chart written?"

Startled, I hesitated as a foggy darkness fell over me. Here was a church pastor open enough to spiritual reality to hold a healing service in his church—yet at the same time affirming a work of the enemy clearly proscribed in Scripture and manifestly opposed to God. *Father,* I prayed, *help me speak Your truth with grace!*

Even as I prayed for wisdom in how to express the truth about astrology, I struggled to affirm his courage in opening to spiritual reality. Nevertheless, I felt very uneasy when we hung up. Shortly thereafter, he wrote me a letter accusing me of being narrow and judgmental in my spirituality, saying that my "rigidness" betrayed "a precarious hold on the reality of God."

Dear ——:

Thanks for staying in touch.

I, too, felt dissatisfied with our phone conversation. I had hoped to be more "confessional" than "instructional." I don't know if *precarious* is the word, but I do know that my "hold on the reality of God" is often not as strong as I—or, indeed, He—would want. After being humbled so many times in my journey with the Lord, I'm thankful that it's not about my hold on Him but about His hold on me.

In fact, part of my humbling has come through my experience

with other spiritualities besides Christian. I've been harmed by that and seen others harmed as well. That experience motivates my response, and I hope someday to have a chance to tell you about it. As a reasonably selfish person, I don't want to suffer that pain, nor, as a reasonably compassionate person, do I want others to do so.

As I've begun to experience Jesus as alive and real, I've come to discover other dark and destructive spiritual forces as well, which use their genuine power to seduce us away from God. In the process, I've come to know Jesus as my only trustworthy Guide in the spirit realm. The discernment of His Spirit, witnessed by the ancient prophets (Isa. 44:24–26; 47:12–15) and stirred in my own prayers, has convinced me that astrology is rooted in those dark forces.

When you ask me to try astrology for myself before speaking against it, therefore, it's like asking me to try adultery before speaking against it. I believe that's a fair analogy, because the ancient prophets (for example Jer. 5:7–9) often used the term *adultery* to describe the people's turning away from God to try other, native spiritualities.

If Hollywood's success in portraying it is any indication, adultery has a genuine power and fascination. But I know it would harm me and the one I love most, so I don't have to try it in order to disregard it as an option. Certainly, I'm still growing in my Christian walk. But I don't have to try something in every case to discern its true nature.

Frankly, what I wish I had said to you on the phone is simply: "What need prompted you in the first place to turn to astrology? What knowledge were you seeking, what healing, what power, what deeper sense of vitality, purpose, direction, or fulfillment?" Whatever your answer, I would only want to ask, "Why didn't you go to

Jesus instead? What made you think that Jesus is not altogether alive, caring, and powerful enough to give you that and everything else you need?"

Being a slave to the stars really doesn't excite me like being a loved son of the Father who created them—and me.

For me at least, the issue here is distrust. When I think of all the different places I used to turn instead of Jesus—philosophies, therapies, spiritualities, and so forth—I feel a deep sadness on my Father's part that I was going everywhere else, when from the very beginning He had everything I needed.

I feel that sadness for you.

It's not, as you charge, that I haven't tried and experienced other spiritual powers. In fact, it's precisely because I *have*—powerfully enough, in fact, to reveal that sooner or later they all lead away from Jesus and into the darkness—that I finally gave up and turned wholly at last to Him. I was really amazed to discover that what I'd been seeking had been right there all along.

Personally, I've experienced the spirit world as a realm of powers far beyond anything I in my human power can match. To venture out into it without staying close to Jesus would be for me to demonstrate a precarious hold on its reality and my own value.

So I don't condemn astrology. But I believe God does. Not because He's a rigid Judge who punishes those who differ with Him, but because He's a loving Father who wants to save His children from deception and harm and fulfill His plan in us. It's not a rigid father who says no when his son chases a ball into a busy street.

I appreciate your feeling that I didn't listen to you when we talked on the phone. It's one thing to judge astrology and quite another to judge you. If in any way I came across as judging you, I ask your forgiveness. I respect your walk. We're each on our own spiritual journey after God's heart, drawing what conclusions we will from our experiences. It's not my place to judge or condemn you. As a brother in the Lord, however, I do want to save you and your parishioners from harm. You may see that as presumptuous, but I'm willing to risk your rejection for that greater goal. If I don't flash the yellow light here, I answer to God.

Since you asked me to teach in your "house," I will offer this: As a pastor and leader in the body of Christ, you walk in the crosshairs of the enemy's gun sights. He wants to bring you down, and any others who follow you. If you entertain the dark spirits that underlie astrology, you've made yourself and your parishioners an easy target. In fact, you've done the enemy's work for him. He doesn't have to break down your church door; you've opened it wide and invited him in.

After this letter, you may well decide you don't want me to come, and I can accept that—partly because, if I were to speak at your church healing ministry, I would bear some responsibility for what might happen there.

The first call of brotherhood is to bless you for opening up to that ministry—and that I've tried to do. But it's another, equally important call to warn you of its dangers. Again, I warn you only because I assume you're as human as I am and, therefore, as vulnerable to spiritual counterfeit as I've been. As I continue to open myself to Jesus, He seems to prune and refine me more and more so the chinks in my armor don't bring me down. In my better moments, I allow, even beg Him to do that, lest I be misled and, in turn, mislead others. I would not be a good friend if I withheld this from you.

In any case, I think we can both learn something from each other. Let's stay connected. Obviously, we'll need to do some more "holy wrestling" together as we go. I'm up for it if you are. Let's work out something for lunch before long so we can at least get to know each other better in between rounds!

Shalom,

Gordon

## LETTER 4

### To a Local Newspaper Columnist Who Had Reported on His Visit to a Psychic

Dear ——:

I am an ordained clergy with a master of divinity degree from Harvard and also a former news reporter (the *Charlotte [NC ]News*) with an MA in journalism from Stanford.

In a recent column, you reported on your visit to a female psychic and fortune-teller in our town. Your "hands-on" feature assignment reminded me of when I was a reporter myself and gave blood for a story on the local blood bank, and when I had a "styled" haircut from the barber I interviewed. In order to write about something with authority, it's natural to assume you have to experience it.

The breezy tone of your story, while appropriate for such features, nevertheless suggests that it may be hard for you to appreciate what I say here—even as it once would have been hard for me. But I write out of considerable experience dealing with occult spiritualities and their harmful effects on the human spirit. Many people who have been harmed after dabbling in psychic phenomena have come to me for help—most of them educated folks like you and me, but nevertheless dangerously uninformed about spiritual matters.

I'm concerned not only for the welfare of your readers, who may be misled by your article either to discount the power in such encounters or to seek it—but also for you, since you have exposed yourself to it.

When I was a boy back in the late 1940s, shoe stores proudly featured upright X-ray machines something like a large speaker's podium with two slots on the floor below and a covered looking-screen on top. To check your shoe fit, you stepped up, put your feet in the slots below, and pushed the X-ray button. Looking down at the top screen, you could see your foot bones outlined within the shoe.

Everyone thought this was a harmless and, indeed, marvelous invention. Further scientific research, however, revealed the serious danger in exposing the customer to such radiation, and the machines were removed at once. Who knows what danger yet remains in the bodies of us who stood there so long, fascinated to see our X-rayed feet?

No matter how innocent your intentions, no matter how entertaining the experience seems, in visiting a psychic and opening yourself to her spiritual wares, you have exposed yourself to a "spiritual radiation" that can have harmful effects not only in your life but in the lives of your family members as well. Many people who have entertained such spiritualities have come to me for prayer about problems that no psychologist or medical doctor could help.

I suspect this may sound as absurd to you today as it once did to me. On the other hand, if you want to contact me for help in this regard, I'm happy to share with you the essentials of Christian spirituality and lead you in a prayer of cleansing.

For many years, like most rational, educated folks, I assumed that things such as psychic readings were harmless, even foolish games. As you did in your column, I snickered at them. A few years ago, however, a traumatic event in my life led me to take Christian spirituality seriously, beyond my vague childhood belief in God.

In a word, I cried out to Jesus. Eventually, as I went back to the biblical accounts, I began to experience the healing power reported there. I discovered not only that the spiritual power in Jesus is real, but also that powers other than and, in fact, contrary to Him operate in the spirit realm. Furthermore, I found that all the good powers of God available to believing Christians in any era—such as knowledge, wisdom, and healing—could be counterfeited by these other powers in a deliberate effort to mislead and destroy.

For example, 1 Corinthians 12:8–9 says that the Holy Spirit "gives one person a message full of wisdom, while to another . . . a message full of knowledge . . . while to another person he gives the power to heal." The book of Acts is filled with examples of this beneficent ministry among the earliest believers (10:19–20; 13:2; 21:11).

Eventually, however, the ministry of God's Holy Spirit by its very nature exposes the counterfeit. And then the battle heats up. Look especially at Acts 16:16 and following, in which the apostles "were met by a slave girl who had an evil spirit that enabled her to predict the future" and who "earned a lot of money for her owners by telling fortunes." Paul and Silas cast the spirit out in the name of Jesus. "When her owners realized that their chance of making money was gone," they "dragged" Paul and Silas before the Roman authorities and had them flogged.

When you read these stories of the ancient Christians, you'll be surprised at how similar their supernatural encounters were to the kind of messages that the psychic you visited peddles today. She likely has no idea that she is a channel for harmful powers.

Please understand me: I am not pooh-poohing psychic messages as a sham. That woman is in touch with quite genuine spiritual powers, which are entirely able to deliver true information *insofar as it suits their ultimate purpose of drawing people away from God, even to destruction.*

As another has put it, these evil spiritual powers will tell you nine truths in order to sucker you into the one lie that destroys you.

Your psychic and the legion of others like her persist today partly because they mediate real power and do, in fact, relay accurate information. But this evil goes free and unchallenged among us because churches have allowed and even fostered widespread spiritual ignorance. Tragically, we Christians today have abdicated our call to teach the truth about spiritual reality, to lead people to encounter the living God revealed in Jesus and experience His saving supernatural power in their lives. While we have busied ourselves playing church—going on Sundays out of habit, serving on committees, planning bazaars, sponsoring youth outings, even doing Bible studies—the powers that actively oppose God's purposes have been jumping in to fill the gap. And very engagingly, as with the psychic you visited.

Meanwhile, we are spiritual creatures, created by a God who is Spirit. When we refuse to acknowledge that and instead turn away from Him, our spiritual hunger remains—and impels us to seek other, false substitutes—such as your psychic. Now, I know she seemed to you like a nice little old grandmother, but in this case, Gramma's hot chocolate is spiked with poison. To the God revealed in Jesus, she is a clear and present danger to the physical and spiritual well-being of us all.

If you'll allow that evil is real and has power to affect us, surely that power is not stupid enough to walk around in a red suit and cape, horned and waving a pitchfork. Rather, it will try to appear altogether harmless—even trustworthy and helpful. As in *Little Red*

*Riding Hood*, a nice grandma will do fine as a disguise for the wolf. Better yet, a polished preacher in a new suit.

If you've stuck with me thus far, thank you. I honestly don't know if I'd have read this far when I was a reporter years ago. At any rate, you're a journalist with credibility in our community, and you have a responsibility to regard all input and investigate carefully what you share with your readers before writing anything harmful or that might lend your credibility to it. My prayer is that this letter might cause you to do that.

If you'd like to call me and talk this issue over, please don't hesitate.

Shalom,

(Rev.) Gordon Dalbey


## LETTER 5

### To the Mother of a Child Molested by Satan Worshippers

Dear Editor:

It's not easy to face the facts in your recent article about Satan worshippers in our community who are molesting children. But I thank you for exposing this evil among us.

As a pastor, I would like to address the distraught mother of a molested five-year-old who asked, "If they [the therapists] can't treat it, it's too late for my son, isn't it?"

In this Easter season, Christians in your story celebrate the fact that God has overcome this and all evil "so that you will know what is the hope to which he has called you" and "how very great is his power at work in us who believe"—in fact, "the same mighty strength which he used when he raised Christ from death" (Eph. 1:18–20). Therapists may not be able to treat the deep wound in your son from this evil intrusion. But as Jesus said, "What is impossible with men is possible with God" (Luke 18:27 NIV).

And so I want you first and foremost to know this: whatever the powers of darkness have done in and to your son can indeed be destroyed, broken, and rendered ineffective by the power of God's Spirit revealed in Jesus. No one, not even God, can erase this awful event from history. But it's never too late for your son to be healed from its effects. In fact, Jesus came "for this very reason, to destroy what the Devil had done" (1 John 3:8).

These words are not just religious fluff. I myself and many other believing Christians today can and often do minister this very real healing power of the Holy Spirit. I can give you several local references if you would like.

Let me reassure you: the God who created us all is a loving Father who wants His children to be healthy physically, emotionally, and spiritually. It's only natural to ask, Then why would He allow such evil to harm a child? I have no magic answer here; many mysteries of life remain unexplained. I do know, however—as you have so tragically experienced—that we live in a world broken by humanity's choice to turn away from God, which has thwarted His purposes and allowed the powers of evil to move among us. And I know from painful and yet glorious experience that the God who created us and this world has not abandoned us to its evil and brokenness, that if we take our wounds to Jesus, God uses even the worst of circumstances to draw us closer to Him and His ultimate purpose in our lives.

God can use a good psychotherapist toward the healing He wants for your son. But the ultimate cleansing and renewal needed from such a spiritual infection will ultimately require the help of someone with the spiritual authority given by Jesus, and a community that is surrendered to Him.

Granted, all this talk about Satan, demons, rituals, and such is foreign to our materialistic way of thinking. We don't like to believe anything is real unless we can touch, see, feel, or otherwise control it. Whether we choose to acknowledge it or not, however, we live in a spiritual world as well as a physical world, and the two are very much a part of each other. What happens in the spirit realm affects us.

Likewise, what we do in our daily physical lives affects our relationship with the spirit realm; people who scoff at the power of spiritual evil to affect their lives leave themselves open to its deceptions and harm.

That's why in the Lord's Prayer, Christians call on God to rule "on earth as it is in heaven." A significant condition to this rule of God in our lives is then indicated with a plea to "deliver us" not just "from evil," as the more sanitized modern translations inaccurately say, but, indeed, "from the evil one."

No matter how educated, professionally competent, compassionate, physically fit, or otherwise strong we may be, our human powers are simply no match for those in the spirit realm. That's why God sent Jesus to protect and guide us in it. And that's why humility is the hallmark of those who know and worship Him. God's full and overcoming power is released only as we let go of our own.

Let me be straightforward here: if you do not have the proper spiritual protection and guidance that God has provided in Jesus, you are as vulnerable to the powers of evil as your five-year-old son. Yes, we can fly to the moon, build skyscrapers, construct the Internet, and make potato chips that stack neatly inside a can, but in the face of spiritual power, both good and evil, we're helpless children. We're saved from evil not by pride in our accomplishment, but by humility before God's accomplishment.

We are engaged even now, as thousands of years ago when the Bible was written, in a spiritual battle that cannot be fought with physical, worldly weapons. Bombs and guns, pills and scalpels, and psychological insights may be called for at times, but the victory we long for in our hearts will always elude us until we turn at last to the spiritual Author of life revealed in Jesus.

In our own community, a growing number of Christians—many from the traditional, oldline denominations and other well-established churches—are beginning to recognize this spiritual warfare as something real. We're busy training together, learning to wield "God's powerful weapons" (2 Cor. 10:4) and walk in His victory.

Once you face this reality, you can see that the Los Angeles area where we live has proclaimed itself through Hollywood and the pornographic film industry as a welcome home for evil spirits of lust and perversion. The beaches, where the child molestations were reported to take place, are a primary focus of that lust, as a ready theater for women in bikinis and men in spandex.

What we are seeing happen to our children is the awful consequence of our supposedly "adult toleration" of such spiritual attack. Tragically, we fancy that our mere human intelligence and good judgment can save us from its effects.

I'm not trying to whip up a frenzy over devils any more than rattlesnakes. But if you go hiking in the Santa Monica mountains, you had better know something about the rattlesnakes there and how to defend yourself in an encounter with one. They're not easy to see, and their effect can be deadly. Similarly, to ignore the reality of

spiritual evil among us is to leave our children and ourselves dangerously vulnerable to its destructive intent.

Sadly, this despicable work of Satan worshippers has thrust you
headlong into that reality. Hate it as you must, your only way out of
this is through it. There is indeed healing for your son. But you must
battle for it.

Overcoming spiritual invasion requires spiritual defense and
spiritual victory. Toward that end, I urge you to give God a chance
to demonstrate the healing He can and wants to do in your family.

You can cooperate with God in this process. Above all, know that
you're not alone in the battle. Seek out a church where people acknowledge spiritual reality and the overcoming work of God's Holy Spirit
today. Read the Bible and trust the ancient witness to that. Gather your
platoon and get others to pray for you. Find a Christian counselor who
moves in the supernatural gifts of the Spirit as described in 1 Corinthians
12. Spend time with Jesus, talking and listening to Him. Take care of
yourself: get physical exercise and rest; eat healthy. Get real with God
and cry out your heartfelt need as Jesus did on the cross (Mark 15:34;
Psalm 22). Tell Him how you feel and what you need. Receive the baptism of the Holy Spirit. Ask Jesus to tell you what specific evil spirits
have entered your child, and in His name, command them to leave.
Stay focused. Remember that "we are not fighting against human beings
but against the wicked spiritual forces in the heavenly world" (Eph.
6:12). Pray, pray, and pray some more. My prayer for you is this:

That you allow your Father God
- to stir in you His hope for your family's healing,
- to use this awful experience to help you recognize and
  confess your own desperate need for Him,

- to overcome your natural resistance to the reality of evil, and
- to experience His power at hand to heal evil's effects.

May you therefore surrender humbly and hopefully to Jesus and let Him teach you by the power of His spirit how to walk out His victory in your portion of the battle that is upon us all.

Shalom,

(Rev.) Gordon Dalbey

## LETTER 6

### To a Seminary Professor Who Asked, "Why Must You Insist on Jesus in Your Healing Prayer?"

Dear Dr. ——:

Thank you for the opportunity to speak before your Psychology and Spirituality program last week. I enjoyed talking with you and the seminarians, as it helped sharpen my discernment regarding what I have experienced in healing prayer. As always, time flew by and I wanted here to clear up some loose ends regarding your excellent question to me afterward.

I appreciate your concern as professor of pastoral care for how to integrate Christ-centered healing prayer with "the larger healing community" that you seek. I value the insights of secular psychology and put much of what I've learned from that discipline to good use in my ministry. I regard it, like medical science, as a gift that can serve God's healing purposes when used according to God's will.

My training in secular psychology and counseling is not as broad as your own, but it has helped me surface issues for clients and gives us a rational basis for understanding their pathology. At the same time, I acknowledge only Jesus as the Healer, and I submit all natural and supernatural gifts to Him so that He can use them according to His will and not mine or my client's.

I do believe that God can act where Jesus is not acknowledged. In fact, I personally experienced His saving power long before I became a believer and could acknowledge its source. Often when I pray with believing clients, Jesus will come and show them how He acted in past events to save them, even when they did not know Him.

One client, for example, was facing a very traumatic situation in her life, and she desperately needed encouragement. When we offered her predicament to God in prayer, a girlhood memory surfaced in which a grade-school classmate almost put her eye out with a sharp pencil. When we invited Jesus into the playground scene where it had happened, in her mind's eye, she saw Jesus come and put out His hand to block the incoming pencil just a bit, pushing it aside from her eye and into the bridge of her nose instead. The doctors had told her that she narrowly escaped blindness; after the prayer, she knew that Jesus had saved her. During the next weeks of our prayers, Jesus came and showed her many other times when He had rescued her from serious injury.

Overwhelmed with humble gratitude, she developed a deep faith and began to trust and allow Jesus to use her present predicament for His larger purposes.

Of course, the question remains, Why doesn't Jesus save the many others who in fact get blinded or otherwise harmed by accidents? I can only say that's one question I plan to ask Him when I meet Him face-to-face! Meanwhile, in this present age, I see through a glass darkly like the rest of us and press on in faith. Not knowing why He doesn't save some does not diminish my praise for His having saved one, nor keep me from doing what I can so He might save more.

While Jesus does act often in situations where He is not acknowledged, it's worth considering that acknowledging Him might give Him more room to do His healing work. I want every healing God has for my client, and I work deliberately to find ways to cooperate with Him in that process.

The apostle Paul suggested this when he wrote that "no one can confess 'Jesus is Lord,' without being guided by the Holy Spirit" (1 Cor. 12:3). The Holy Spirit honors those persons and occasions where Jesus is acknowledged as Lord. Indeed, the Spirit works most freely and powerfully where Jesus is worshipped, praised, adored, exalted, loved, and glorified.

I can only say that this has been my experience. Amid all our theological questions, it's helpful to remember that we're talking not formulas but relationship here. A normal father will naturally do what he can to help his child. But his heart is especially moved by the one who dearly loves and honors him.

It's understandable for you to ask whether one might invoke other names for the healing agent, such as "burning bush," "image of light," or "inner mind." Avoiding the particular name of Jesus might foster a broader perspective and thus a more nonjudgmental, tolerant, and inclusive ideology. A major problem with this "call-it-whatever-you-want" approach, however, is that the very name of Jesus has a particular meaning in Hebrew—"God saves." Accordingly, it refers to a particular man in a particular historical context with a particular mission to save people from a lost and broken world—even as it manifests in their own personal lives.

Ironically, science may offer the best resolution to this issue. A research chemist, for example, seeks the exact chemical elements and conditions that produce a desired result. The researcher tries a wide variety of chemical combinations until discovering which particular one has the properties that cause the reaction. In fact, the specificity of elements used in the reaction is a major focus of research, which aims at replicating the desired effect by combining the particular optimum conditions that have been shown to cause it. If sodium makes the reaction work, the chemist does not say, "In order not to offend those on a low-sodium diet, we could call it uranium or calcium instead of sodium."

The basic question arises: What is the appropriate goal of healing prayer that would allow one to say, "It worked"? From a human-centered view, the answer is clear—if it cures the cancer, clears the arteries, removes the migraine, and so forth.

The God revealed in Jesus, however, has a greater goal beyond physical healing. As someone else has said, we believe not because it works, but because it's true. A healed body, that is, does not imply a healthy relationship with God or that you're living according to God's will. Nor does living according to God's will guarantee a healthy body.

The true and larger purpose of healing prayer is to draw closer to the God who created you and thereby become more equipped and encouraged to fulfill His purposes for your life. I don't mean here to minimize the anguish of illness, but to maximize the joy of walking out your created destiny. This is precisely what Jesus came to do, and when He is worshipped, the Holy Spirit moves to make this happen—whether you're physically changed or not.

The major obstruction to God's purposes is the proud pursuit of our own. Paul asked, "Do you not realize that God's kindness is meant to lead you to repentance?" (Rom. 2:4 NRSV). Healing, therefore, is designed to humble us and make our hearts more open to what God is doing.

Not everyone prayed for in the name of Jesus is healed. If God is both omnipotent and loving, this confirms that God's purpose for us is greater than our immediate physical healing. When the healing we want doesn't occur, that doesn't mean God has abandoned us. It means He wants to use the pain and fear to draw us to Him so He can shape us for our destiny. The Sculptor's chisel hurts, but it brings forth the work of beauty.

The truth—both sad and frustrating for God—is that happy times often are not as effective as suffering in stirring our self-centered human spirit to cry out for God to come closer. "I will abandon my people until they have suffered long enough for their sins and come looking for me," as God said. "Perhaps in their suffering they will try to find me" (Hos. 5:15).

When healing does occur, we agree that there is, in fact, a healing agent. The question then would be, to borrow again from scientific research: How do we identify that agent sufficiently to replicate its power in future times of need? If your heart is open and you truly want to draw closer to God and His purposes, what agent best accomplishes this goal? This is an old question, one the apostle Paul faced in talking to the Athenians about their statue labeled "To an Unknown God" (Acts 17).

My own answer, born out of considerable personal loss and pain, is simple and practical.

If I'm sick enough to seek healing prayer, I don't want to toy with any variety of ostensibly benign images, any more than I want "just any nice doctor" when I go to the hospital. I want the best specialist. I want to be ministered to by the One who dealt with my physical, emotional, and spiritual brokenness on the cross, conquered there the powers of death, rejoined me to my Creator, Father God, and thus opened the floodgates to His healing power and His purpose in my life. When I need help, I want the One named Y'Shua, that is, "God saves," on my case.

I don't want an amorphous philosophical or even theological idea. I want the promised Great Physician who lived, died, and was resurrected in history and is demonstrably active and present to me even now in the Holy Spirit.

Finally, and most convincingly to me—though this may be the most difficult of my points for you to accept, even as it was at first for me—we must face the fact that spiritual reality encompasses far more than the most intelligent of human minds can grasp, including evil. Not all things spiritual are good, and if we are to entertain the spirit realm with any positive expectation, we must know the true well enough to recognize the false. Mere good intentions, such as a desire to see someone's body healed, are no substitute for the discernment of evil. That's why Jesus urged us to be not simply innocent as a dove but also wise as a serpent.

The terminal drawback of all other substitute images is that they do not account sufficiently for the power of spiritual evil, which takes advantage of our brokenness to turn us away from God and abdicate His purposes for us. I'm not saying that all sickness is caused by demons, but I am saying that dark spirits are as palpably real as the Holy Spirit and, as such, quick to foster and capitalize on illness for evil ends. Thus, Jesus "went around doing good and healing all who were under the power of the devil" (Acts 10:38 NIV).

In biblical faith, evil is a spiritual entity with a distinct personality and independent will—a fallen angel, a spiritual counterfeit, or pretender, to God's throne. As a supernatural power, this evil can perform some healings—but precisely in order to shift the focus of glory away from Jesus, its chief and victorious rival. Unlike Jesus, its goal is not to fulfill, but rather, to sabotage your God-created purpose in life. Knowing and experiencing this reality leads to the tough but necessary conclusion: I am committed to praying for healing in myself and in others. But I'd rather suffer in sickness surrendered to Jesus, crying out to Him and thereby drawing closer to my Father and His larger purpose in my life, than be made physically healthy by a demon and miss God's plan for my life.

Today, like the Snake from the very genesis of human life, evil would misrepresent God and thereby seduce us away from our divine destinies. My extensive experience has convinced me that any spiritual power, no matter how "healing," that does not relate directly and victoriously to the power and personality of evil can in the end only serve evil and foster its destructive ends. Furthermore, those who proclaim explicitly the presence and power of Jesus are eligible to wield His authority and break the work of evil in their own and others' lives. "The Son of God appeared for this very reason, to destroy what the Devil had done," as John said (1 John 3:8b). "The Spirit who is in you is more powerful than the spirit in those who belong to the world" (1 John 4:4).

NO ONE HAS EVER FULLY CAST OUT A DEMON IN THE NAME OF the "burning bush" or the "healing light." But many others, myself included, who have prayed in the name of Jesus have been set free from oppressive evil spirits—and the lifelong emotional bondages and physical illnesses they foster.

Jesus is the only One with power and authority to deal conclusively with the very real and destructive power of evil. Christians are privileged to know and experience this truth. Indeed, anyone who doesn't acknowledge the reality of evil cannot fully appreciate the reality of Jesus and His saving power. You can't proclaim Jesus' presence and power without sooner or later engaging evil.

Thus, the very first one to recognize Jesus as the Son of God is not a faithful believer but a demon (Mark 1:24). When Jesus arrives, the powers of darkness know the kingdom of God is at hand and their time is short. Like cornered beasts, today as in biblical times, they are wily and vicious. As one who has personally suffered their counterattack, I simply cannot afford to let the healing work of Jesus in my life be co-opted by another spiritual power, no matter how nice the name that disguises its destructive goal. The older I get, the more I want to get on with what God created me to do, and after many regrettably uninformed explorations down spiritual rabbit trails, I've experienced the power of Jesus to get me there.

Jesus is the element who makes the "chemical reaction" go—the One with the bonding properties that unite and restore human beings to God and thereby to our created purpose.

Unfortunately, like so many other clergy, I was not taught spiritual reality in seminary. But what was once unfortunate is today tragic in its consequences. Ignorance of a thief's presence only gives the thief freedom to steal.

Those of us who want to minister God's healing to a broken world must begin to face and educate ourselves about full spiritual reality. Thankfully, we're not left without a reference text. It's all portrayed in the Bible and demonstrably real to anyone humble enough to name Jesus as Lord and claim the overcoming power of His Holy Spirit.

Again, I'm grateful for the opportunity to speak at your program. I hope this letter answers your question—or at least stirs a few more. If so, please give me a call. I'd enjoy sharing with you some of my experiences that have shaped my view—and hearing your own.

Shalom,

(Rev.) Gordon Dalbey

## LETTER 7

### To the President of a Church-Affiliated College Hosting a Conference on Occult Practices

Dear President ——:

Recently, I saw the program for a conference on spirituality scheduled on your campus. Since your college was founded by and today claims explicit [denominational] roots, and you have regular Sunday services at your campus chapel, I wanted to let you know something about the nature of the conference sponsors. I assume you have chosen simply to rent your facilities for this event; I don't know if you or your staff have examined its programs, but if you haven't, I urge you to do so immediately.

As one who has ministered in Southern California now for several years, I count myself qualified to respond to a wide variety of spiritually oriented activities. Whatever you're looking for, from the most traditional to the most bizarre, you can find it here.

In fact, I have noticed that precisely to the extent that I have taken my own Christian spirituality seriously, I have encountered those pursuing some other spirituality. I'm not sure exactly why that's true, but it seems to parallel the Bible stories of the early church's out-in-the-open competition between the Jesus-believers and the host of pagan spiritualities in the marketplace.

Many prospective church members whom I visit have dabbled in a wide range of activities beyond the borders of historic Christianity. Those activities are not mere theological debates, but palpable encounters with supernatural power. These people do not ask me, "Does your church have a better youth program, nicer sanctuary, friendlier people, etc.?" but "Does this Jesus you talk about have any real power today, and if so, is He more powerful than the other spiritual realities we've experienced?"

I probably don't have to tell you that seminary didn't prepare me for that kind of question. Sure, I had read all the best German theologians, memorized the ethical arguments, and learned the scholarly exegesis. But to think that this Jesus Christ whom I talked, sang, preached, taught, and read about had any real power now to make a palpable difference in my life—or in anyone else's life—well, that was a little too much for me to entertain.

Looking back, I see that I was simply proud and just didn't want to give up my sense of being in control with my trained, rational mind. I allowed Jesus only as much power as would fit into my own construct—which, I confess, turned out to be precious little power for Him. With righteous eloquence, I used to prophesy against "those middle-class folks" who could only tolerate a "domesticated Jesus" after their own image. But I eventually had to confess that in my own walk, I was one of them.

When I looked at myself that honestly, I became tired of merely preaching at sick people and comforting them in their distress, without being able to offer them any real power to overcome it. I was awakened to the reality of Jesus' presence and the power of the Holy Spirit by a number of fellow oldline–denomination clergy who had determined to investigate and experience the Christian heritage of healing prayer.

Eventually, I began to experience what could only be called miraculous results as parishioners were healed through prayer. Indeed, I discovered that the spirituality described in the Bible is accurate even now, that the Holy Spirit who engineered the healing then is alive and well today, working "signs and wonders" among those willing to submit their lives to Jesus and seek only His power and authority in their lives.

I found the best biblical outline of how this power of the Holy Spirit works in 1 Corinthians 12, which lists many of the "spiritual gifts" that function among those surrendered to Jesus. One of these gifts is "the ability to tell the difference between gifts that come from the Spirit and those that do not" (v. 10). This is sometimes called the gift of "discernment," and I have had considerable experience exercising it in recent years.

I trust you can see why this gift is so important to any church— or church-related college—that would move in authentic Christian spirituality. As long as you operate in this world that has fallen away from its Creator, you'll sooner or later find yourself competing with other spiritualities. When that happens, you need to know when the phony comes your way; otherwise, you'll be led astray into a variety of dangerous and damaging spiritual provinces. I can tell you that I've made my own share of mistakes in this arena and grieved the resulting harm to myself and others. I can only ask God's forgiveness for turning away from Him, trust in His mercy, and pray He'll use the whole ordeal to help others avoid the same mistakes later.

Many spiritual powers operate in the world with real and demonstrative effects. But not all of them come from the God who loves us and works to bring us into our full potential to love one another.

The many that do not come from the God revealed in Jesus are as determined to mislead us as God is determined to lead us. In a word, evil is real. In fact, the major stratagem of these powers is to turn people away from the God revealed in Jesus, who has exposed and wholly defeated them.

Certainly, evil personified would be clever enough not to walk down the street in a red suit with horns and a pitchfork. More likely, it would be attractively dressed and geared for public esteem—and thus the more seductive. Among well-educated folks, certainly it would present some ostensibly benign research-oriented credentials, as for example "Fellowship" or "Center for the Study of . . ." or, indeed, the deceptively enticing name of your conference. Such an agent of evil would operate most effectively where people denied or avoided the true spirituality of Jesus, in the presence of whom their nature would become evident by comparison. Ominously, that describes most churches today—and apparently your college.

Without belaboring the point, I must tell you that my own experience has demonstrated clearly that all the "seminars" and activities described in your conference booklet purvey spiritualities that Christian discernment recognizes as patently evil and therefore dangerous both to the participants and to your campus community as host. Their contacting the dead, astrology, divination through ESP and tarot cards, spirit guides, and the like are explicitly proscribed in the Bible to anyone who would follow the true God revealed in Jesus (Deut. 18:9–13; Acts 16:16ff.).

Not uncommonly, I see in my healing ministry people who have engaged those practices and later need emotional and/or physical healing from the effects—which damage the human spirit and lead people away from the God revealed in Jesus. I'd be happy to share with you my considerable firsthand experience with such clients.

I therefore urge you to disassociate your college from such activities. The ancient prophets called them "fornication," insofar as they caused the people of God to break their covenanted spiritual focus on God alone. When you host such a conference on your campus, you become a purveyor of spiritual pornography, which brings disgrace on a Christian institution. Worse, to lend the good name of your college to such activities allows them to be viewed as acceptable to and even endorsed by Christians. This can seduce others in your community into their practices who have not been properly warned and trained in authentic Christian spirituality.

My experience suggests that such counterfeits flourish only because we in the church have abdicated our own true spirituality—which when embraced is fully as exciting and adventurous a "frontier" adventure as any of those. What's more, the Holy Spirit is authentic to the crying need of us broken and lost creatures of God. We don't need to dabble in the occult. We have all we need in the risen, living Christ and His Holy Spirit—whose power and goodness unmask your conference for what it is: a sham, both farcical and patently dangerous.

I didn't learn much about spirituality in seminary. But I did learn about integrity—and you sacrifice yours when you allow something like this on your campus.

If you've hung in here with me thus far, I thank you sincerely.

Please do give serious thought to what I say and respond when you get a chance.

Shalom,

(Rev.) Gordon Dalbey

## LETTER 8

### Second Letter to the College President After He Rescheduled the Occult Conference

Dear ———:

I note that you have once again invited the occult spirituality conference to your campus this year. I'm struggling with how best to express to you my sadness and dismay at your decision to do so.

Last year, I tried to explain as clearly and directly as possible why such a program is a disgrace to your college and to our common Christian witness. Your letter last year responding to mine was gracious. But grace is no substitute for truth.

Please understand that in no way do I intend my letters as a personal attack upon you. You are not the enemy; you are the victim. The true spiritual enemy is at work through such occult activities as this conference, just as inimically as through his more obvious manifestations such as racism and war-making, which your larger fellowship has so courageously fought from its beginnings.

If you will not listen to me, I urge you to listen to and respect your own heritage. Read seriously the seventeenth-century journals of (the founder of your movement), who along with your forebears so courageously braved prison and faced death in order to witness this very reality of Jesus I affirm here. The compassion and discernment of God's living Spirit was the foundation of his and their devotion to racial harmony and peacemaking.

The founding fathers and mothers whose faith birthed your college would be deeply wounded to see you associating with other, occult spiritualities and frankly would disown you in an instant.

As I have searched for some reason you chose to dismiss my warning and your own heritage, I can only imagine two possibilities.

First, you remain ignorant and simply don't know what you're dealing with.

As I granted in my last letter, such ignorance is sadly not unusual, as oldline–denomination churches have too often flatly abdicated responsibility to recognize, teach, and practice authentic Christian spirituality. As a consequence, we have failed to experience and warn of the dangers in entertaining other, occult spiritual powers as espoused by this conference's sponsors.

Again, I'm not judging your ignorance but lamenting it, as I shared in it myself until relatively recently. As the president of a Christian college, however, you are responsible to educate yourself on this issue in order to protect not only your college's good name, but the welfare of its community as well.

I would not presume to say these things to you without offering every resource at my disposal to help you. I would welcome the opportunity to speak on your campus at no charge. If not myself, I can recommend several, more local resource speakers.

As for books, many highly respected oldline–denomination church leaders have written from this orthodox Christian perspective. I believe you would appreciate psychiatrist Scott Peck's *People of the Lie*. Episcopal priest Dennis Bennett's *The Holy Spirit and You* has an excellent introductory chapter on the occult in relation to Christian spirituality. Former Catholic priest Francis MacNutt's *Deliverance from Evil Spirits* is especially thoughtful and well balanced.

A second possible reason for your ignoring my warning is that, in fact, you understand what I'm saying, but you lack the courage to confront the organizers of this event with your Christian convictions.

Here again, I'm no one to judge, as I have certainly known that fear myself—especially when I wrote my letter to you last year! Authentic Christian spirituality, in its supernatural power and manifestations, has only recently been rediscovered among the historic churches, and then only by a minority—albeit a growing one. Much as our first-century forebears, Christians who would espouse and live out spiritual reality today take a genuine risk both personally and professionally. Once again, I want you to know that should you ever be willing to take that risk, you have my fullest support in any public way that you might want me to express it.

Meanwhile, I must tell you that coming to this truth in my own life has cost me considerably, and I am not free to turn away from it. The more hard-wrought the truth, the more compelling its voice. Insofar as we're each responsible to share the measure of truth entrusted to us, I will continue to do so, even with you.

I don't blame you for balking. I know very well—again, from my own sin—that those who share the full reality of Christian spirituality do so at times not only with disorderly enthusiasm, but also with snobby judgment. I have done that myself and have sought God's forgiveness. I don't presume to harbor all Christian truth; I'm a broken vessel with much yet to learn, and those closest to me can testify best to that. But my sin does not exempt me from sharing what I have, in fact, experienced to be true, and the biblical record that confirms it.

The biblical prescription for reconciliation is to go first to your brother and talk directly together. If he does not listen to you, then bring others with you for a second confrontation. Since you have dismissed my personal word, I am writing to your denominational magazine editors about what's happening on your campus and contacting your regional denominational officials to inform them as well. I am also writing to your college's board of trustees in hopes of alerting them.

Because I know all too well in myself how handicapped we "modern, rational" folks are in recognizing spiritual power, I will continue trying to awaken you and others to the evil that you are entertaining in your midst.

And so I will offer one more consideration.

Without a moment's hesitation, I hope you would refuse to permit on your campus a weeklong rally for the Ku Klux Klan to promote their anti-Christian program. Why, then, do you welcome anti-Christian occultists? That you see no contradiction in that marks you—like most of us—as a tragic victim of the dogmatic materialism of our European/Western culture.

Unlike third-world peoples, we are so determined to control our lives and the world around us that we are blind to the powerful spiritual realities that literally surround, infuse, and, indeed, manipulate us.

Not only have educated, worldly, intelligent Christians abdicated the proclamation of Christian spirituality to the rigid fundamentalists and the sensationalist "faith healers," but we stubbornly refuse to allow and experience the true spirituality of Jesus ourselves. We entertain instead such counterfeits as you host on your campus.

To frame it as the ancient prophets might, we who have been

given the very keys to the kingdom of heaven are hanging out in spiritual flophouses; we who have been called to dine at the King's table are rushing off excitedly to the garbage pits; we who have been covenanted into fidelity to the living God by the sacrifice of Jesus have gone a-whoring with false gods.

Let me emphasize: I respect the occultists. I do not scoff at their offerings as mere superstitious nonsense. Indeed, they are calling upon and mediating genuine spiritual power that manifestly affects people's lives—primarily to turn them away from the God revealed in Jesus and to sabotage His purposes in us.

I therefore don't want to spend my best energies on them and their deceptions, but rather on Jesus—who, after all, did not condemn the pagans but focused His anger instead on the religious leaders, who should have known better. If we Christian leaders had been doing our appointed task faithfully, not only would these occultists be recognized as a dangerously misleading counterfeit, but your campus would be too busy studying, experiencing, and proclaiming the reality of Jesus and the Holy Spirit to have any space on your calendar for them.

As the enemy attacks your most vulnerable spot, so it is only too characteristic of God's enemy to slip into an "open-minded" and "inclusive" community like yours through the occult. Insofar as you allow your college to be used by that enemy of God, I am bound as your Christian brother to call you into accountability for the safety of your community.

My brother, I must tell you that when I saw the conference flyer for this year again on your campus, I felt patronized by your response letter to me last year. Yes, you graciously "appreciate my concern," but you do nothing about it. If you respond to this letter, please don't thank me again for taking the time to write you. I don't want you to appreciate my effort. I want you to listen to what I'm telling you.

The ultimate victory of evil would be for you and me to end up fighting each other. I have no desire to disrespect, diminish, or discount you personally or professionally. I trust you can receive my taking time to write you as a gesture of respect for you and your position, as well as for your college.

Accordingly, my experience, my spiritual gifts of discernment and teaching, my blunders and my learning, are all at your disposal. I know personally how hard it is for us rational, educated folks to acknowledge spiritual power—and I know the dangers in failing to do so. Tell me how I can help and I'll be there for you.

Shalom,

(Rev.) Gordon Dalbey

# EPILOGUE

It seems strangely fitting to close this book by noting that, except for the question from my parishioner, my letters were not answered or affirmed.

I'm human enough to feel angry when the hard-wrought lessons of my suffering are ignored or rejected. Certainly, the consequences of dismissing the truth are real and destructive, and I don't want others to suffer them as I did. In my more faithful moments, however, I know my job is simply to speak the truth as I have experienced it, and it's the Holy Spirit's job to cause others to embrace it (John 16:13).

Such truth-talking is fruitless without grace-walking. Balking at the truth doesn't mark someone for condemnation as an enemy, but rather for compassion as a fellow human being, afraid to trust God and anxious to stay in control—even as I was in the opening events of this book and, yes, even today in other ways.

"Everthing that goes into a life of pleasing God," Peter wrote, "has been miraculously given to us by getting to know personally and intimately, the One who invited us to God. The best invitation we ever received!" (2 Peter 1:3 MSG). In the life, death, and resurrection of Jesus, that is, God has invited us all to exchange the illusion of our control for the reality of His power. This book is my attempt to extend that invitation to you.

Whether I extended it or not was an issue between me and God.

Whether you now accept it or not is an issue between you and God.

And so, as the best of invitations, it concludes with this hope: RSVP.

# SELECTED RESOURCES

**Books**

Andrews-Dalbey, Mary. *The REST of Your Life*. Atlanta: CarePoint Ministries, 2007.

Ankerberg, John, and John Weldon. *Encyclopedia of New Age Beliefs*. Eugene, OR: Harvest House, 1996.

Campbell, Ron. G. *Free from Freemasonry*. Ventura, CA: Regal Books, 1999.

Evans, Michael and Wholeness Ministries. *Learning to Do What Jesus Did: How to Pray for Physical, Emotional, and Spiritual Healing*. Bakersfield, CA: Archer-Ellison, 2003.

Dalbey, Gordon. *Fight like a Man: Redeeming Manhood for Kingdom Warfare*. Wheaton, IL: Tyndale House, 1996.

Greven, Philip. *Spare the Child: The Religious Roots of Punishment and the Psychological Impact of Physical Abuse*. New York: Vintage Books, 1992.

Lewis, C. S. *The Screwtape Letters*. London: G. Bles, 1942.

MacNutt, Francis. *Deliverance from Evil Spirits*. Grand Rapids, MI: Chosen Books, 1995.

————. *Healing*. Notre Dame, IN: Ave Maria Press, 1974.

Martin, Walter R., and Ravi Zacharias. *Kingdom of the Cults*. Rev ed. Minneapolis, MN: Bethany House, 2003.

O'Mathuna, Donal, and Walt Larimore. *Alternative Medicine: The Christian Handbook*. Grand Rapids, MI: Zondervan, 2001.

Peck, M. Scott. *People of the Lie*. New York: Simon & Schuster, 1983.

Penn-Lewis, Jessie, and Evan Roberts. *War on the Saints*. Cathedral Station, NY: Thomas E. Lowe, 1973.

Sandford, John and Paula. *Healing the Wounded Spirit*. Clarks Summit, PA: Victory House Publishers, 1985.

Sears, William. *Christian Parenting and Child Care*. Nashville: Thomas Nelson, 1991.

Sherrill, John L. *They Speak with Other Tongues*. New York: McGraw Hill, 1964.

Sklar, Dusty. *The Nazis and the Occult*. Rev ed. New York: Dorset Press, 1990.

Wallis, Arthur. *God's Chosen Fast*. Ft Washington, PA: Christian Literature Crusade, 1968.

**Healing and Deliverance Ministries**

Christian Healing Ministries (Jacksonville, FL) www.christianhealingmin.org

Elijah House Ministries (international, based in Spokane, WA) www.elijahhouse.org

Ellel Healing Ministries International (based in UK, world-wide including Orlando, FL) www.ellel.org.uk

Genesis Process Ministry (Auburn, CA, emphasis on addiction recovery) www.genesisprocess.org

Lutheran Renewal Ministry (St. Paul, MN) www.lutheranrenewal.org

Presbyterian Renewal Ministries International (based in NC) www.prmi.org

Wholeness Ministries (Bakersfield, CA) www.wholeness.org

# NOTES

*Introduction: Bad Angels*
1. Jovial Bob Stine, *101 Wacky Kid Jokes* (New York: Scholastic Inc., 1988), 63.

Chapter 5: Jesus, the Warrior King
1. Elie Wiesel, *A Jew Today* (New York: Random House, 1978), 170.
2. Ibid., 176.
3. Ibid., 178.

Chapter 6: Meeting the Enemy: A First Skirmish
1. G. Dalbey, "The Great White Son Turns Left," *Christian Century*, June 9. 1971, 716.
2. Francis MacNutt, *Healing* (New York: Bantam Books, 1977), 145–146.
3. Ibid., 189.
4. Ibid., 209.
5. Ibid., 155.

Chapter 7: The Bible as a War Story
1. Bernard W. Anderson, *The Unfolding Drama of the Bible* (Chicago: Folet Publishing, 1971), 47.
2. C. S. Lewis, *The Screwtape Letters* (New York: Collier Books, 1961), 62-63.

Chapter 8: My Battle Partner, the *Paraclete*
1. Francis MacNutt, *The Nearly Perfect Crime* (Grand Rapids: MI: Chosen Books, 2005); rereleased as *The Healing Reawakening* (2006).
2. Bob Whitaker, "Gifts of the Holy Spirit" (teaching series), 1984.
3. Don W. Basham, *Ministering the Baptism in the Holy Spirit* (Monroeville, PA: Whitaker Boooks, 1973).

Chapter 13: The Weapon of Fasting
1. Richard J. Foster, *Celebration of Discipline* 9San Francisco: Harper & Row, 1978), 48.

Chapter 14: Norwegian Bivouac: Of Heritage and Destiny
1. C. S. Lewis, *Mere Christianity* (New York: Macmillan, 1978), 51.